DRIVING
ECO-INNOVATION

D R I V I N G
ECO-INNOVATION

A breakthrough discipline
for innovation and sustainability

CLAUDE FUSSLER

WITH PETER JAMES

PITMAN
PUBLISHING

London · Hong Kong · Johannesburg
Melbourne · Singapore · Washington DC

PITMAN PUBLISHING
128 Long Acre, London WC2E 9AN
Tel: +44 (0)171 447 2000
Fax: +44 (0)171 240 5771

A Division of Pearson Professional Limited

First Published in Great Britain in 1996

ISBN 0 273 62207 2

British Library Cataloguing in Publication Data
A CIP catalogue record for this book can be obtained from the British Library.

10 9 8 7 6 5 4 3

Typeset by Pantek Arts, Maidstone, Kent
Printed and bound in Great Britain by Biddles Ltd, Guildford and King's Lynn

The Publishers' policy is to use paper manufactured from sustainable forests.

CLAUDE FUSSLER is the vice president of Environment Health & Safety, New Businesses and Public Affairs for Dow Europe SA, based in Horgen, Switzerland.

A French national, Fussler is a chemical engineer by training. He is a founding member and past president of the European Partners for the Environment, EPE. EPE is a multi-sectoral group working to bring about a sustainable Europe. Fussler was also a founder of a group called SPOLD dedicated to the advancement of life cycle analysis.

In 1995 Fussler received *Tomorrow* magazine's first-ever Environmental Leadership Award.

PETER JAMES is director of the Sustainable Business Centre. This conducts and disseminates research on how organisations can integrate sustainable development into their activities. It has particular expertise in the areas of environmental change management, environmental performance measurement, environmental benchmarking and environmental accounting. Peter is also an associate of Ashridge, the management college, where he was employed whilst writing this book. Prior to joining Ashridge, Peter held positions at Stirling, Warwick and Limerick business schools, latterly as Professor of Management.

If you would like to comment on or discuss any of the concepts raised in this publication, please contact:

Dow Europe
Bachtobelstrasse 3
8810 Horgen
Switzerland
Tel: (+41) 1-728-2401
Fax (+41) 1-728-2097

Contents

Part 3: HOW TO CHANGE?

Part 4: THE ECO-COMPASS

Part 5: USING THE ECO-COMPASS

Part 6: AT THE GREEN EDGE?

The concept of eco-efficiency was created by the member companies of the World Business Council for Sustainable Development (WBCSD). "Eco-efficiency is reached by the delivery of competitively priced goods and services that satisfy human needs and bring quality of life, while progressively reducing ecological impacts and resource intensity throughout the life cycle, to a level at least in line with the earth's estimated carrying capacity". In *Driving Eco-Efficiency* Claude Fussler shows business leaders how to chart the course to a successful and sustainable future.

This work represents a significant contribution to the crucial debate on this topic. Therefore, the WBCSD is pleased to recognize it as the first in a new series of publications – *Eco-Forum: business perspectives for sustainable policies and practices*. This will comprise books and articles published by others but endorsed by the WBCSD on works which add particular value to the dialogue on the conduct of business towards sustainable development.

The WBCSD is a coalition of 120 international companies united by a shared commitment to the environment and to the principles of economic growth and sustainable development. Its members are drawn from 33 countries and more than 20 major industrial sectors. The WBCSD also benefits from a thriving global network of nine national and regional business councils and four partner organizations.

The WBCSD provides a powerful and unified business voice on sustainable development issues and plays an important role in developing closer cooperation between business, governments and others and in encouraging high standards of environmental management in business itself.

Its work program – comprising a number of working groups with company representatives – deals with policy development and environmental management issues. The WBCSD is also involved in a number of field projects in developing countries and countries in transition.

Bjorn Stigson
Executive Director
WBCSD

We will be interested to see where librarians shelve this book. With due respect, we hope it poses a dilemma.

In this text we examine environmental trends in considerable depth but this is not essentially an environmental book. It is, first and foremost, a book about innovation – innovation which in this case is fuelled by environmental issues. The truth is we hope they buy a copy for both their business *and* ecology sections. It is not that we want to sell more copies, we simply believe the issues we address are relevant to both audiences.

A perfect merger

The themes of innovation and environment marry well. The need to operate the global economy at levels where society exists off the earth's dividends and not its resource capital will induce profound changes in existing markets. Business is and will become an increasingly important factor in the sustainable development equation – an equation we examine in considerable depth in this book.

If you are a marketing professional you have probably heard this before. But what you probably haven't heard are concrete answers to three fundamental questions that may determine the pace of your entry into these markets:

- When, where and how are these markets emerging?

- Will I be able to make a profit – short and long-term– in these markets?

- How do I innovate to create the right products to meet my customers' needs in these markets?

Our goal is to provide answers to these questions. Some trailblazing companies (which we profile in later chapters) have done the work for us by setting solid examples. They are providing products and services that are environmentally efficient and economically profitable – eco-efficient, as we say. They have also found that markets for environmentally efficient products are viable today and are growing rapidly. They have all approached innovation in different yet effective ways. Each one has something to teach us.

A template for breakthrough innovation

We have taken their experiences and combined them with new thinking on the development of eco-efficient products and processes to create a template for breakthrough innovation. We call this template the eco-compass. We describe its development and application in Chapters 15 and 22.

The one recurring theme in this book is that the time to begin developing eco-efficent products is *today*. While incremental improvements in environmental performance are ongoing, the lag between the inception of a quantum breakthrough (the types that create new markets) and its wide application and acceptance is measured in years and often decades.

To know where you are going, it is important to know where you came from: in the next few chapters we take a broad look at the issues and trends that are shaping the markets for eco-efficient products and processes.

As the saying goes, all good ideas have 1000 parents. That's certainly true of many of the concepts in this book. While I can't name all 1000, there is a core of people without whom the publication would not have been possible. Among these, I include three special groups, the *Conspirators*, the *Inspirational Leaders* and the *Supporters*.

But there is one person in particular who I must single out for his extraordinary contribution, my co-author, Peter James. Peter brought to this project his brilliant writing and organizational skills, his insight as a business and environmental academic and an outstanding wit. His personal dedication brought to life a book out of the patchwork of concepts, approaches and background facts that filled hours of inspired discussions.

Throughout the writing process Peter and I committed that case studies would illustrate the book's themes more vividly than any theory or chart. I'd like to say a special thank you to the eco-innovators profiled in the cases. We understand how busy you are turning the concepts in this book into reality. We appreciate the cooperation and the lessons we learned as you shared your experience. We wish you continued success and many more breakthroughs.

The Conspirators

The Conspirators are my Dow colleagues who powered the production of the book with intellect and sweat equally. David Russell, Hans Stäuber, Bob Sylvest, Scott Noesen and Manfred Wirth invented the eco-compass and keep perfecting it, workshop after workshop. Robert Lensch had the idea of the book in the first place and probed business colleagues for their needs and wants in the area of Innovation. Anita Mueller, Kai Hockerts, Christian Ulrich, Daniel Halder, a commando of bright young students, chased the case studies material. They corrected many flaws in the early eco-compass tests.

Paula Gasparin and Sylvia Horlacher saved us from chaos by skillfully piecing together all the details.

We all have other jobs and many, higher priorities. This book could have taken forever without Mike Kolleth, the coach who kept us on track with energy and enthusiasm. Of all the members of the Conspirators group, none has lived with this project as closely as my wife, Martina. Instead of just giving up the necessary free time she dove into the research material, was a precious support, and provided a fresh valuable perspective when I was missing the obvious in the final reviews.

The Inspirational Leaders

I was naive to many sustainability issues in 1991 with my business and manufacturing experience. Some exceptional people shaped the ideas upon which my actions and many of the concepts in this book are now built. I am particularly indebted to John Elkington, Peter Winsemius, Ernst Ulrich von Weizsäcker, Jacqueline Aloisi de Larderel, Friederich Schmidt Bleek, Stephan Schmidheiny and Laurens Jan Brinkhorst.

In Dow David Buzzelli and Yves Bobillier show the way, provide challenge and encouragement.

I am continuously learning from these leaders.

The Supporters

And there is the Supporters group, too large to all be named. I am particularly thankful for the dialog, the workshops, the partnership experiments, the tough questions. In one way or another they have made a substantial contribution to the eco-innovation approach and influenced what have I learned so far. Thanks to all and particularly to: the WBCSD eco-efficiency cadre: Frank Bosshardt, Bjorn Stigsson, Jan-Olaf Willums, Al Aspengren, Ben Woodhouse, those who made the policy realm approachable: Bob Hull, Paul de Jongh, Domingo Gimenez-Beltram, Geneviève Verbrugge, Paul Hofseth, Tom Burke, Bill Long, Rebecca Hamner, Jeremy Eppel, Robert Donkers, the dedicated believers in EPE: Raymond van Ermen, Michel Miller, Frank Schwalba-Hoth, Hans Alders, Garsett Larosse, Maria Berrini, Peter Hindle, Nick de Oude, Kees Lugtmeijer, Konrad Otto-Zimmermann, David Rehling, Sasha Kranendonk and all the other partners in EPE, Wouter van Dieren, Ashok Khosla, Walter Stahel and the Factor 10 Club, Maria Buitenkamp, Joachim Spangenberg, Nick Robins, Bob Ayres, Pat Delbridge, Louis Jourdan, Jacqueline Kramer, Ezio Manzini, Julia Hailes, the members of the Dow Environment, Health and Safety Councils and The Dow Corporate Environmental Advisory Panel and a few more colleagues at Dow who pioneer quality management systems and eco-innovation and have provided support for this project: Harry Spaas, Antonio Lorenzo, Bruno Krummenacher, Paolo Lucchini, Suzanne Kremeier, Alan Poole, Frank Mark and Peter Flückinger.

I remember the summer months of my early childhood in post-war Strasbourg. They brought out a fleet of small electric vans from the town Ice Works. The drivers picked the long logs of ice layered on jute bags and delivered them to the front doors. The housewives smashed them into smaller pieces to haul to their ice box. We kids would steal and suck on the shreds. It was a neat business. The river provided the water for the ice, moved the compressors of the ice machine and the turbine that recharged the vans' batteries.

But housewives tired of hauling the ice, draining the water from the box and depending every day on the ice man for cool and safe food. They got a refrigerator.

The Ice Works and the ice box business died in a few seasons. I wonder if either of them ever thought of moving into the refrigerator market.

Your business success depends on how well you serve your customers. But you do not know what these customers will need five or ten years from today. Is your competition designing a new offer that will solve a future problem? How could they see it while you and most of your customers are satisfied with a stable, efficient and profitable relationship?

The initiative is yours to take. You can anticipate the changes that will delight your customers, provoke your competition and return profits from your skills, your time and your capital. Change is fundamental to business success. It opens the opportunity to make the next right move. But it is risky too. You could make the wrong move or altogether miss your chance to move.

You will find in this book an approach to help increase your performance in new business development. And save time. How can it claim this? It looks at fundamental trends you may not see. Or you may be too busy now to stop and reflect as many of us are. Yet these trends will shake up your customers and your business during the next 30 years. Thirty years – this is well beyond your normal business planning cycle. But companies with normal planning cycles are easy prey for companies with vision. This is natural selection in the business realm.

The next 30 years will be fierce. We will live through demographic pressure like never before. Three billion more people. This is as much as in the last 45 years, a period rich in change and crisis. The information boundaries will continue to dissolve. There will be few physical obstacles to migration from rural areas towards cities and from poor countries towards rich countries. The pressure will be relentless. The issues of poverty, equity and security will erupt onto the corporate agenda.

This pressure will hit us while we are losing our innovation stamina. Technological progress is costly and slow. It continues to slow down. When did we last see a major breakthrough? Yes, information technologies and biotechnology are stunning exceptions. But remember that even DNA decoding, integrated circuits, lasers and fiber optics stem back to the 1950s and 1960s. Since then the change in our world has been in rapid incremental steps. But the refrigerator of today is not very different from the first model that pushed the old ice box out of my grandmother's kitchen. This model will not rust, the door seal will not dry out and crumble, the compressor does not stir the china, it's harmless for the stratospheric ozone shield, but it still wastes a lot of heat keeping our food fresh.

The yearly collections of designer clothes, watches, car models, home appliances may give an illusion of innovation. They are merely the battleground for the purchasing power of a minority in a saturated market. Product evolution and proliferation is not innovation.

This book is a tool to enable us to regain our innovation capacity.

I believe that we are facing extraordinary opportunities. The imperatives of quality of life and equity on a planet that gets more crowded by the day will bring them to the farsighted. The eco-innovation method is therefore aligned to the objectives of sustainable development. It integrates the long-term trends that will transform consumption, value creation and material processes. It helps you to see far and high. It allows you to reflect on how your customers' needs, your resource base may change in abrupt ways. It will point to the areas where your unique set of skills will find growth, and in particular value growth.

We are on a learning curve. The "nuts and bolts" of the eco-innovation approach are presented in various levels of detail for your own hands-on experiments. The book is packed with extensive case studies. They will stimulate ideas from the examples of other eco-innovators, who have decided that status quo is not an option and that value can be created on the way to sustainable development.

I know that the notion of sustainable development is not yet in day-to-day business language. But it continues to gain a share of the mind. I got many of the insights for this book from two networks: one is the European Partners for the Environment where environmental, business and policy experts explore together new avenues towards sustainability in Europe. The other is the World Business Council for Sustainable Development, a group of large transnational corporations. Since 1992 they have set themselves the goal of eco-efficiency. This is the simultaneous pursuit of environmental care and economic value creation.

Eco-efficiency now finds its place in the business agenda. I believe that it translates sustainable development at the operational level – provided that it is linked to radical goals of improvement. We expect here to create wealth with four- to ten-fold less resource intensity within a generation. A bold claim. Recent developments that prove best our innovation power still took 20 years or more from discovery to first market impact – from DNA de-coding to man-made insulin, transistors to integrated circuits, or lasers to optical compact disks.

You will quickly realize that without breakthrough improvement in mind, eco-efficiency would only be a new word for the optimization of current business practices. It would not bring you much – certainly not innovation and value.

It would ignore the other fundamental dimensions that confront us all at the beginning of the new millennium.

- the importance of social justice and equity in the interest of our common security and peace;

- the empowerment of individuals to fit their personal development scenario to the global needs of sustainability;

- the thrill of leaving a legacy.

In Parts 4 and 5 you will find a compass and a map to eco-innovation.

The seas ahead will be rough. We will be more and more tossed among these three currents in business: short cuts in our traditional value chains, information intensity and environmental overload. Steering forth is imperative and possible. Those entrepreneurs who meet the turmoil with novel solutions will thrive. The best skippers win when the wind gets difficult.

Claude Fussler
14 April 1996

Part 1

LOSE OR WIN?

The business challenge of sustainable development

How will innovation happen over the coming decades and what will drive it?

Chapter 1 answers this by discussing the nature of innovation. New technologies tend to follow an "S" shaped performance curve. They start with a phase of trial and error. After many years of slow improvement they take off in a succession of breakthroughs. They finally slow down in a phase of incremental improvements. Many current technologies are stalled in this last phase. They will eventually be replaced by new ones still in the early stages of their curve. The successful companies of the next millennium will be those which recognize this now and make the transition in good time.

This recognition is not easy but Chapter 2 identifies three techniques which can be helpful – back casting, identifying key drivers and developing scenarios.

Three key drivers for the millennium will be demographics, environmental stress and changing patterns of value creation. They are discussed in Chapters 3 to 5.

Chapter 6 describes three possible scenarios all of which will require radical change by business.

In reading these chapters you will get:

- *an insight into why business is losing its innovation stamina and how this can create competitive advantage for those who have a long-term vision;*

- *a model of long-term technology development and adoption;*

- *methods for considering long-term trends;*

- *information about three key drivers which will determine the future – demographics, environmental stress and value creation.*

Chapter 1

The need for "super innovation" and the key role of eco-innovation

The world needs change and yet everything seems to stay the same.

It is June 1992. In the heat of Rio de Janeiro delegates gather for the "Earth Summit" – the United Nations Conference on Environment and Development (UNCED). They see a record number of heads of state for an international gathering, a unique mix of representatives, from diplomats to displaced peoples, and from environmental activists to executives of multinational companies. And they meet after months of unprecedented media and public discussion about the topic of the conference – sustainable development.

▶ SUSTAINABLE DEVELOPMENT – THE RIO BREAKTHROUGH?

The conference produces, or provides the venue for signing, three major initiatives:

- 'The *Rio Declaration on Environment and Development*. Its 27 principles define the rights and responsibilities of nations as they pursue human development and well-being.

- *Agenda 21*, a blueprint on how to make development socially, economically and environmentally sustainable.

- A statement of principles to guide the management, conservation and sustainable development of all types of forests, which are essential to economic development and the maintenance of all forms of life.[1]

Most governments also sign two international agreements negotiated in parallel to the summit process:

- The *Convention on Biological Diversity* which requires signatories to conserve living species and ensure equitable sharing of the benefits of biodiversity.

- The *United Nations Framework Convention on Climate Change*. This requires signatories to stabilize emissions of greenhouse gases to levels which will not destabilize global climate.

The initiatives represent compromise and so do not satisfy everyone. Many want more action, more quickly. But, as delegates head for their planes, almost all believe that a major step has been taken towards creating a greener and fairer world.

Rio's wishful thinking?

Four years later, their optimism can often appear as wishful thinking. True there has been some progress. The Montreal protocol is phasing out the chlorofluorinated hydrocarbons (CFCs) which damage the ozone layer. And many cities and rivers are becoming cleaner. True as well that the Climate Change Convention has been in force since March 1995 and is now ratified by more than 150 nations.

But the basic trends which led to Rio continue. Population is expanding and the world economy is growing. Consumption of land, energy and materials continues to increase as does output of wastes and potentially damaging substances such as carbon dioxide. These large-scale trends negate any local successes. We are, at best, merely running to remain stationary.

One problem is recession and job insecurity in many industrialized countries. Environmental care can seem a luxury in such conditions. And a spate of "contrarian" books and articles challenge the basic assumption of Rio – that the world is facing an unprecedented environmental and social threat.[2]

The contrarians attack what they see as sloppy thinking or extreme pessimism by environmentalists. But few contrarians doubt that population growth and economic expansion create environmental pressures which must be managed. The debate is usually about the means and urgency of action.

▶ INNOVATION LETHARGY

The sniping between environmentalists and contrarians conceals the real cause of our lack of progress. It is an "innovation lethargy." Sustainable development requires radical improvements in products and services. They must provide customer satisfaction with much lower levels of environmental impact. But in practice the established technologies and lifestyles which create unsustainable development still maintain their dominance. Take the case of the automobile: the symbol of high technology, affordable to a large section of the population, 35 million are produced yearly by a dozen large manufacturers. But how efficient is it?

Cars are inefficient ...

The Swiss do not themselves manufacture cars and drive a broad cross section of imports. The Touring Club monitors the average energy efficiency of this fleet. It has improved by 18% in the past 21 years. Hardly impressive even if one takes into account more safety and comfort devices added regularly to the models and a shift to heavier and more powerful models. This is an example of technology lethargy. Average fuel efficiency is stuck, and stuck on very low.

Why do we need cars? To move around for leisure, to work, bring the kids to school and the shopping back home. Delivering this service is extremely inefficient. As Figure 1.1 shows, only 2% of the fuel energy you put into your car provides the final service of personal mobility while 75% is lost in waste heat (exhaust gases, radiation and cooling water). If we apportion the energy residual which actually provides momentum between the car and the average 1.5 individuals it carries (on the basis of mass) we arrive at the figure of 2%. The remainder is expended on moving the weight of the vehicle and running its engine.

● **FIGURE 1.1**
Car energy efficiency

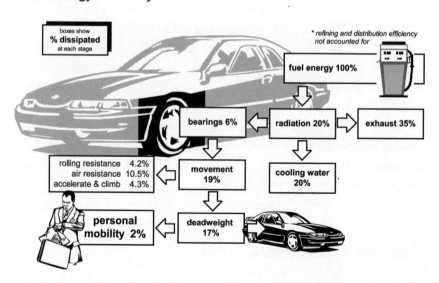

There are several ways to look at this. With all its technological might the car industry has not yet produced the fuel efficiency breakthrough. But high fuel efficiency mobility systems are a sure opportunity in the long run. The most obvious paths are low weight-high occupancy systems. The breakthroughs then will be in designs that fit personal behavior and use smart structural materials.

And so are buildings ...

Buildings are still built to traditional designs using traditional materials. As a result, there are only slow rates of improvement in their energy efficiency. And continuing environmental impacts from their construction and operation.

Barry Commoner observes that, since the fall in real energy prices in the early-mid 1980s, "there has been little or no further improvement in residential or industrial energy efficiency in the United States." He contrasts this with studies by the American Physical Society which demonstrate the potential for a ten-fold improvement in residential energy efficiency.[3]

> *There are only slow rates of improvement in the energy efficiency, material requirements and environmental impacts of established technologies.*

Most domestic processes are inefficient

In a 1989 study, Robert Ayres looked at energy efficiency for the major end uses in the USA.[4] He challenged the conventional wisdom that energy should just correlate with GNP growth. Major conservation efforts can completely decouple GNP and energy. With a study of the American Physical Society he established the following service efficiencies:

Air cooling	0.7 to 5% depending on design of the building
Cooking and hot water	0.3 to 3%
Lighting	0.7% – when poor use efficiency is accounted for 7.0% – electricity to light in perfect use conditions
Residence	0.4%

Every key end use is stuck at the bottom of the scale. Its performance is a compound of incremental technology development and dumb functionality. Our systems light empty rooms, heat open windows and consumers seem not to mind. In every category there are leading models that significantly beat the average and make the case histories and technical news. Whether the business designs to deliver to market or the technical reliability or the costs to use them are a hindrance, they do not really affect overall consumption yet. Breakthroughs are needed.

And many new products create problems

Even products or technologies which offer substantial improvements in environmental performance in one dimension can create problems in others. Mobile phones, for example, require much less energy and fewer materials than land communications. But there are toxic materials in their batteries. And the more successful a product is, the more that improvements in the performance of an individual unit can be offset by an overall increase in demand.

Energy consumption shows this effect. The energy needed to generate one dollar of world GDP has declined by about 1% per annum. This trend should continue. So we are becoming more energy efficient. However, this is more than offset by the effects of population push and GDP growth. The International Energy Agency forecasts that absolute world energy consumption will increase by 2.1% a year to 2010.[5] This will mean a 50% increase in carbon dioxide emissions over the 1990 levels, even though scientific opinion and international treaty obligations require a stabilization or fall in these emissions. Breakthroughs in energy efficiency and fossil fuel substitution are urgent.

A general innovation lethargy?

Innovation lethargy is not just an environmental issue. Outside the special case of information technology, much of business relies on incremental improvement rather than fundamentally new product development. Business strategist Gary Hamel has spoken of "corporate anorexia." He sees that years of cost cutting and reengineering undermine the vision and the will to develop new products and build new markets. There are many causes of this. In the West there is risk aversion caused by regulation and strict liability regimes. Growing development costs can be afforded by only a few players. Ageing workforces and job insecurity erode creativity. Another factor in many Asian – and some European countries – is low investment in fundamental research and development.

Radical innovation will happen

Don't be deceived: our innovation lethargy will end. Research into technical change by Eric Elias, James Utterback and others shows that phases of incremental improvement normally alternate with radical innovation.[6] The US National Science and Technology Council on the business opportunities of sustainable development summarizes it in this way:

> The technology landscape is characterized by incremental changes in products and processes punctuated by breakthroughs that radically alter our lives. Continual competition between "new" and "old" approaches shapes this technological terrain. This landscape cannot be understood, navigated, or managed effectively with short-sighted policies. The long view is absolutely necessary

because technologies can take years or decades to travel from initial idea to commercially viable products.[7]

> *"The long view is absolutely necessary because technologies can take years or decades to travel from initial idea to commercially viable products"*

▶ THE S-CURVE

Almost all technologies follow a characteristic pattern:

- a first phase of trial and error, which can take several decades;

- a second phase of rapid improvement, with multiple breakthroughs;

- a final, mature phase of incremental improvement and consolidation.

Graphing this gives a characteristic shape – the "S-curve." Figure 1.2 shows the S-curves for two different forms of lighting, incandescent lamps and fluorescent lamps.

It shows too how a new technology can create a step improvement in performance. Fluorescent lamps had reliability and other teething troubles in their early days. But their energy efficiency soon made them the most cost-effective means of high intensity lighting. The softer light of incandescent lamps gives them a role in home lighting but they now occupy only one niche in the overall market.

As with incandescent lamps, most mature technologies will die or shrink into a niche. Newer technologies at the beginning of their S-curve will replace them. But this can be a slow process. Often, an apparently mature technology has a final burst of performance improvement as an emerging technology introduces competitive pressure. The heyday of sailing ships occurred with the "China

● **FIGURE 1.2**
The lighting S-curve

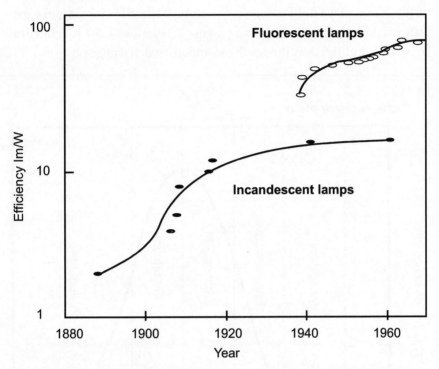

Source: Betz. F. Strategic Technology Management: McGaw-Hill: New York, 1993: Engineering and Technology Management Series

Clippers" of the late nineteenth century. This was several decades after the first steam ships. The innovation burst produced beautiful boats which sailed, literally, like the wind. But it merely slowed rather than prevented their replacement by steamships.

Building markets is also slow

Technologies cannot move up the S-curve if there is no demand for the products which incorporate them. The "adoption curve" – which measures the percentage of potential customers adopting new technologies and products – is similarly "S"-shaped. There is often a lag with radical performance improvements. Innovators are always in search of the new but they are only a small proportion of the population. Others are more wary and take time to familiarize themselves with things they could not even dream of. Take off comes when early adopters are ready to try things, and accelerates as it reaches the majority. Figure 1.3 estimates the number in each category.

● **FIGURE 1.3**
   Patterns of adoption

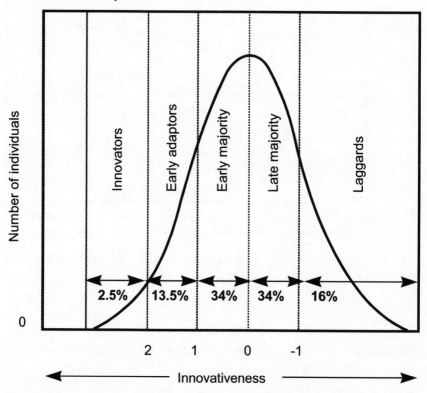

Source: Midgely, D. New Products Marketing; Halsted Press: New York, 1977

   Putting the performance S-curve and the demand S-curve together creates the pattern shown in Figure 1.4. The first stage is one of rapid experimentation resulting in many designs. Obsessive entrepreneurs will be figuring out how an uncertain technical potential can connect with unformed customer needs. Their counterparts are the early adopters, seeking the newest, most advanced innovations.

● **FIGURE 1.4**

The S-curve – innovation and adoption

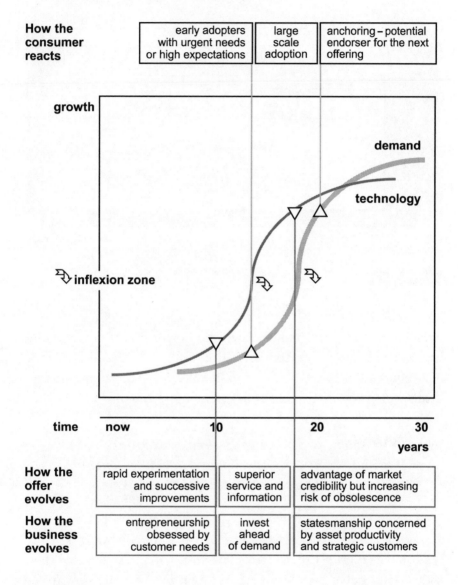

The need to create both effective technology and consumer demand means that all innovation is difficult and time consuming. It can be especially so for "super innovations" – the technologies which reshape economic and social possibilities by

● **FIGURE 1.5**

The technology development timetable

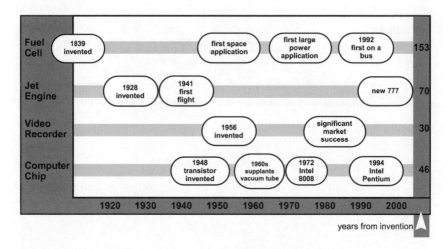

Sources: A Bridge to a Sustainable Future, US National Science and Technology Council; Bill Gates, *The Road Ahead*. Viking, 1996

creating a new performance curve and new forms of demand. For them, the period between invention and widespread use – the first plateau of the S-curve – can be decades. The jet engine and transistors provide two examples (see Figure 1.5).

> *The jet engine was invented in 1928, took its first flight in 1941 and was only widely deployed in military aircraft during the 1950s and civil aircraft in the 1960s*

Computer chips are singled out as the example of dynamic innovation (see Figure 1.6). Moore's law stated that they double their power and halve their size every 18 months. They are now in the vertical part of the S-curve and will change our world. But it took 25 years from the discovery of the transistor to the first real integrated circuit, the Intel 8008 microprocessor.

● **FIGURE 1.6**
Computer chips

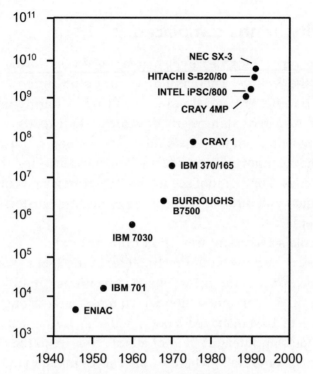

Source: Vaclav Smil, Energy in World History, Boulder, Co: Westview, 1994, p.204

Fast growth creates an industry paradigm

The rapid growth section of the S-curve comes with large scale adoption. Economies of scale become possible and competition more intense. The typical result is concentration into a few companies – General Electric, Pratt and Whitney and Rolls Royce in the case of jet engines. These achieve ever greater focus of their technical and managerial skills on continuous improvement in performance, reduced costs and better service. They invest massively ahead of demand to maintain and strengthen market dominance. The result is ever tighter linkages between them-

15

selves, "strategic" customers and suppliers, and a shared industry culture about the right way to do things.

Maturity brings complacency

Yet these very strengths can be a great weakness during the final stage of the S-curve. There is a drive for optimization within the narrow parameters of a dominant culture. A tightly knit inner circle of industry "statesmen" develops. Their focus is on asset productivity and strategic customers. The result is technical blindness. They cannot see the risks of obsolescence for their core technologies. They cannot see the early warning signs of innovations which will offer superior ways of meeting customer needs and so replace them.

Motorola's successful transition from AM radio to FM radio in mid century and to cellular technology in the 1980s is an exception which proves the rule. Few organizations can build a new business around an innovation which makes an existing technology obsolete. IBM managed it once, with a shift from tabulators to mainframe computers. It did not adapt so easily to the challenge of personal computers, where Apple and Compaq made the running and Intel and Microsoft captured the value.

▶ SURFING THE S-CURVE

The points where the S-curves change direction, points of inflexion, are the signposts for alert business (see Figure 1.7). The successful "surfers of the S-curves" will be those who are ready to respond to such signposts. But change of pace is difficult to detect in the here and now. Surfers will follow the maxim: move before you have to. Replace current products ahead of the competitors, with new ones which address fundamental long-term needs.

Those who wait for clear signals of the senescence of a technology will be too late. One lesson from technological history is that

● **FIGURE 1.7**
Surfing the S-curves

desired competitive innovation scenario

•*address the fundamental long term needs*
•*reinvent the winners before they slow down*
•*replace them before competition does*

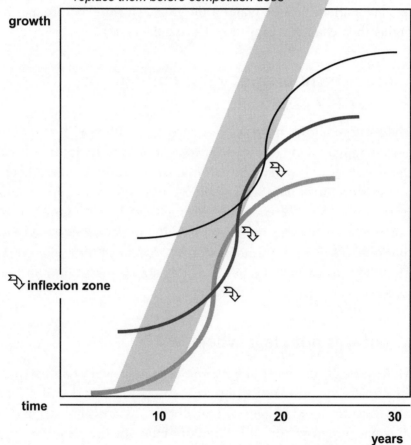

it is indeed hard to spot inflexions as they happen. Who in the mid 1980s would have predicted the rapid phase out of CFCs? Although the environmental storm clouds were building, the products were profitable and widely used and appreciated. Yet within a decade their legal uses in the industrialized world are a few niches where no substitutes exist.

Because of the slow incubation of radical new ideas successful innovators must have an inventory of options available to seize the opportunity provided by turning points. Such options can only succeed when inspired by a long-term view of future customer needs and problems. The better they solve such needs and problems the less innovations need to wait for the elusive turning points and the higher their chance to prevail and shape the market.

Current technologies will eventually be superseded ...

The S-curve allows us to see our current position with regard to sustainability. Many of our current technologies are in their final, mature stage. All will eventually be superseded by newer technologies on the initial stages of the S-curve. When it happens, this transition can be a rapid one. The converse is that mature technologies which seem well established can suddenly lose their markets. IBM's mainframe business seemed set for exponential growth in the early 1980s but had stalled and moved into decline within a few years.

... But it is not clear when

That is the good news. The bad news from a sustainability perspective is that innovation lethargy can persist for decades. The transition from old to new will never be automatic. It is driven by the energy and vision of innovators who see the potential and make it happen. Today's innovators have the opportunity to force the pace of sustainable development. If it is taken, the transition to technologies offering better business and environmental performance could happen over the next ten to twenty years. If it is not, the shift will be slow and painful.

Business as usual ... or radical innovation?

So there is an act of faith about radical innovation. Of course, it is always worth studying customer needs and industry trends as long as you understand they will seldom give a complete picture. But in today's circumstances you face two choices: keep on with business as usual, make the best of assets and react to new trends as they become irresistible: or anticipate the changes and embrace a strategy of innovation and entrepreneurship to outsmart competitors stuck in the business-as-usual mindset.

> *There are two choices. Business as usual or embracing a strategy of innovation and entrepreneurship to outsmart competitors.*

▶ SUCCESS REQUIRES LONG-TERM VISION

The business literature sings the praises of companies which anticipate events. But how do they do it?

They combine a consistent long-term sense of direction with a culture of continuous change and improvement. This is how they win over competitors who believe they can react in increments to the rising tide but who lack a long-term perspective and lose their grip on events that accelerate away from them.

One differentiator between radical and business-as-usual approaches is the willingness to cannibalize successful product ranges with new ones. In the short term this can limit sales. But in the longer term it maintains technological and market leadership, provides multiple options and fosters a culture of energy and innovation.

Joseph Morone shows this in his book, *Winning in High-Tech Markets*. He studied Corning, GE Medical Systems and Motorola, three of the small number of US companies which have been successful in international hi-tech markets. His conclusion is unequivocal:

> These businesses built and renewed, and continue to build and renew, their competitive advantage through radical and generational innovations. They sustained that advantage over time through more incremental product line improvements and extensions, but it is on the basis of the riskier, failure-laden, expensive, and time-consuming efforts to pioneer new businesses and new generations of technology that their competitive advantage was and still is established.[8]

Taking a strategic approach

He also contrasts their long-term, strategic focus with a short-term, entirely financially driven approach. He maintains that:

> Financial considerations are constraints on general management decision making rather than its determinants. In every case, once a course of action is deemed strategically necessary or desirable, financial considerations determine the pace and approach, and they are the ultimate measures of performance. But the decisions about whether to set out on or to continue the course of action are shaped by strategic considerations. For any major potential investment, the driving question is: "Given that we are committed to this area of business, what steps must we take to stay ahead?" rather than, 'Given that we must achieve a certain rate of return from our investments, is this a wise investment?"[9]

But there is another driving question for companies that want to succeed in the longer term. We suggest that much of their business will be shaped by the aspiration for sustainable development. The irresistible forces of population growth and consumer aspirations are meeting the fragility of our planetary systems and resources. The only solution is radical shifts in values, technologies and patterns of consumption and production. This will mean the "sunset" of unsustainable products and processes. It will also create boundless opportunities for the entrepreneurs who can match cost-effective capabilities with the needs for cleaner products and processes.

Another driving question – make products and processes sustainable

Leading thinkers on sustainable development believe that these cleaner products and processes must better the resource and environmental impacts of existing ones by a "factor of ten." Take this as a working assumption. The business opportunity is to do this in ways which improve rather than diminish customer service and satisfaction. Hence the new driving question is:

> *Given the need for sustainable development, how can we change our products and processes to enhance customer service while radically reducing environmental impacts and improving quality of life?*

Notes

1 Keating, M. *The Earth Summit's Agenda for Change.* Geneva: Centre for Our Common Future, 1993, p.viii.

2 Hagan, M. "Enter the Contrarians," *Tomorrow*, Oct–Dec 1993, pp. 10-23.

3 Commoner, B. "Making Things Work Better," in Scientific American, *Triumph of Discovery.* New York: Henry Holt, 1995, p.77.

4 Ayres, R. *Energy Inefficiency in the US Economy: A New Case for Conservation.* Laxenburg, Austria: International Institute for Applied Systems Analysis, 1989.

5 International Energy Agency *World Energy Outlook.* Paris, 1995.

6 Elias, E. *Innovation and Obsolescence.* Menlo Park: SRI International, 1995. Utterback, J. *Mastering The Dynamics of Innovation.* Boston, Mass: Harvard Business School Press, 1994. This chapter makes considerable use of their ideas and insights.

7 National Science and Technology Council *Technology for a Sustainable Future.* Washington DC, 1994.

8 Morone, J. *Winning in High-Tech Markets.* Boston, Mass. Harvard Business School Press, 1993, p.217.

9 Morone *op cit.*, p.221.

Chapter 2

Thinking about the future

S till not convinced? We will soon tell you more about the drivers of these changes. You are excited by the potential of a breakthrough innovation but still want information on how it will fit with long-term business trends? You are convinced but uncertain about how to "surf the S-curves" and develop new sustainable technologies while maintaining an existing business? Let us look at what drives change. Let us look as well at techniques that integrate rapid changes into your business development game.

▶ ENVISAGING THE END GAME

No-one can predict the future but futurologists and forecasters have their methods for gaining insight. How can we achieve this insight? By borrowing from chess, according to Peter Winsemius. This former Dutch Environment Minister is now a partner at McKinsey & Co. advising many top management teams on sustainability issues and business strategies. He counsels . . .

> First, set a direction and an aspiration level, and then tailor actions accordingly. The grand masters of chess, when presented with a complex board position, search for patterns which allow them to envisage the best possible end-game. Working their way backward from this mental model of what the future could be, they choose the

most appropriate move that takes them one step closer to realising the ideal end game.[1]

In some cases such "back casting" can be relatively straightforward. Microprocessor suppliers have simply extrapolated past improvements in chip performance into the future to provide the "end game" of a performance target. They then use this to guide their research and development decisions. But setting a direction through complex changes with 30 year time scales is more difficult.

Winsemius gives examples of how an end game perspective can translate into short-medium strategies in an organization . . .

> If the anticipated global warming measures pose a serious threat to a company, top management could define medium-term change objectives that include a stabilization of the CO_2 emissions of a corporation's processes and products by a given year. Similarly, if a mandatory chlorine cutback looks likely, top management could decide to phase out PVC in short life cycle applications such as packaging materials. Waste disposal pressures might produce a practical objective of a 90 percent reduction in a company's total process and product waste. [2]

The ultimate end game: sustainability

The concept of sustainability should provide a long-term mental model of what the future will be like. Back casting from it can therefore illuminate the pathways which business should, and will ultimately be compelled to, follow. Part 3 analyzes the business implications of sustainable development in greater detail.

▶ IDENTIFY DRIVERS AND BUILD SCENARIOS

Futurologist Peter Schwartz suggests two further approaches to thinking about the future:

- identify and understand a few key drivers which will be of critical importance

- then use alternative trends in these drivers to construct two or three scenarios of the future.

At the very least one is prepared for, and can therefore react quickly, to a range of contingencies. And any elements they have in common have a high probability of occurring.

Three drivers: demographics, environmental stress, value creation

The following chapters discuss three key drivers of, or constraints on, sustainable business development:

- *demographics* – population growth and structure and its socio-economic implications

- *environmental stress* and the limits it might impose on human activities

- changing modes of *value creation* by business.

Scenarios help decision making

First a little more on scenarios. Peter Schwartz believes these . . .

> are a tool for helping us to take a long view in a world of great uncertainty. The name comes from the theatrical term "scenario" – the script for a film or play. Scenarios are stories about the way the world might turn out tomorrow, stories that can help us recognize and adapt to changing aspects of our present environment. They form a method for articulating the different pathways that might exist for you tomorrow, and finding your appropriate movements down each of those possible paths. Scenario planning is about making choices *today* with an understanding of how they might turn out.[3]

Schwartz learnt his trade while working for Shell. The company is well-known for its scenario building. It uses them to consider possible trends in energy production and prices and the factors which will influence them. The box describes a less well known, but arguably even more successful, example of scenario utilization in South Africa.

● SCENARIO PLANNING FOR A NEW SOUTH AFRICA

The Anglo-American Corporation dominates South Africa's economy. In the early 1980s it became concerned about growing unrest in the country. Opposition to the apartheid regime was mounting and becoming more violent. This was a threat to Anglo's business interests.

In 1984 it developed scenarios of two possible South African futures – the high road and the low road. Both scenarios assumed that South Africa would be under growing international pressure to scrap apartheid and that unrest would continue until it happened. They also assumed that whites would not "unconditionally surrender".

The high road scenario envisaged accommodation between blacks and whites, with power sharing, federalization and greater spending on black people's education and welfare. This virtuous circle would lead to higher living standards. In the low road scenario compromise proved impossible. It saw a continuation of violence even after the formal abolition of apartheid. This vicious circle would damage the economy, creating falls in living standards and continued discontent.

Does the high road sound familiar? It is more or less the story of the last decade. But there have always been plenty of temporary or local lurches towards the low road to remind everyone how easy it would be to stumble down it.

Many believe that the Anglo scenarios played a major role in South Africa's democratic transition. According to Paul Schoemaker:

> They were powerful means of shaping the debate and influencing the agenda for political action in South Africa. Anglo apparently recognized, after examining the various scenarios, that its future would be very bleak under the low road scenario. Consequently, executives decided to share their views and insights (via lectures, a video, and a book) in an effort to embark on the high road. The Anglo scenarios had much impact in South Africa and continue to frame internal debates.[4]

Anglo's recognition means that its business remains intact in the new South Africa. It has sufficient good will among black leaders to neutralize radicals' criticism of its power. Its willingness to think long term, and back cast from it has paid off.

Avoid mental blind spots

The central message of scenario planning is to avoid mental blind spots. These develop when prejudice or arrogance lead to an excessive confidence in stability and the continuation of present trends. Business then relies on a single line forecast and it is usually complacent and optimistic. The discovery of the ozone layer shows how easily such mental blind spots can occur. The Nimbus-7 satellite which was monitoring atmospheric conditions sent back data about falling ozone levels after 1978. But the computer analyzing it was programed to ignore low readings as being "rogue data," impossible by definition. It all went into an electronic waste bin until 1985, when other measurements in the Antarctic revealed the problem.

It is easy today to have a similar blind spot about sustainability. The world goes on, media interest has waned. And most politicians are more concerned about jobs and goods in the shops than problems of environmental degradation or social inequity.

But do not treat evidence that these problems are worsening as "rogue data." Sooner or later they will affect you. The next two chapters examine how.

Notes

1 Winsemius, P. and Guntram, U. *Towards a Top Management Agenda for Environmental Changes*. Amsterdam: McKinsey & Company, 1994, pp. 9-10.

2 Winsemius *op cit.*, p. 12.

3 Schwartz, P. *The Art of the Long View*. New York: Doubleday, 1991, pp. 3-4.

4 Shoemaker, P. "Scenario Planning: A Tool for Strategic Thinking," *Sloan Management Review*, Winter 1995, p. 36.

Chapter 3

The three key drivers I: Demographics

▶ POPULATION GROWS INEXORABLY

The future of the world is being created in unexpected places: the pulsating backstreets of Canton and Shanghai, the ever-expanding suburbs and shanty towns of Mexico City and Sao Paulo, the burgeoning hi-tech centre of Bangalore. It is in these cities, and the countries and continents of which they form part, that population growth is greatest and the hunger for prosperity the most compelling.

This population growth and prosperity hunger is hard-wired into the next century. There will be more people with most of them seeking higher standards of living. The only questions are how great the population increase will be and how future generations will define prosperity.

Unprecedented population increases

Population data are difficult to obtain and sometimes unreliable.[1] But the general trend is clear. Human population is increasing at an unprecedented rate.[2] World population in 1750 was around 1 billion. It took under two centuries for a second billion to be added, by around 1930. The third billion arrived between about

1930 and 1960, the fourth from 1960 to 1980. The fifth was more or less added in the 1980s. Current world population is around 5.7 billion. The sixth billion will have arrived in under a decade.

In 1994 alone world population increased by 88 million people. This is a greater number than live in Germany and five times the population of Taiwan.

The rate of growth is slowing. The 1994 increase of around 1.5% compares to the 2.2% increase in the most fertile year of all, 1964. The evidence is that the rate of increase will edge downwards. But only slowly, so that overall population will still increase for many decades.

A 50% increase in the next 30 years

The most quoted forecasts are those prepared by the United Nations (see Figure 3.1). Its median forecast is that world population will almost double from the present 5.7 billion to around 8.5 billion in 2025. The growth will be the equivalent of six Europes. In this median scenario, the numbers on the planet will grow further until the end of the twenty first century. Even the "low growth" projection envisages that there will several billion more people on the planet in coming decades.

The UN's median estimate of world population is that it will increase from the current 5.7 billion to around 8.5 billion in 2025.

Birth control makes little immediate difference

Are you puzzled by these projections? Are birth rates not falling in most countries? Do not the Chinese say that every couple may have only one child? If so, will population level off sooner rather than later? We often get asked these questions, and always give the same three answers.

Birth rates are indeed falling, but still remain high in many large countries such as India and Nigeria.

What is falling even more quickly is mortality, particularly among children. Between 1950 and 1992 average life expectancy in the industrialized world rose by nine years, from 66 to 75. In the developing world, the increase was 22 years, from 40 to 62. The main cause was a surge in survival of children but all ages have benefitted from health improvements. Compared to any other period in history we are a world of Methuselahs. Jeanne Calment has just released a CD of music and wise words at the age of 121 and there still seems plenty of scope for the lessons of the longest lived in countries such as Japan to be applied elsewhere.

High fertility and falling infant mortality over recent decades create populations with a high proportion of fertile teenagers and young adults. Most of these want and have children. These children can expect that their parents and even some of their grandparents will be alive for many years, and witness the births of their children's children. So overall population will continue to grow for many decades after a bulge of young people. Even in China where the birth rate is now lower than in the USA this demographic momentum will increase the population from 1.2 billion now to 1.4 billion in 2010.[3] The fact that so many generations are alive at once also creates high demand for housing, infrastructure and essential amenities.

The world becomes more African, Asian, Hispanic ... and urban

Maps of the world look very different when country size is based on population rather than area (see Figure 3.1). Asia, Africa and Latin America are the dominant continents and China and India the leading countries. Europe is a small appendage whose proportion of world population is constantly shrinking.

By 2025 the European Union will account for only 7% of world population – about the same as West Africa or East Africa.

● FIGURE 3.1

World population: the shape of things to come

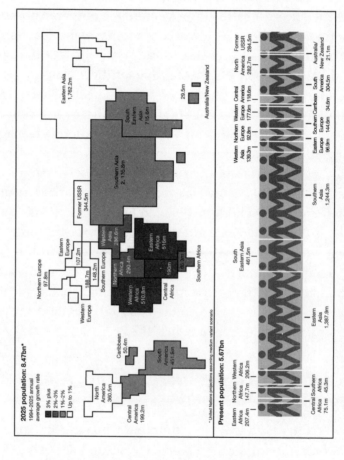

2025 population: 8.47bn*

1994–2025 annual
average growth rate

■ 3% plus
■ 2%–3%
▨ 1%–2%
□ Up to 1%

* United Nations projections assuming medium variant scenario

Present population: 5.67bn

Source: United Nations Population Fund (taken from the *Financial Times* 30 September 1994)

Jingxin, China, Teapa, Mexico. Reni, India. Never heard of these towns? Nor had we until we found them in an atlas. They are individually insignificant except to those who call them home. But it is in the tens of thousands of small towns and villages like them that most of the world's new inhabitants will be born – to run. Whether as children moving with parents, or teenagers and young adults seeking a new destiny, the majority will move to new homes.

Most will migrate to towns and cities. In 1950 one in every three people lived in an urban area. Now it is almost one in two. By 2025, the UN predicts, it will be nearer to two out of every three individuals. A large proportion of these will be in large cities of over a million people. Providing transport, waste disposal and other infrastructure for such cities, and preventing illness from disease and pollution, will be one of the most difficult challenges of sustainable development.

The pressure of migration

In the past, high population growth and poverty has created long distance migration. Some have moved to richer countries. Others have colonized frontier regions. Both these trends will continue and probably intensify.

Legal immigration into the USA is already at similar levels to the peak years of the "melting pot" in the early twentieth century. It exceeds them when illegal immigrants are taken into account. One result is that white Caucasians and Afro-Americans will be in a minority at the start of the next century. Hispanic and Asian Americans will be the majority.

There are similar numbers of aspiring entrants to other prosperous areas of the world. According to the World Resources Institute:

Given relative population growth rates and incomes, migration pressure appears likely to be strong from North Africa into southern Europe, from Latin America into the United States, from East and Southeast Asia into North America and possibly Japan, and from the southern tier of former Soviet republics into Russia. [4]

Most of these regions have graying populations and could make good use of young, energetic, individuals. But large scale immigration usually creates social tension. Especially when it is of the desperate and destitute rather than the optimistic and skilled.

But no more new frontiers ...

The other traditional safety valve for population growth is migration to frontier regions. Agricultural land can be created there by cutting down forests or draining wetlands. The pace of this has increased rather than diminished with time. There was a greater expansion of cropland between 1950 and 1980 than in the century and a half preceding 1850.[5] Almost everywhere, the best land is now in use. That which remains unused is usually fragile, such as hillsides, prone to soil erosion, or tropical forests whose soils initially give high yields but are soon stripped of nutrients. Bringing these into cultivation reduces biodiversity for no real agricultural gain.

▶ PROSPERITY HUNGER

Population growth is not necessarily bad. More people mean more creativity and a greater collective intelligence to apply to environmental and other problems. But every new person on the planet is an additional demand on resources and an additional source of environmental impact. The higher their economic aspirations, the greater this resource demand and impact will be.

As China's experience demonstrates, the developing world wants more prosperity. Even in the industrialized world, political debate focusses on how we can restore or increase economic growth.

> *"The prospect of one fifth of humanity suddenly entering the consumer age will force industrial countries ... to face up to the unsustainability of their current practices"*
> *Megan Ryan and Christopher Flavin on China [6]*

● CHINA: A MIDDLE WAY FOR THE MIDDLE KINGDOM?

In any scenario, China is the key to sustainable development.[7] Its 1.2 billion people comprise almost a quarter of the world total. And by 2025 there will be around 1.5 billion individuals living in the country.

Over the last fifteen years the Chinese economy has grown by over 8% in every single year. Its economy doubles in size every eight years. Even in 1992 83% of urban households had washing machines, 75% color televisions and 52% refrigerators. According to the World Bank, greater China (including Hong Kong and Taiwan) will overtake the USA as the world's largest economy early in the next century.

The resource requirements and environmental impacts created by this combination of large population and rapid growth are colossal – and becoming ever more so.

At present rates, energy consumption will double and grain consumption rise 50% by 2015. These requirements must be met from a resource–poor country. China has only 7% of the world's cropland and fresh water and 2–3% of its forests and oil reserves. Economic growth is turning it into an importer of food and raw materials. Its demographic pressure will be felt in all world markets.

Air quality and water quality are also declining. China now accounts for 16% of global man-made sulphur emissions and 11% of carbon dioxide. Within a few years it will overtake the USA as the leading contributor to many global environmental problems.

Chinese scientists and policy–makers are beginning to see ecological and resource security as the major constraint on China's economic growth. Megan Ryan and Christopher Flavin summarize the crossroads which China is at:

> The country which invented paper and gunpowder may now have the opportunity to leapfrog the West and show it the way to a sustainable economy. If it succeeds, China could become a shining example for the rest of the world to admire and emulate. If it fails, we will all pay the price.[8]

The problem arises if everyone aspires to the material and energy intensive lifestyles of the most affluent billion on the planet. If China moved to US levels of car ownership and utilization, around 20% of its cultivated land would go for roads and parking space.

Global inequality

In 1991 the world's richest 20% had 61 times the income of the poorest 20% – compared to a multiple of "only" 30 in 1960.[9] Per capita incomes in Africa actually fell during the 1980s. Figure 3.2 illustrates the extent of these inequalities. Many cities and countries have a similar profile.

All over the world the well off are consuming, surfing the Internet and generally enjoying rich, "Northern", lifestyles. Down the road are millions without jobs and in grinding poverty. Of course the poor have always been with us but now there is a major difference. They know more about the world and their place within it than in the past. They can watch the same TV programs as the rich and aspire to the same lifestyles. And if their hopes are thwarted then there is likely to be massive social unrest and large scale migration to better-off nations.

The ordinary workers of the population rich countries will be serving the North's growing appetite for the products their low wages make possible. And making European, Japanese and North American workers more insecure as a result. They and their children will be better educated and in better health than in the past. The result? The ambition and the capacity to change the established economic and political order.

▶ THE GLOBAL TEENAGER

Geologically, the earth is aging. Demographically, most of its nations are becoming younger. Almost half of the world's popula-

● **FIGURE 3.2**
  Hourglass

Distribution of economic activity, 1989–percentage of world total
(Quintiles of population ranked by income)

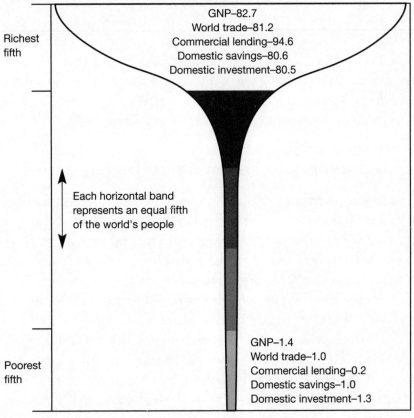

Source: United Nations Development Programme, *Human Development Report 1992*, Oxford University Press, 1992

tion is now under the age of 20. In Egypt 42% of its 60 million citizens are under 15.

In general, these youngsters are better educated than any comparable generation in history. Three quarters receive primary education. Just under half go to secondary school. Not sufficient by any means. But still enough to give the world a greater stock of human capital and a greater potential for frustration and discontent if their raised expectations are not met.

Two billion teenagers

This is especially true of a new demographic phenomenon – the global teenager. The teenage population is growing rapidly in most regions except western Europe and Japan. By the year 2000 there will be two billion of them. Their energy and hormones create the usual adolescent mix of curiosity, vitality and sense of rebellion. Futurologist Peter Schwartz predicts that they will have a similarly transforming effect on world culture – and the nations in Africa, Asia and Latin America – as their forebears had on European and American culture in the 1950s and 1960s.

Gray panthers and Asian tigers: friends or foes?

The global teenager is generally concerned about sustainability. But, for all the surface differences, they also share their parents' desire for better lives. Their youthfulness and exuberance contrasts with the graying societies and values of the industrialized world, particularly Europe. Its aging populations are becoming ever more concerned with financing pensions and health care and making a world fit for comfortable retirement.

These trends are problematic and potentially destabilizing for the rich North and its present way of life. Sustainability advocates argue that, even if growth in developing countries becomes much cleaner, it must be supported by considerable resource and pollution cuts in the North to preserve the planet's carrying capacity.

Friedrich Schmidt-Bleek of the Wuppertal Institute argues that sustainability requires a halving of current energy and material flows (see Figure 3.3). To make room for the aspirations of the developing world, he believes that industrialized countries need to dematerialize their economic processes by 90% to achieve a "factor 10" improvement.[10]

The following chapter examines the environmental stress which will occur if radical changes are not made.

● FIGURE 3.3
The Factor 10 challenge

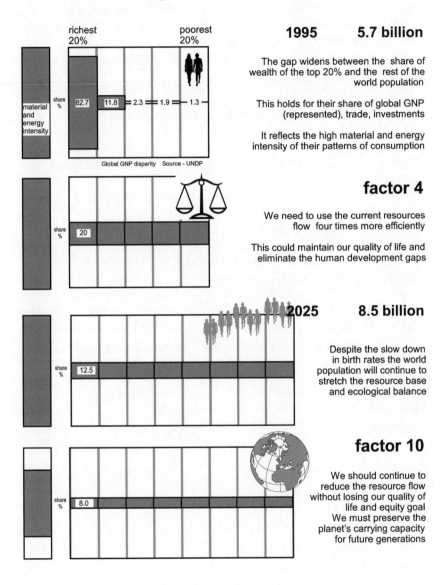

1995   **5.7 billion**

The gap widens between the share of wealth of the top 20% and the rest of the world population

This holds for their share of global GNP (represented), trade, investments

It reflects the high material and energy intensity of their patterns of consumption

richest 20%   poorest 20%

material and energy intensity

share %   82.7   11.8   2.3   1.9   1.3

Global GNP disparity   Source - UNDP

factor 4

We need to use the current resources flow four times more efficiently

This could maintain our quality of life and eliminate the human development gaps

share %   20

2025   **8.5 billion**

Despite the slow down in birth rates the world population will continue to stretch the resource base and ecological balance

share %   12.5

factor 10

We should continue to reduce the resource flow without losing our quality of life and equity goal
We must preserve the planet's carrying capacity for future generations

share %   8.0

Notes

1 Nicholas Eberstadt provides a useful discussion in "Population, Food and Income" in Bailey, R. *The True State of the Planet*. New York: Simon & Schuster, 1995. However, he does not challenge the basic proposition that population will grow considerably over coming decades.

2 This chapter is based on two sourcebooks about population and other environmental issues. One is Brown, L.; Lenssen N.; and Kane, H. *Vital Signs 1995: The Trends That Are Shaping Our Future*. New York: Norton/Worldwatch Institute, 1995. The second is World Resources Institute *World Resources 1994-95: A Guide to the Global Environment*. Oxford: Oxford University Press, 1994. Both are essential items for anyone interested in environmental and population issues.

3 Brown, L. *et al. State of the World 1995*. New York: Norton/Worldwatch Institute, p.115.

4 World Resources Institute *World Resources 1994-95*. Oxford: Oxford University Press, 1994, p.31.

5 Richards, J. "Land Transformation," in Turner, B., Clark, W., Kates, R. *et al.* (eds) *The Earth as Transformed by Human Action*. Cambridge: Cambridge University Press, 1990. Cited in World Resources Institute.

6 Ryan, M. and Flavin, C. "Facing China's Limits," in Lester Brown *et al. State of the World 1995*. New York: Norton/Worldwatch Institute, 1995, p.129.

7 Ryan. M. and Flavin, M. "Facing China's Limits," in Lester Brown *et al. State of the World 1995*. New York: Norton/Worldwatch Institute, 1995, p.131.

8 This discussion draws upon Ryan, M. and Flavin, C. "Facing China's Limits," in Lester Brown *et al. State of the World 1995*. New York: Norton/Worldwatch Institute, 1995.

9 United Nations Development Programme (UNDP) *Human Development Report 1994*. Oxford: Oxford University Press, 1994.

10 Schmidt-Bleek, F. *The Fossil Makers*. New York: Springer, forthcoming.

Chapter 4

The three key drivers II: Environmental stress

Some scientists and most environmentalists believe that even present levels of population and economic activity are unsustainable. Many more see projected rates of population and economic growth as too much for our planet. Even "contrarians", the environmental skeptics who believe that much environmental science is flawed and the scale of environmental problems exaggerated, generally concede that there are real issues to be addressed.

The contrarian counterattack against environmentalism is useful. It draws attention to the uncertainty attached to many environmental problems and the ways in which they can be exaggerated. It is vital that environmental debates – and the science they rest on – becomes more discriminating. Even so, the balance of scientific opinion is clear. A number of environmental issues are already serious and will "go critical" over coming decades if preventive action is not taken.

▶ WHAT ARE THE KEY ENVIRONMENTAL ISSUES?

There are many ways of classifying these environmental issues. The European Environmental Agency identifies eleven key themes:

- *climate change,* such as global warming
- *ozone depletion* in the upper atmosphere
- *acidification of soils and surface water* as a result of emissions of acid-forming gases such as sulphur dioxide and nitrogen oxides
- *air pollution and quality*
- *waste management*
- *urban issues* such as land use patterns, congestion and noise
- *inland water resources*
- *coastal zones and marine waters*
- *risk management* of potential accidents, incidents and natural disasters
- *soil quality*
- *nature and biodiversity.*[1]

The changing environmental agenda

Over time, public and policy attention shifts between these themes. In the 1950s attention focussed on the human health effects of industrial processes. Britain's 1956 Clean Air Act was a response to lethal air pollution. One notorious London "pea-souper" killed over 4000 people in a single December week. Unfortunately, the main solution was building higher chimneys to dilute combustion gases. This only turned the problem into acid rain in Scandinavia and upland Britain. Japan had its Minamata and other disasters involving heavy metal contamination of water supplies around the same period.

In the 1960s Rachel Carson extended the concern to ecosystems when she published *Silent Spring*, an account of wildlife damage by pesticides.

Club of Rome forecasts energy/resource crisis

The focus in the 1970s was depletion of energy and mineral resources. Their tone was set by *Limits to Growth*, a report published in 1972 by the Club of Rome. The Club brought together systems analysts, scientists and others to model future resource requirements. Their intention was to warn by creating a "worst case" scenario of the future. This predicted that many key resources would become more expensive as stocks were depleted.

In practice, the scenario was interpreted as a forecast. But there have been no shortages. So the report, and all concern about excessive resource consumption, became discredited. Indeed the real price of most resources fell in the 1980s. Look at the most economically critical resource, crude oil. Its real cost is no higher than in the 1960s. The high levels it reached after the Yom Kippur war and Iranian Revolution are now only a bad memory.

1980s: decade of disasters

In the 1980s attention switched to the health and ecological implications of core industrial activities: chemical manufacture, nuclear power generation. The debate was shaped by a series of disasters such as Three Mile Island, Seveso, Love Canal, Bhopal, Chernobyl, Schweizerhalle and the *Exxon Valdez*.

As the decade progressed, concern extended to the risks of climate and ecological changes caused by human activity. CFCs and stratospheric ozone depletion, extinctions and loss of biodiversity and global warming came into the mainstream.

Are there natural limits?

All these issues remain prominent in the 1990s. But leading environmental thinkers are linking them into an integrated analysis of the "natural limits" on human activity.

For some the real limit to growth is not pollution or energy resources. Rather, it is the earth's ability to provide the food, water and materials needed for basic sustenance. Lester Brown, president of the Washington-based Worldwatch Institute, believes that:

> Nature's limits are beginning to impose themselves on the human agenda, initially at the local level, but also at the global level. Some of these, such as the yield of ocean fisheries or spreading water scarcity, are near-term. Others, such as the limited capacity of the atmosphere to absorb excessive emissions of carbon without disrupting climate, will manifest themselves over the longer term.[2]

"Nature's limits are beginning to impose themselves on the human agenda" – Lester Brown

Is food the real limit?

Brown's main worry is food shortages. One indisputable fact is that world grain stocks are at their lowest level for decades – about 62 days' supply in 1995. He thinks three factors are slowing the growth of world food production:

- the decline of world fisheries
- water shortages
- diminishing returns from fertilizer application.

Malthusians have been wrong before

There are two possible criticisms of Brown's views.

1 They are old wine in a new bottle. The original vintner was Thomas Malthus. In 1798 he published his *Essay on Population*. This too argued that population growth was outstripping food resources. But the last two centuries defy his predictions. The area of cultivated land and its yield rose in line with population. Humanity has always been at the

edge of hunger and malnutrition. But there has only been local rather than global famine.

2 Any problems will be handled by market forces and technology. If marine fish becomes more expensive it can be farmed. Or people can substitute cheaper animal protein. Or become semi-vegetarian. If cereals cost more there is land being "set aside" because of low produce prices. We can cultivate this again. And genetic engineering can create less thirsty and pest-prone varieties of plant.

But Brown's points are more subtle. He is not crying doom but pointing out that present trends carry two dangers. The first is that a system near its limits is sensitive to disruption. A few major crop failures could cause widespread hunger and chaos in the world grain markets. Many people might die before market and technological reactions come into play.

The second danger is the corrosive effects of a world in which animal and fish protein – part of traditional culture in most areas of the world – is reserved only for the rich or for special occasions. There could be no more graphic illustration of global inequality, and nothing more likely to stir the fires of social discontent in poorer parts of the world. Brown's writings are not a cry of doom, they are more a plea for innovation to manage natural resources more efficiently and share them more equitably.

Are materials the limit?

Schmidt-Bleek also believes in natural limits. However, he stresses the unsustainability of material movements. By his calculation humanity moves double the mass shifted by geological forces at the earth's surface.

Less than 20% of all materials originally moved end up in products and infrastructure.

Why does this matter? Firstly, because the winning, movement and transforming of materials is the most important use of energy and the main generator of pollutants and wastes. Secondly, because the same processes are directly damaging to biodiversity. Schmidt-Bleek believes that:

> In Germany, some 70 tonnes of solid natural materials is put in motion annually per capita, without considering erosion, to create the kind of material welfare to which people are accustomed. In addition, more than 500 tonnes of water is moved per capita. If eight billion people copied what the advanced industrial nations are doing, a rapid ecological collapse would be the inescapable consequence.[3]

As with Brown, Schmidt-Bleek's purpose is not to be a Cassandra but to persuade governments and individuals to innovate to reduce material burdens. He estimates that a sustainable level of human-made materials movement is one which equals geological flows. This is about half of present levels. Equity requires that the developing world has a greater proportion of this flow than at present. The implication for the industrialized world? Reduce material flows (including those induced in the developing world to provide imports) by a factor of ten (see page 159). The implications for business? A tremendous innovation opportunity for processes, goods and services of low energy and material intensity.

▶ LIVING IN ECO-SPACE

Biologists have always had a concept of limits, which they call carrying capacity. This is the maximum population of a given species that can be supported indefinitely by a defined habitat. If exceeded, per capita resources decline and the population eventually crashes.

Eco-space is stocks of resources and sinks for wastes

The concept is very useful in managing game, wildlife or livestock at a local level. But it is much more difficult to apply to large, multi species, habitats. However, the concept has been adapted by scientists such as Horst Siebert and Hans Opschoor into one of "environmental utilization space" or "eco-space."[4]

The environment contains a "stock" of resources for us to exploit and "sinks" to absorb our wastes. Eco-space measures the sustainable "carrying capacity" of these stocks and sinks. Are resources only partially exploited or sinks only partly used? Then eco-space is considerable and need not constrain human activities. Are resources fully exploited and sinks unable to absorb more wastes without being degraded? If so, there's no spare eco-space anymore. Consumption and pollution must be curbed.

Assessments of eco-space are based on both biophysical data and political judgement – for example, about the acceptability of river pollution which is environmentally damaging but does not threaten life support systems.

The concept of eco-space has inspired the European branches of Friends of the Earth. They have calculated the eco-space of the Netherlands and Europe. For global resource or waste issues this involves an estimate of world eco-space. Countries and continents get their shares on the basis of population. The conclusion reached was that Europe has a negative eco-space and must drastically reduce its resource consumption and environmental impacts (see overleaf). The technique is in its infancy and it will be improved. But it does provide a quantified approach to back casting and a range of ambitious targets for the innovative enterprise which wants to surf the S-curve to long term success.

▶ THE PRESSURE OF LIMITS

The arguments about limits have gone on for centuries and will surely continue. We are not trying to persuade you that "limitarian" views are correct. Make your own mind up about that. But do understand that innovative environmental thinkers are think-

● FAIR SHARES OF CARBON DIOXIDE?

Friends of the Earth Europe has made its own calculations of the continent's eco-space.[5] In the case of CO_2 it takes the global reduction targets proposed by the Intergovernmental Panel on Climate Change (IPCC). Then it calculates western Europe's "fair share" based on its proportion of world population. The result is a per capita "allowance" of 5.4 tons of CO_2 emissions in 2010 and 1.7 tons in 2050. The current level is around 7.3 tons. The authors accept that the 2050 target may be impossible to achieve. But they still urge governments to base their policies on coming as near to it as possible.

ing in terms of limits – *and that their ideas are beginning to influence governments*. There are few European policy-making conferences these days, for example, which do not consider the notion of limits to consumption or an equitable balance between the needs of developing countries and the affluence of the OECD nations.

Ecological taxes could make resources and pollution more expensive

The proposed carbon tax indicates that limits are back on the agenda. It also demonstrates one important difference between now and the 1970s. Most limitarians today favour market-based initiatives, which influence more by altering prices than by prescriptive measures. The European Commission looks at a tax reform in which the price of energy is raised while taxes on labor are dropped. Similar suggestions have been made by the World Business Council for Sustainable Development and the US President's Council on Sustainable Development.[6]

If you are in business, what will this tax reform do to your costs and sales? Force you to completely change your products and processes. This is the answer that policy makers want to hear. It may not be welcome but eco-innovators must incorporate the possibility into their business development plans.

Notes

1 European Environmental Agency *Environment in the European Union 1995*. Copenhagen, 1995.

2 Brown, L. *et al*. *State of the World 1995*. New York: Norton/Worldwatch Institute, 1995.

3 Schmidt-Bleek, F. "Increasing Resource Productivity On The Way To Sustainability," *UNEP Industry and Environment*, Oct–Dec 1995, p.8.

4 See special issue of *Milieu* (Netherlands Journal of Environmental Sciences), 9, 1994/95, especially J. Opschoor and R. Weterings, "Environmental Utilisation Space: An Introduction," pp.198-205. This section is also based on the discussion in Organisation for Economic Co-operation and Development, *Clarifying the Concepts – Workship on Sustainable Consumption and Production*, Paris, 1995.

5 Friends of the Earth, *Towards Sustainable Europe*, Brussels, 1995.

6 Schmidheiny, S., and Zorraquin, F. *Financing Change*. Cambridge, Mass.: MIT Press, 1996. US President's Council on Sustainable Development *Sustainable America*. Washington, DC: US Government Printing Office, 1996.

Chapter 5

The three key drivers III: Value creation

The rationale of business is to create value for customers. Until recently most economic value as recorded by our current wealth indicators was created by large western organizations. Their customers were seen (and often behaved) as acquisitive individuals seeking as many material possessions as possible. But now the distribution and form of added value are changing rapidly. Value is migrating:

• between continents and countries

• within value chains

• within and between organizations.

▶ THE PACIFIC CENTURY

The nineteenth and twentieth centuries were the Atlantic centuries. It seems inevitable that the twenty first will be a Pacific one. Over a third of the world's population and many of the fastest growing economies are in East Asia. On present trends, the Chinese economy seems set to overtake Japan within a decade and the USA within two. In many ways the Pacific era is already upon us. As of 1996 the world's tallest building is no longer the Sears Tower in Chicago but the Petromas building in Kuala Lumpur, Malaysia. Simon Winchester dates the transition to 1989 when more jumbo jets flew across the Pacific than the Atlantic ocean. If India joins China as an economic superpower the shift of economic strength and dynamism from West to East will be complete.

Value chains are restructuring

This economic dynamism is partly a response to local demand. It also reflects the restructuring and dispersal of many value chains. We have a value chain wherever a sequence of economic transactions and physical operations take basic resources into final consumer goods and services. Not only new entrants but existing providers of goods and services challenge the traditional organization of value chains to capture a larger economic advantage.

The integration of the world economy and improved communications permits relocation of activities sensitive to labor costs to low wage countries.

Better communications and new approaches to management also mean that many large organizations are fragmenting. Most chains now involve a complex web of linkages between a large number of players. What captures the greatest value in this world? Not physical activities such as manufacturing but knowledge-based inputs such as systems integration and customer service. The change is clearest in computers. The fortunes of the once-mighty IBM have waned as those of Intel and Microsoft have waxed (see opposite).

Adrian Slywotsky uses the term value migration to describe this process.[1] Value migrates when customer priorities change. This makes existing business designs obsolete and creates opportunities for new ones. He argues that:

> For decades, many successful industry leaders employed a single, dominant business design that represented their key choices and assumptions: integrated manufacturing, in-house R&D, direct sales force, broad product line, a command and control organizational hierarchy, and a value-recapture mechanism based on a per-unit price.[2]

Now there is more competition between business designs. Innovators such as Microsoft, Nucor in steel or Southwest Airlines in air transport are constantly inventing new ones to better match customer priorities. And the new business game runs at the speed of squash rather than golf. Five strategic moves or fewer can be all it takes to destroy a dominant design and establish a new one.

> *The new game of business is founded on different assumptions:*
> - *profit rather than revenue*
> - *share of market value rather than share of market*
> - *customer power rather than product power*
> - *business design rather than technology*
>
> Adrian Slywotsky,
> author of Value Migration

● VALUE MIGRATION FROM IBM TO MICROSOFT

For quoted companies, market capitalization measures the speed and direction of value migration. IBM's fortunes rose because of a business design which perfectly matched the needs of large corporations in the 1960s and 1970s. The design was based on centralized mainframes, long-term leasing and technical back-up and the economies of scale which this predictable world made possible. By 1983 IBM had a market capitalization of over $90 billion. It was thought to be the best managed company in the world.

By 1994 its capitalization had fallen to $43 billion and the company's revenues were little higher than a decade previously. Contrast this with one of IBM's suppliers, Microsoft. Its market capitalization of $36 billion almost matched IBM's. Even though revenues were only $5 billion. Why? Because investors believed that value was migrating from hardware to software. And that Microsoft's business design – based on supplying only software and licensing its operating system to anyone – would capture more of this than IBM.

Microsoft's success also contrasts with the recent problems of Apple. It has the software strengths to take advantage of the value shift. Yet it faltered because it kept its operating system proprietary and maintained a low-value hardware operation. This created a war on two fronts, against a highly focussed Microsoft for software and low cost manufacturers of IBM clones for hardware.

▶ THE HOLONIC ENTERPRISE

Value migration becomes easier as organizational patterns become more fluid. Jessica Lipnack and Jeffrey Stamps call the emerging pattern of teams and small groups connected through networks a world of "teamnets." They write:

> Most organizations are operating in the Age of the Network, whether they know it, like it or want it. One obvious indicator is the proliferation of connections with other organizations. They take many names – "strategic alliances," "joint ventures," "outsourcing partnerships," and "flexible business networks," to name a few – linking customers, suppliers and competitors. When executive, staff and line colleagues form multiple, overlapping teams, they too are exploding in numberless cross-functional projects, horizontal corporations, and virtual enterprises.[3]

The box on the following page describes their five key principles for success in this New Age.

The ultimate network is the "virtual company" or what Patrick McHugh, Giorgio Merli and William Wheeler call the "holonic enterprise." This is . . .

> a set of companies that acts integratedly and organically; it is constantly re-configured to manage each business opportunity a customer presents. Each company in the network provides a different process capability and is called a holon.[5]

Business advantages

They identify numerous advantages for such an enterprise:

- *leverage*, from shared services and the synergies from combining the best capabilities of many operations;

- *speed*, as a result of streamlined decision making;

- *flexibility*, particularly the ability to change service or product capabilities to match rapidly changing market requirements or add holons to face increased demand;

- *shared risk*, between the different participants;

- *independence*, with each "holon" being free to leave;

- *faster growth and increased profits*, because of greater customer responsiveness;

● PRINCIPLES FOR SUCCESS IN THE NETWORK AGE

Jessica Lipnack and Jeffrey Stamps identify five key principles.

- *Unifying purpose.* Purpose is the glue and driver. Common views, values, and goals hold a network together. A shared focus on desired results keeps a network in synch and on track.

- *Independent members.* Independence is a prerequisite for inter-dependence. Each member of the network, whether a person, company or country, can stand on its own while benefiting from being part of the whole.

- *Voluntary links.* Just add links. The distinguishing feature of networks is their links, far more profuse and omnidirectional than in other types of organization. As communication pathways increase, people and groups interact more often. As more relationships develop, trust strengthens, which reduces the cost of doing business and generates greater opportunities.

- *Multiple leaders.* Fewer bosses, more leaders. Networks are leaderful, not leaderless. Each person or group in a network has something unique to contribute at some point in the process. With more than one leader, the network as a whole has great resilience.

- *Integrated levels.* Networks are multilevel, not flat. Lumpy with small groups and clustered with coalitions, networks involve both the hierarchy and the "lower-archy", which leads them to action rather than simply to making recommendations to others.[4]

- *sustainable customers*, who gain value from the flexibility and responsiveness of the system;

- *less capital requirement*, because equipment is used more intensively;

- *quick failure recognition*, because of the multiplicity of holons;

- *increased ability to deal with inevitable change*, as a result of the flexibility of the organizational arrangements.

▶ SUSTAINABILITY – THE BRIDGE TO THE FUTURE

How does this chaotic, turbulent world of value migration and ever-changing networks relate to sustainable development? One implication is that the status quo is not an option. Whether sustainable development happens or not, the world is not going to stay the same.

Turbulence creates opportunities for all new business designs. This compares to the dynamics of evolution in nature. Under stress the successful mutants adapt and prevail faster. The difference in the business world is that you do have the option of design. Here the notion of end game and a general sense of what sustainable development should be like become all important. By definition unsustainable goods and services will fail in the long run. The innovator looks beyond the turbulence, for the fundamentals of sustainability and takes advantage of the turbulence to adapt to new value capture designs.

Often sustainability can be designed into new products and services at relatively low cost, compared to the high expense of retrofitting existing ones. The flexibility of the new value order also makes it easier to break down the rigidities of mature industries and their industry paradigms. Nucor has shown how to do this in steel, Nike in running shoes. The same opportunities are there for creative entrepreneurs who can create competitive and sustainable business designs.

Stay close to customers ...

The big message is stay close to customers so that business designs are matched to *their* priorities. Doing this means going beyond the conventional needs that are tracked by market research. Consumers often do not know what they want, and cannot, therefore, imagine it. What do the video recorder, fax machine, Federal Express and Cable News Network have in common? All had negative market research findings yet went on to commercial success.[6] You too, have the opportunity to create new markets for eco-innovations by demonstrating that they are possible.

... And focus on their long-term needs

The lesson for innovators is to understand what customers will need in future. This is where a sustainability perspective provides a bridge to the long term (see Figure 5.1). One rail of this is the demographic drivers (three billion more people and the global teenager) which are changing customer values and wants. The other is the likelihood that products will be reshaped by rising resource and environmental costs as we press against the limits of our planet.

In coming decades, value will migrate to the products which respond to these pressures and:

- make long-term consumer need an innovation priority;
- provide new solutions through technology;
- create value through new, sustainable, business designs.

Taking a 20–30 year view gives you insight into, and early warnings about, the implications of sustainable development. And it increases the chance that value will migrate to you.

● **FIGURE 5.1**
Demographics drive business opportunities

2025   8.5 billion

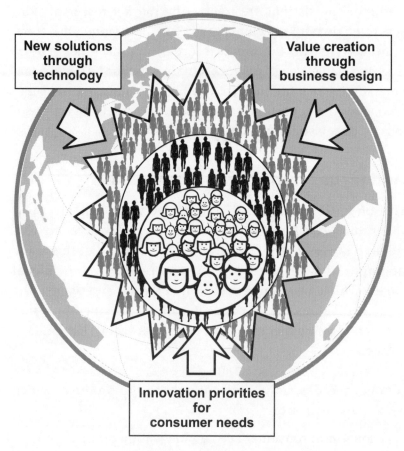

1995   5.7 billion

Notes

1 Slywotsky, A. *Value Migration*. Boston: Harvard Business School Press, 1996.

2 Slywotsky *op cit.*, p.28.

3 Lipnack, J. and Stamps, J. *The Age of the Network*. Essex Junction, Vermont: Omino, 1994, p.16.

4 Lipnack, J. and Stamps, J. *op cit.*, p.18.

5 McHugh, P., Merli, G. and Wheeler, W. *Beyond Business Process Engineering*. Chichester, UK: Wiley, 1995, p.4.

6 "Ignore Your Customer," *Fortune*, 1 May 1995, pp.121-26.

Chapter 6

Sustainability scenarios and their implications

What future will emerge under the triple push of demographics, environmental stress and value migration? We are at the crossroads to three possible scenarios suggest the European Partners for the Environment (EPE).[1] Their views are especially interesting because they come from an unusual if not unique collaboration between business, government and NGOs (see box). EPE's mission is to accelerate Europe's course towards sustainability through a triple win of business success and jobs, environmental care and quality of life.

EPE's three scenarios can be summarized as:

- *No limits* – Global environmental degradation has not materialized. Rapid technological innovation and economic growth based on new clean industries, services and information technologies have generated the wealth to pay for a safe and clean Europe.

- *Orderly transition* – Environmental problems are serious. They are addressed with strong integrated economic and environmental policies. The EU role increases in setting targets, steering scientific programs and ecological tax reform. Business is proactive and works closely in partnership with stakeholders.

- *Values shift* – Scientific evidence and a series of environmental disasters lead to radical industrial and economic change. A

EUROPEAN PARTNERS FOR THE ENVIRONMENT

The European Partners for the Environment (EPE) is the first multistake-holder organization in Europe that fosters debate about, and shared responsibility for, sustainable development.

EPE is based in Brussels. It had founding support from the European Commission, the Dutch and French environmental ministries and early members included SustainAbility, Wuppertal Institut, Hunton & Williams and Ambiente Italia. It now has more than 60 member organizations, including companies, NGOs, national and international agencies and unions. Its current board has representatives from:

United Nations Environmental Programme, Geneva

International Council for Local Environmental Initiatives, Freiburg

European Environmental Bureau, Brussels

Danmarks Naturfredningsforening, Copenhagen

WorldWatch Europe, Brussels

An Taische, Dublin

Elliniki Etairia, Athens

Regional Environmental Center, Budapest

European Trade Union Confederation, Brussels

Orée, Paris

Dow Europe, Horgen

Ecover, Westmalle

Elf Aquitaine, Paris

Novo Nordisk, Bagsvaerd

Procter & Gamble, Brussels

bottom-up approach takes over where governments are ineffective. Social and ecological concerns are paramount and inspire a more caring, fair and vibrant community life.

The following pages provide detailed summaries.

● SCENARIO 1: NO LIMITS

Key words	*Rapid change, technological innovation, adaptation, no limits, cultural diversity, maximizing quality of life at individual level.*
Summary	Environmental concerns of 1990s were greatly overstated. Global environmental degradation has not materialized, and economic growth based on new clean industries has generated the wealth to pay for a clean and safe environment in Europe.
The economy	Liberalization and privatization have continued apace. World-wide free markets drive innovation and growth. Role of governments is redefined and focussed on ensuring markets function efficiently, eg through strict anti-monopoly laws and making central banks independent.
Industry	Great diversity of scale, form and sectoral structure. Skills and learning of central importance in information/knowledge economy. New technologies emerge, especially in communications, biotechnology, robotics and nanotechnology areas. Computing and cognitive technologies provide basis of added economic value.
Energy	Diverse sources of supply, notably clean fossil fuels, also renewables and new, inherently safe nuclear technologies. Carbon dioxide emissions are not a problem, as research has confirmed that global warming will be minimal and nondamaging. In any case, the new economy needs much less energy than the old.
Transport	Private modes dominate, remaining public networks are privatized. Clean vehicles coexist with cycles and pedestrians. High-tech communications are ubiquitous, work is largely electronically based, through multimedia, teleconferencing and fully interactive virtual reality.
Tourism	Market acts to conserve natural, cultural and historical value, as people are willing to pay to preserve their quality of life. Tourism is increasingly based on appreciating cultural and biological diversity. Old fashioned idea of getting a tan is more easily achieved through technological and biotechnological means.
Agriculture	Large increases in productivity through new chemical and biotechnological approaches, open up large areas of North for nature restoration and conservation. Increased carbon dioxide emissions lead to climate change and benefit agriculture.
Barriers	Threats are from lack of ability to change or innovate, because of regulatory barriers, social resistance, or tendencies to protectionism. Another danger is growing unemployment, divisions between rich and poor, and increasing social tensions, leading to crime, violence and insecurity.

● SCENARIO 2: ORDERLY TRANSITION

Key words *Sustainability, stewardship, managerialism, targets, steering, scientific expertise, international negotiation, optimization, carrying capacity.*

Summary Environmental problems are serious, but can be solved with strong, integrated economic and environmental policies. Result: a growing EU role and responsibility to coordinate and integrate policies. Partnerships are common in defining and implementing policy.

The economy Environmental issues are fully integrated into World Trade Organization and national economies. Internalization of costs occurs through ecological tax reform; a significant proportion of national tax revenue is now from environmental sources.

Industry Transition to cleaner energy sources and low waste production is driven by tax reform and tougher regulations. Focus is on optimization and efficiency, including industrial ecology. Regular sustainability assessments and audits take place. Multinationals grow in economic and social importance, working closely with stakeholders and forming center of most people's lives.

Energy Widespread efficiency improvements, coupled with a move from fossil fuel-based systems to renewables and hot fusion. Energy systems are centralized, including combined heat and power. Europe launches R&D program for sustainable energy to compete with Japan's *New Earth 21*.

Transport Strategies for mobility management and cleaner transport emerge, with an optimally structured mix between individual transport and public transport systems. Investment in transEuropean networks. Cost internalization has reduced traffic and helped to localize economies.

Tourism After a decade of growing damage in 1990s, tough policies to protect resorts are based on eco-efficiency regulation and incentives. There is a growth in eco-tourism with high user fees to ensure environmental protection.

Agriculture Role of farmers expands, including not just food production, but also guardianship of countryside. Cost internalization has promoted less polluting, more economical rational agriculture, as well as restoring the competitiveness of low-input and organic farming.

Barriers Risks arise from uncontrollability and disorder, whether from environmental disasters, economic instability or inability to build societal consensus for necessary changes, such as ecological tax reform.

● SCENARIO 3: VALUES SHIFT

Key words	*Prevention, urgency, participation, new relationship with nature, decentralization, equity, community, caring, spirituality.*
Summary	New scientific evidence, following a series of environmental disasters, shows environmental problems are truly serious, necessitating radical industrial and economic change. Growing dissatisfaction with government and business catalyses a bottom-up approach. Social and ecological concerns are paramount, as people recognize the value of fairness and community life.
The economy	Steady-state economies are essential. There are major changes in consumption patterns to keep within environmental limits and share global environmental space equitably. Local economies and self-sufficiency are central, non-market activities increasingly important.
Industry	Business and industry focus on meeting needs – eg mobility, comfort, joy, communication, knowledge, rather than producing goods and services *per se*. Technologies are designed to fit closely with local surroundings rather than being globalized. There is a return to traditional skills, insight and craft work.
Energy	Carbon dioxide reductions of 80–90% in Europe are needed. Demand is greatly reduced through triple glazing, insulation and high efficiency boilers. Reduced energy demand in production and use of products. Small scale, low capital intensity, decentralized energy sources dominate. Wind and solar energy replace most fossil sources. Large changes in energy and transport systems..
Transport	Physical transport is minimized, and an international flight is becoming a once-in-a lifetime experience. Trade is greatly reduced and limited to high value products. Land use patterns change to accommodate reduced mobility. Bicycle-based urban planning is common.
Tourism	Transport – and especially flight, on which much tourism used to depend – is enormously reduced. Sectors that were based on unsustainable transport and development fall away, but not before widespread destruction has been caused. Tourism is now local, based on sustainable transportation.
Agriculture	Land degradation is avoided through traditional techniques, diets are largely vegetarian with fish and aquaculture for protein. Communities depend mainly on local food sources, with land management based on strict principles of sustainability. There are significant population migrations where people find the land cannot support them.
Barriers	If environmental problems turn out to be not so serious, most of the changes in the scenario would not materialize, because the assumption is that they would be environment-driven. People may not help each other or cooperate, or be willing to sacrifice short-term interest for longer term social good.

▶ ALL SCENARIOS ENVISAGE MORE PRESSURE ON BUSINESS

Any one of the three scenarios is plausible at this point of time. They are vastly different yet some actions by governments, business and other organizations would be of value in any scenario. Most actions involve the capability to think long-term, integrate social needs, maintain a readiness to change and have the capacity to implement quickly and flexibly.

All the scenarios envisage increasing pressure to innovate and take social responsibility.

- In the *no limits* scenario the driver will be competition from other companies as they introduce and build market leadership for their products and services.

- For *orderly transition*, government will be an equal if not more important driver. As well as strengthening conventional regulation it will create a regime where many environmental costs are internalized. Companies will get a mix of positive incentives and tough penalties to achieve environmental improvement.

- The *values shift* scenario is inherently hostile to business. Only those which can, through innovation and social responsiveness, demonstrate their care for the new values will win and maintain a licence to operate.

By this point you might be feeling depressed. Surely the picture is one of a hostile world, filled with minimalist customers and even more minimal profits? Probably, if you are interested in business as usual. But if you are willing to dream of new products and services the future is more inviting. There will be growth, but of a different kind. There will be customers, but with different values. And there will be profits, but based more on service and intelligence than moving mass. The next section provides a map to those who feel these are the times to differentiate and build competitive advantage while contributing to a better future.

Notes

1 European Partners for the Environment *Towards Shared Responsibility*. West Malle, Belgium, 1994.

Part 2

CHANGE TO WIN

Many people in business see sustainable development as a threat to markets and profitability.

In Chapters 7 to 9 we discuss how they will certainly affect these and redefine national and corporate accounting. However, there will still be economic development, and therefore increasing markets for many products and services. These should be highly profitable.

Some may think that there is plenty of time to respond to these opportunities. In Chapter 10 we argue that this is unlikely and that changes, when they occur, will be rapid and will only benefit those who have prepared for a long time. Business will be wise to develop its own equivalent of the precautionary principle.

In this section you will:

- *gain a perspective on how fundamental trends will affect customers, markets and profitability;*

- *appreciate that economic growth will continue, particularly value growth for innovators;*

- *gain information about environmental accounting and how it can be applied to business;*

- *understand the precautionary principle and its relevance to business.*

Chapter 7

Will there be growth?

Did the Indonesian economy grow by 7% a year in the 1970s and early 1980s or by 4%? Conventional sources suggest the former, the World Resources Institute (WRI) the latter.[1] The discrepancy arises because the conventional calculations ignore costs of environmental damages and permanent depletion of resources. WRI calculated the costs of depleting oil reserves, reduced forest worth because of unsustainable forestry practices and soil erosion. It then deducted them from the conventional figures.

Eventually such deductions will be routine rather than exceptional. The creation of "national accounts" to measure a country's economic activity (Gross Domestic Product (GDP) as it is usually called) is surprisingly young and still evolving. It began in the 1920s and became standardized after the war. Statisticians make tough decisions to define and produce them. One of the most crucial is to base the accounts on actual monetary transactions rather than estimated values. (There are two exceptions: estimates are made of what owner-occupiers of buildings would pay in rent, and what the food eaten by farmers is worth.)

GDP excludes unmonetized costs

There is a problem with this approach. Anything which does not have an clear monetary value does not appear in the national accounts. Housework and the loss of species from unsustainable forestry are only two examples.

On the other hand, monetary transactions which are "bads" rather than "goods" do appear in the accounts. GDP is swollen by the costs of cleaning up land contamination or building flood control schemes to counter greater water run-off from deforested hillsides, or medical care programs to alleviate poor water sanitation in the world. Yet these only rectify past mistakes rather than make any original contribution to economic welfare.

The absurdity of such outcomes is illustrated by the GDP implications of the 1995 Kobe earthquake. According to the World Wildlife Fund:

> Japan will actually make money out of the catastrophe. Five thousand five hundred people were killed, 33,000 injured and the bill for damage has already exceeded $110 billion. Yet the income generated by the huge rescue and clean up effort means that, according to calculations based on Gross Domestic Product (GDP), the earthquake will turn out slightly positive on balance.[2]

Conventional GDP calculations show that Japan has benefited economically from the 1995 Kobe earthquake.

These distortions impede the original purpose of national accounting – to provide better information for economic management. As WRI's work on Indonesia demonstrates, including the cost of unsustainable development can alter the picture completely. The same point is made by other studies, including one examining the US economy. The authors conclude that air, water and noise pollution cost 2% of GDP. Long-term degradation of soil, biodiversity and other forms of natural capital cost a further 15%.[3]

GDP does not measure welfare

The distortions are even more significant when GDP figures, that is economic data, are used to measure welfare. A nation whose economic activity expands by 6% is then "better off" than one growing by 2%. But individual and social "well-being" is a complex state. It depends upon far more than wealth. Good health, work satisfaction, opportunities for learning and other non-economic factors contribute to it.

Are all these not more likely to be achieved when you are rich or at least financially comfortable? An Erasmus University researcher suggests this is not necessarily the case. His studies of the relationship between income and subjective happiness show that, beyond a minimum level, there is no clear correlation (see Figure 7.1). Money cannot buy happiness. Culture and social models are more important.

Getting a better picture of well being means either modifying or replacing GDP. Bodies such as the UN and World Bank have

● **FIGURE 7.1**
Income and happiness

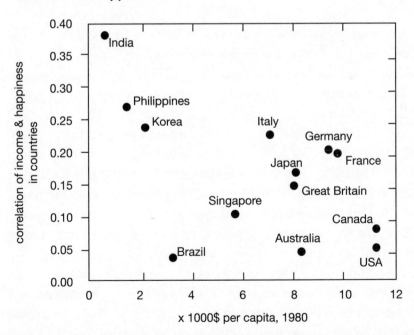

(The y-axis is the correlation between the level of income and happiness (as expressed in interviews) within a country. The x-axis is mean income per capita in a country).
Source: Veenhoven, 1993 (cited in Friends of the Earth, *Towards a Sustainable Europe*; Brussels, 1995)

accepted the case for modification and are developing new techniques to deduct environmental costs from GDP. The WWF is
campaigning for all countries to measure "true GDP" by end 1999.

Herman Daly's steady state economy

For economists such as Herman Daly the end point of this debate
is a "steady state" economy. He means by this . . .

> an economy with constant stocks of people and artefacts, main-
> tained at some desired, sufficient levels by low rates of
> maintenance "throughput," that is, by the lowest feasible flows of
> matter and energy from the first stage of production ... to the last
> stage of consumption ... It should be continually remembered that
> the steady state economy is a physical concept.[4]

A steady state economy would not have quantitative growth –
that is, an increase of stocks or throughputs. But it could develop
and create value, by providing increased service from a given
amount of resource. This allows "qualitative growth" – that is
increase in GDP, adjusted for environmental and other costs, without any increase in resource use.

Daly's steady state economy seems unlikely to materialize in the
short-medium term. Its implications stretch our technology and
social innovation capability. We have already seen that population
growth continues inexorably and that much of the world's population still hungers for prosperity and equity. It seems inevitable that
the world's physical "stocks" (of buildings, basic equipment, transport and other infrastructure) will grow in area and mass for many
years. We will therefore continue to harvest wood and cotton,
pump oil and gas, electrolyze salt, cast glass and metals, kiln
cement and push nature back in many places. This makes it even
more essential to greatly reduce "flows" or "throughput" of energy,
materials and wastes. Even so, and in spite of the likely damaging
environmental consequences, there is probably going to be physical
as well as qualitative growth over coming decades.

Although the environmental consequences will be damaging, population growth and prosperity hunger mean that there is probably going to be physical as well as qualitative growth over coming decades.

Influence on policy

Why then take seriously the ideas of Daly and other "limitarian" economists? For these reasons:

1 They make as much sense in setting ambitious targets as zero defects or zero accidents in business. They tell you to pay attention to the limits and fragility of the natural systems that sustain our wealth.

2 They influence the environmental movement and thereby, to a degree, policy makers. The ideas of Daly – and other bold environmental thinkers such as Opschoor – are sufficiently important to be discussed in detail at an OECD workshop and a UN ministerial conference on sustainable production and consumption.[5] Such gatherings clearly influence policies that will set the true cost of resources and pollution.

Revised national accounts are one incremental response to their ideas. Such accounts will require data on environmental damage and expenditure. These will be both estimated and derived from companies and will provide political ammunition to green lobbyists for duties or levies on environmentally damaging activities. WWF is already on a campaign:

> To make the new system work, public regulations on energy use, pollution and water use will be necessary. This could have knock-on effects that improve the quality of life, such as tax reform to reduce resource use and increase employment by decreasing tax on human labor. Industry forced to pay spill-over costs for the environmental damage it causes would think twice before inflicting it.

There would be winners and losers with a nature-adjusted GDP. Countries would see environmentally damaging industries go out of business, while sectors that enhance the environment would increasingly contribute to economic growth. Financial institutions would then alter funding policies to encourage good businesses and discourage the bad.[6]

In such a world it will be easier to calculate the costs of environmental damage created by a company's processes and products. If the costs are high it will become impossible to market certain goods and services.

On balance, this is good news for eco-innovators. There will be economic development – but in added value more than in physical stocks and flows. Within this envelope, value should migrate from creators and transformers of mass to service enhanced and "dematerialized" products. These innovations will be economically advantaged over resource and waste intensive traditional solutions. But will these products meet consumer needs and make money? They will, as the next two chapters show.

Notes

1 Repetto, R., Magrath, M., Wells C., Beer C. and Rossini F. *Wasting Assets: Natural Resources in the National Accounts*. Washington, DC: World Resources Institute, 1989.

2 WWF – World Wildlife Fund *The GDP Effect*, Geneva, 1995, p.1.

3 Cobb, C. and Cobb, J. *The Green National Product*. Lantham, Maryland: University Press of America, 1994.

4 Daly, H. *Steady State Economics* (2nd edn). Washington, DC: Freeman, 1992, p.17.

5 Organisation for Economic Co-operation and Development *Clarifying the Concepts: Workshop on Sustainable consumption and Production*, Paris, 1995 Ministry of Environment – Norway Oslo *Ministerial Roundtable: Conference on Sustainable Production and Consumption*, Oslo, 1995.

6 WWF – World Wildlife Fund *The GDP Effect*. Geneva, 1995, p.2.

Chapter 8

What kind of markets?

Even in a world of redefined GDP, there should be growing markets for products and services. But their nature and the means used to advertise and distribute them will be very different. There will be a shift from:

- supply to demand

- product to service

- product proliferation to lean service

- quantity to quality

- articulated to unarticulated needs.

▶ FROM SUPPLY TO DEMAND

John Elkington is the founder and chairman of the environmental consultancy SustainAbility. With his colleague, Julia Hailes, he wrote the bestselling *Green Consumer Guide* which brings sustainable development to the supermarket checkout and directs business attention to its marketing opportunities as well as its threats.

The green consumer movement has been buffeted by recession and controversy about product environmental claims. Nonetheless, Elkington, Hailes and their SustainAbility colleague, Geoff Lye, in a special report for Dow Europe, believe that the environmental focus is shifting:

– The 1970s focus was on "doomsday scenarios" and assessment of large scale projects.

– This shifted in the 1980s to plants and processes.

– This production orientation has been joined in the 1990s by an emphasis on products and their life cycles.

– The next focus, they predict, will be on sustainable consumption and lifestyle patterns as part of a broader move to sustainable economies.[1]

The next focus will be sustainable consumption and lifestyle patterns.

Sustainable lifestyles

Sustainable lifestyles are now appearing on policy agendas:

• *Agenda 21* discusses it, as does the European Commission's Fifth Environmental Action programme, *Towards Sustainability* (although neither has concrete proposals to achieve it).

• "Changing consumption patterns" forms part of the mission of the UN Commission for Sustainable Development (see box opposite).

• The Dutch government states that its environmental goals require fundamental change in lifestyles.

The latter knows what a sustainable lifestyle in the Netherlands will be like. It commissioned a pioneering report[2] which identifies

● **DEFINING THE SUSTAINABLE CONSUMPTION AGENDA**

The 1994–95 Oslo Ministerial Round Table brought together a worldwide group of government ministers and representatives from international agencies, NGOs and business. Its brief was to make recommendations for the UN Commission on Sustainable Development's work program on sustainable production and consumption. It placed particular emphasis on:

● building partnerships for sustainable consumption between different sectors of society, and reinforcing the values that support sustainable consumption;

● establishing the policy framework for sustainable consumption, for example, by moving towards environmentally sound pricing and ecological tax reform;

● extending producer responsibility for the environmental impacts of goods and services;

● setting a government example in sustainable consumption through environmentally sound public procurement and administration;

● empowering individuals and households to adopt more sustainable consumption patterns (for example, by providing information and support networks).[2]

four key areas where consumer lifestyles make a significant contribution to environmental damage:

● *domestic energy consumption*, which accounts for a quarter of the Dutch total and creates emissions of nitrogen and sulphur oxides, carbon dioxide and other environmental impacts;

- *personal transport*, which has similar effects to domestic energy as well as generating noise and disturbance. 88% of Dutch vehicles are privately owned and the Netherlands has some of the highest traffic densities in the world;

- *purchase of products and packaging*. These generate waste (about 14% of all landfill) and emissions and other effects from use;

- *high consumption of meat and dairy products*. Intensive livestock farming consumes energy, water and materials and generates emissions of the greenhouse gases carbon dioxide and methane. It also creates 15 million tons of manure per year (over 1 ton per person!).

> *A Dutch government report identifies four principles for achieving sustainable lifestyles – rationalizing access, acting communally, closing material loops and buying services not products.*

Overcoming barriers

The report identifies many opportunities. But it also identifies barriers, including:

- low consumer motivation, with insufficient financial, social or moral incentives to change attitudes and behavior;

- insufficient understanding of linkages between behavior and environmental impacts;

- insufficient opportunity, because of lack of availability of sustainable products or services.

The Dutch government is now putting solutions into place. Its initiatives include more education and information, especially on products, price incentives for environmentally favorable activities, new facilities to foster waste separation and low-impact transport.

● FOUR PRINCIPLES FOR SUSTAINABLE LIFESTYLES

In its 1993 report for the Dutch government, consultants ERM identified four core principles for sustainable consumption:

Rationalize access: many inefficiencies exist in the way that people, goods and services are brought together. The consequences include increased fuel consumption in travelling, traffic congestion, air pollution and land take for roads and car parks. In many cases it should be possible to reduce access and transportation journeys by, for example, bulk deliveries of goods to consumers in their homes. In other cases, the need for access can be removed altogether, for example, people working from home do not need to commute.

Act communally: a long-term trend towards greater privacy and individual ownership has increased the requirement for products and services. For example, while the population of the Netherlands has remained static, the number of households has increased as more people choose to live alone or in smaller family units. This has led to an increase in the number of domestic appliances, furnishings, motor cars etc required to serve the same number of people. However, some communal activities remain socially acceptable and popular – dining out, drinking, visiting cinemas. The social acceptability of acting communally could be built upon to increase the frequency and extent of such activities in order to increase efficiency of materials and energy consumption.

Circulate goods: material and energy resources are squandered and environmental impacts increased when consumer products (and their packaging) are discarded and replaced at frequent intervals. Short product life can result from built-in obsolescence, improved technology, or people's desire for change and novelty stimulated by affluence and advertising can also play a role. There is great potential for reducing resource waste through the establishment of product repair and exchange services to keep goods in circulation. Consumers need not be exhorted to consume less if they can reconsume. ▶

> ▶ *Buy services not products:* material and energy saving can also be made from applying economies of scale. Using a publicly or privately provided service, rather than purchasing the product/appliance that performs the same function will reduce the requirement for individual products. Examples include commuting by public transport rather than driving a private car, using a laundry service rather than buying a washing machine, employing a decorating firm rather than buying do-it-yourself equipment.[4]

▶ FROM PRODUCT TO SERVICE

What is the difference between a product and a service? The product is a means to an end – providing customer value. But a customer's long-term loyalty is not to individual products but to the need for service. The point was first made by marketing guru Levitt in 1960.[5] He examined the rise and fall of American railroad companies. They declined because they defined their business as about a product, the railway. But customers wanted a service – quick, convenient and cheap transport – and abandoned the railway for roads and cars when these could provide it more successfully.

Of course, it is good business to take pride in a product. But "factor 10" dematerialization means that many existing products are dinosaurs. New niches will develop for innovators who are entrepreneurs free from a specific product orientation. They identify with the service their business provides.

Eco-innovators imagine and implement smarter, lighter and more sustainable means of providing service while enhancing customer value.

Many US electric utilities are doing just this. They found it difficult or impossible to build new generating capacity in the 1980s and as a result, they introduced Demand Side Management approaches to influence the size and timing of their customers' electricity needs. The cost to them of helping customers save electricity is significantly lower than building and operating additional generator capacity. They now appreciate they are providing services such as warmth and motive power rather than kilowatts of electricity. Sometimes the improved efficiency can deliver the service more effectively than additional power purchases. The current deregulation of the US electricity industry is changing the situation. But, until now, the utilities who have gone furthest down this "megawatt" route have been among the most profitable in the sector. To make demand side management work, they have had to better understand their customers' needs and in so doing, provide further opportunities to create additional value by designing new products and services for them.

▶ FROM PRODUCT PROLIFERATION TO LEAN SERVICE

It is important that these new products do not exacerbate the problems of product proliferation. The number and variety of products on the market show that creativity and vision can be a curse as well as a blessing. They allow us to imagine and desire better, even perfect, products or services and to innovate towards them. Henry Petroski, professor of civil engineering at Duke University, North Carolina, has shown the power of this mechanism in the evolution of such commonplace objects as the pencil, the fork or the paper clip. In this pursuit of the better product form follows failure. As Petroski puts it . . .

> Here then is the central idea: the form of made things is always subject to change in response to their real or perceived shortcom-

ings, their failure to function properly. This principle governs all invention, innovation and ingenuity.[6]

This has profound implications on the way products proliferate, draw resources and stimulate consumption. Let us look at a new product. In the early stages it brings useful features. But very quickly the first generation models show their shortcomings. The first fax machines were slow, produced smudged flimsy documents that kept rolling up and falling under the desk. The first customers' *needs* quickly become *wants* for more performance.

The classic marketing drama

Various suppliers, as well as new entrants to this promising market, draw lessons from the failures and design new forms. They use different approaches around each other's patents or specific advantages. Some target specific niches. But most go for economies of scale and must produce in volume to cover their fixed costs. These are the basic rules of the marketing domain: match capabilities to needs, manage costs below the market value (see Chapter 23).

The result is that supply capacities usually exceed demand. The fight for market share becomes therefore a success and survival issue. This is a classic marketing drama. It unfolds as the front line business person fights their way to customers with the double barrelled weapon of Price and Promotion. The customer now gets attention, information and choice. Advertising reveals hidden wants of self-esteem, security or fulfillment that may be addressed by the latest fax system. Wants prevail over needs. In Petroski's words . . .

> whereas the shortcomings of an existing thing may be expressed in terms of a *need* for improvement, it is really *want* rather than need that drives the process of technical evolution. Thus we may need air and water, but generally we do not require air conditioning or ice water in any fundamental way. We may find food indispensable, but it is not necessary to eat it with a fork. Luxury, rather than necessity, is the mother of invention: every artifact is somewhat wanting in its function, and this is what drives its evolution.[7]

Half spoiled, half longing

Incremental innovation, the sort that fills a few wants and leaves consumers half spoiled, half longing, is a strong catalyst for rapid obsolescence and repurchasing of the next model.

Employees and financiers committed to the new product lines and capacity have an obvious interest in driving consumption. But so, too, do today's consumers.

Sustainability and consumption will be difficult partners. The debate has started in the most advanced policy circles of the northern Europe countries. It is a difficult debate that must avoid the virtuous calls to curb production. It may affect the poorest first. Needs and wants will grow with population and access to information. The debate will be about a consensus of measures that continue to support equitable consumption yet significantly reduce its environmental burden. Figure 8.1 maps the relationships of this complex debate and identifies three broad solutions:

- business becoming better at identifying and meeting customer needs

- more information about and regulation of product offers

- positive and negative incentives for consumers to buy or use fewer products.

Identifying and meeting customer needs more effectively

The business solutions require technology breakthroughs, not smooth incremental evolution. The aim is not just better service but *lean* service. Part 5 describes a broad method for achieving this. Some more specific options are:

● FIGURE 8.1
The model of product proliferation

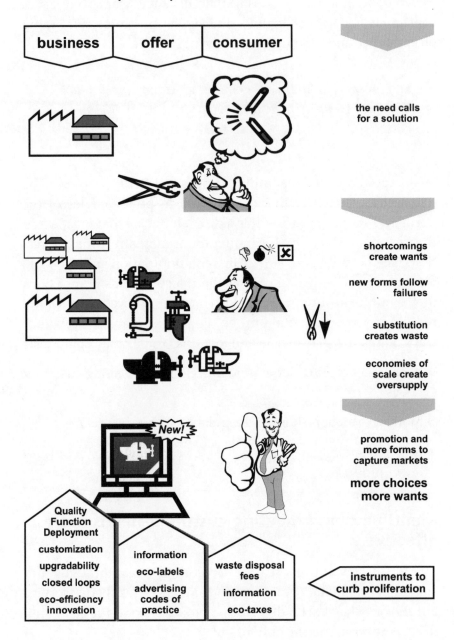

- *Customization and Quality Function Deployment(QFD).* Better needs analysis, and a design approach integrated with small-scale, modular production systems, can deliver low-cost and high-quality personalized consumer goods. Economies of scale become less critical.

- *Service life extension.* Better designs that last and antique with a special emotional quality. Timberland shoes or the return of the Volkswagen "Beetle" come to mind.

- *Precision technologies* to meet customer needs more effectively and with less environmental impact. The box discusses one example, nanotechnology.

● THE POTENTIAL OF NANOTECHNOLOGY

Nanotechnology will replace probabilistic chemistry that relies on high pressure and temperature followed by sorting on-spec molecules and recirculating the rest. Nanotechnology, in theory, assembles molecules atom by atom (they are measured in nanometres, one billionth of a meter), and clips them together into perfect materials. It disassembles them the same way for perfect recycling. The potential for sustainable material loops is daunting.

Nanotechnology is today where integrated circuits were at the discovery of the transistor, 48 years ago. But we already have nanopincers that push atoms around. The IBM researchers in Zürich clipped atoms together, one by one, for a photo of the company logo that made all the scientific magazines. That was in 1991 and the pincers operated at –270 °C. In 1996 they can already operate their pincers at ambient temperature, another breakthrough on the early phase of the S-curve.

Information and incentives

Sustainable consumption and the new technologies that enable it will be further encouraged by policy instruments to provide better information and effective incentives, such as:

- *Internalization* of environmental costs to producers and consumers, for example, by stringent waste collection fees (see Chapter 9).

- *Codes of practice in advertising*. Advertising is seen by most advocates of sustainable consumption as the driver of wasteful purchases and transfer of frivolous lifestyles to developing economies and new generations. The charge has some basis but flies in the face of freedom of information and the explosive ramification of electronic information networks. Stop advertising and you will do close to nothing to change needs, wants and purchases. You will affect market share and create other curiosity and information channels. But policy makers will increasingly demand balanced information in advertising on the sustainable development aspects of products and businesses.

- *Eco-labels*. The attempt in the European Union to provide an eco-label in many product categories demonstrates how difficult it is to implement policy instruments that would directly favor the market share of a few product designs at the expense of the majority. It is particularly difficult when one gets stuck between a complex technical analysis of the products and a broad democratic process to set the labeling criteria. Many will be tempted to paint the criteria greener than the market can deliver, to make it tighter and more detailed than the analysis can verify. They argue about the rules of the end game but have no players and no prizes for the first games. This simply stalls the process. Remember the S-curve? This tells us that technologies move slowly in their initial stages but accelerate steeply as confidence and experience builds. We need to get started on a "good enough" basis in order to achieve medium-term acceleration.

Then labeling and information provided on the sustainable development impacts of products should be a powerful tool to disseminate the reasons, incentives and desire to change consumption behavior.

Any business that takes the long-term road to success will need to take account of the dynamics of product proliferation and search for solutions beyond incremental product evolution.

> *Eco-innovators can make skillful use of the technology resources available today to match needs and wants more closely at a lower environmental burden.*

▶ FROM QUANTITY TO QUALITY

The post-war baby boomers of the industrialized world had a "no limits" credo. They created a lifestyle model based on consumerism and consumption which fueled resource-intensive economic growth.

Postmodernist diversity

Today's teenagers and young adults are more eclectic. Many seek a different image. In the 1970s SRI developed a Values and Lifestyles (VAL) classification of consumer attitudes and behaviors which marketers found invaluable. But James Ogilvy, VAL research director, has described how it became increasingly ill-matched with behavior in the 1980s and 1990s:

> People were no longer staying true to type. Men who behaved like Achievers by day would become Experientials at night. Women would shop for expensive fashions one day, then go to a discount store the next day. The coherence and consistency that had characterized lifestyles in the past was breaking down.[8]

He concludes that consumers are becoming postmodernists, creating their own pot pourri of values which change over time. In his words:

> From art to architecture to ethics and fashions we are finding that it is possible to embrace many different values: not one set of absolute values, nor a nihilistic rejection of all values, but a complex mixture of different values.

This postmodernist world emphasizes quality of life. Goods and services are purchased according to their fit with individually chosen lifestyles and values which are not necessarily sustainable. If your quality of life depends on regular travel to all parts of the globe, you may be part of the problem rather than the solution.

But there is one near-constant in this postmodernist diversity.

Some derive this sense from ecology, others from religion or tradition. Western retailers and consumer goods manufacturers such as Levi's, Body Shop, Benetton and Esprit are already tapping into these values with their product positioning.

From Iran to Ireland, Java to Japan, there is a growing sense of planetary limits and unity.

The sense of planetary unity is often built on a yearning for community. Many find that their personal and working lives are ever more individualized and stressed. American and British social gurus speak of the "anxious class." A longing for friendliness, neighborliness and social interaction comes through in consumer surveys and political opinion polls alike.

The desire to understand the world and be interconnected with it is now being played out in the hurried development of electronic highways and networks. Armed with affordable and shareable technology, global teenagers and others exchange their ideas and aspirations on globe-spanning computer networks. The initial effect is to create diversity and more knowledge of consumption possibilities. But in the long run, they will surely generate a collective mindset and new values that support sustainable development.

▶ IDENTIFYING UNARTICULATED NEEDS

How can you link with these value shifts? Move beyond today's business and innovate for future opportunities. That's the message of business gurus Gary Hamel and C.K. Prahalad. They scorn over-reliance on market research to identify customer needs. Often customers don't know what they want until ideas and opportunities are provided. And they advocate "out of the box" thinking to identify new types of customer who are not currently being reached. The outcome is summarised in Figure 8.2.

Today's business is only a small share of the total field of options. The real opportunities lie in currently unarticulated customer needs and unserved customers. Many of these needs will be driven by the imperatives of sustainable development. And the unserved customers include the billions of poor people who need sustainable products and services which are compatible with their budgets.

● **FIGURE 8.2**
Unexploited needs

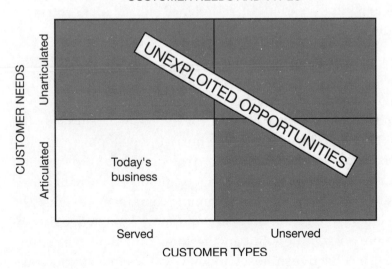

Source: Hamel, G. and Prahalad, C., reproduced in SustainAbility, *Who Needs It?*, London, 1995

What is sustainable marketing?

For many environmentalists the marketing manager is public enemy number one. The charge? Creating unsustainable and unnecessary desires by playing upon people's ego, insecurity and weakness. Whether guilty of this or not, sustainable marketing is likely to be different from today's variety. Elkington, Hailes and Lye see tomorrow's objectives as being to:

- help consumers make the transition to more sustainable lifestyles and consumption patterns;

- replace psychological marketing with an emphasis on real, tangible benefits;

- focus on value to customers rather than on volume of product shipped;

- switch to informing before selling;

- respect rather than play upon human weakness;

- be sensitive to all stakeholders;

- shift from traditional chemical, synthetic and short-life products to natural – and to better designed and smarter synthetic – alternatives.[9]

Some will see these prescriptions as new "marketing ethics." Others will doubt the feasibility in their own lifetimes, if ever. The report's authors admit that there is no guaranteed timetable. But they also give a warning.

"Successful companies, however, will rarely wait for all the answers to be in, or for someone else to set the timetable. Instead, they will set out to create the markets of the future." – SustainAbility[10]

The need test

Where does sustainable marketing start? By asking: is my product really necessary? To answer you need to consider six supplementary questions. The following boxes provide the questions and answers for a sample product, air conditioners.

You may have passed the test, but where did the value come from? You may have an unexpected ally: government. As the next chapter shows, more and more governments evaluate the merits of restructuring taxes and other determinants of profit and loss to steer markets towards sustainable production and consumption. It will create strong differentiation between your innovation and your competitors that are entrenched in discounting the environment.

● THE NEED TEST

The Diagnosis

1 What is the primary function of your product or service?

2 What other benefits does the product or service offer?

3 Is there likely to be a long-term need and/or demand for the product or service?

4 What is the value:impact ratio for the product or service today?

5 Would this product or service be sustainable in an equitable world of 8–10 billion people?

6 Are there more sustainable ways of providing the same function, or of meeting the same need?

The Prognosis

7 On the basis of 1–6 above, what threats and opportunities will there be for the product or service during the sustainability transition? What are the smart innovation opportunities?

● THE NEED TEST FOR AIR CONDITIONING

The Diagnosis

1 What is the primary function of air conditioning systems?
To cool, heat and otherwise condition air in buildings.

2 What other benefits do air conditioning systems offer?
A more stable and predictable internal environment, coupled with a higher sale or resale price for buildings equipped in this way.

3 Is there likely to be a long-term demand for the primary function?
Yes, in hot parts of the world, but not necessarily elsewhere. The level of the requirement all depends on two key factors: 1) the expectations of those who live and work in buildings; and 2) the extent to which urban areas and buildings are designed to encourage natural air-conditioning. The need has also been driven by the growing numbers of heat-generating computer and other forms of office equipment.

4 What is the value:impact ratio for air-conditioning systems today?
Problematic, both in terms of energy consumption and ozone depletion. The fans, pumps and refrigeration plant soak up huge amounts of energy – as much as 20% of a building's power bill.

5 Would this approach be sustainable in an equitable world of 8–10 billion people?
As currently designed and operated, no.

6 Are there more sustainable ways of providing the same function?
Yes. Some developers argue that many buildings are over specified in relation to their air-conditioning needs. The reason: electronic equipment only accounts for 10% of overall office heat and is becoming more efficient, although designers continue to build in hefty safety factors.

The Prognosis

7 On the basis of 1–6 above, what are the prospects for air conditioning systems? What are the smart innovation opportunities?
In tropical climates, good. In temperate climates, less so. Anyone who works out how to design buildings which are naturally air conditioned will not only help protect the environment, but also save heavily on investment and ongoing energy costs.[11]

Notes

1 Elkington J., Hailes, J. and Lye, G. *Who Needs It? Market Implications of Sustainable Lifestyles*. London: SustainAbility, 1995.

2 Environmental Resources (ERM) *The Best of Both Worlds: Sustainability and Quality Lifestyles in the 21th Century*. Den Haag: Netherlands Ministry of Housing, Physical Planning and the Environment, 1993.

3 Ministry of Environment, Norway *Oslo Ministerial Roundtable – Conference on Sustainable Production and Consumption*, Oslo, 1995.

4 Environmental Resources *The Best of Both Worlds: Sustainability and Quality Lifestyles in the 21st Century*. Den Haag: Netherlands Ministry of Housing, Physical Planning and Environment, 1993, pp.III–IV.

5 Levitt, T. "Marketing Myopia," *Havard Business Review*, July / August 1960, pp.45-56.

6 Petroski, H. *The Evolution of Useful Things*. London: Pavillion, 1993, p.22.

7 Petroski op cit., p.22.

8 Ogilvy, J. :The Postmodern Consumer," in *The Deeper News* special issue, *Values and the Corporation*, Emeryville, Ca: Global Business Network, 1994, p.7.

9 Elkington, J., Hailes, J. and Lye, G. *Who Needs It? Market Implications of Sustainable Lifestlyes*. London: SustainAbility, 1995, p.48.

10 SustainAbility *op cit.*, p.49.

11 SustainAbility *op cit.*, p.37.

Chapter 9

Will there be profits?

"I'm fed up with environment. You can never do enough, it's constantly eating into the bottom line and it's a treadmill for life" one business leader complained. Is he right? There may be customers but will there be margins where the cost of regulation and resources rise regularly?

▶ BOTTOM LINE ENVIRONMENTAL ACCOUNTING

For many companies the answer will be no. Unsustainable performance will damage profitability in a number of ways. But dematerialized, smarter ways of providing customer service will enhance it. Either way we'll need better accounting methods to identify and quantify the bottom line costs and benefits of sustainability.

What are these benefits? They include:

- savings on raw materials and energy

- elimination of expensive end-of-pipe solutions

- increased competitiveness through use of new and improved technologies in process and products

- reduced risks from on- and off-site treatment, storage and disposal of toxic wastes

- improved health and safety of employees

- less pressure from environmental restrictions or prohibitions on business activities

- improved public image

- business health and staying power.

Actions for sustainability are not always win–win. But the scale of the benefits is likely to increase as costs are internalized and liability regimes tighten.

> *Most environmental costs aren't allocated to products or processes but are hidden in overheads. Companies therefore have a distorted view of their financial structure and environmental savings potential*

Environmental costs can be high

Until now there have been only *ad hoc* calculations of the costs and benefits of environmental initiatives. But this is changing. The World Resources Institute (WRI) undertook six comprehensive analyses of environment related product or process costs in US companies.[1] They comprised:

- nearly 22% of non-feedstock operating costs at Amoco's York town refinery

- over 19% of the manufacturing costs of a Du Pont agricultural pesticide

- 2.4% of the net sales of a S.C. Johnson Wax consumer product.

The latter may not seem large. In fact, the environmental costs are higher than the operating profit. In all cases, the costs far exceed initial estimates, largely because they are lost in overheads.

The German textile company, Kunert, also calculates that environmental costs comprise over 10% of the total costs of its Mindelheim mill (see box).

● WASTE COSTS AT KUNERT

Kunert makes hosiery and other textile products. Its Kunert, Hudson, Burlington and Silkona brands are sold across Europe. It is also a pioneer of eco-balancing. This identifies and quantifies all the material and energy flows of a plant or a company. The result? An accurate picture of the environmental footprint. And clarity about areas of waste and opportunities for improvement.

An eco-balance of Kunert's production of tights at its Mindelheim plant found that only 47% of input materials went into products. About 35% was for packaging, and 18% waste. The eco-balance identified the costs of these wastes as 11% of total production costs. Most of this is the purchase and financing costs of raw materials not utilized in products.

The leverage of such an analysis to reengineer material flow and improve profitability is significant.

Understanding costs and benefits leads to better decisions

Underestimation of the costs of unsustainable performance makes it harder to justify eco-innovation. If they are not recognized, how can the reduction which breakthrough innovations can achieve be properly understood?

The World Resources Institute identifies a number of business uses for better environmental cost information:

- *guiding product mix* and *pricing products* so that decisions are made with accurate information about the real costs and profitability of product lines

- *choosing manufacturing inputs* to avoid materials with high control and disposal costs

- *assessing pollution prevention projects* and *evaluating waste management options,* so that any potential savings "hidden" in overheads are made visible

- *comparing environmental costs across facilities* to identify good and bad performers and opportunities for improvement

- *capital budgeting* to understand future environmental benefits, costs and liabilities

- *product design*; in order that the whole-life costs of products – including disposal – are built into design decisions.

The two last uses are especially relevant to eco-innovation. Unsustainable processes and products will gradually become more expensive. Quantifying some of the potential costs in advance tilts the balance in favor of breakthrough improvements.

The process of understanding the business benefits and costs of sustainability is also important. Simply establishing a dialog between accountants and potential eco-innovators creates benefits. The former begin to see the bottom line importance of sustainability and the latter become adept at justifying their ideas in the mainstream language of the business. Certainly Bill Blackburn of Baxter, which is the leader in the field of practical environmental accounting, sees this as the most important gain from their activities (see box).

● BAXTER'S ENVIRONMENTAL BALANCE SHEET

The American corporation Baxter International is a leading producer, developer and distributor of health care products and services worldwide. It produces an annual "balance sheet" of the costs and benefits of its environmental actions.

Its 1994 balance sheet has three main items:

- costs of $27.6 million, mainly from operation and depreciation of pollution control equipment and expenses of environmental staff

- benefits of $23.4 million from 1994 initiatives. These are mainly savings in packaging and waste disposal costs resulting from waste minimization measures

- continuing benefits of $51.2 million from previous year's waste minimization and other environmental initiatives.

The net result is an annual "profit" of almost $50 million per annum.

The balance sheet also contains estimated costs of future opportunities, such as further reductions in packaging. It excludes any benefits from enhanced customer perceptions of Baxter. The company believes these to be considerable. It is currently working with customers to identify opportunities to change its products and packaging to provide benefits and savings to both.

Bill Blackburn, Baxter's Vice President for Corporate Environmental Affairs, finds the balance sheet to be invaluable. It convinces skeptics that environment can make a bottom line contribution. By calculating future cost savings, it guides environmental strategy. Above all, it creates an ongoing dialog between environmental and business managers. Bill Blackburn believes that it:

> enables these professionals to focus on common opportunities using a common language – the language of business – money. It has been the ultimate tool for integrating our environmental programme into our business.[2]

Accounting for externalities

Current business environmental accounting focusses on a company's internal costs. But many of the environmental costs created by economic activities are externalities. That is, they are borne by society as a whole rather than the organization or individual creating them. These external costs can be considerable. In the case of road transport, for example, economists argue that the external costs are such items as road infrastructure, accidents and accident prevention, congestion, pollution, repairs and so on and estimate them to be 100–200% greater than the actual cost to a car or truck operator.

This imbalance is unlikely to persist. Government policy is more and more based on the "polluter pays" principle. Through taxes, stringent liability regimes and other means, policy makers are gradually internalizing many external costs as the only path to steer the economy towards sustainable development and the markets towards innovative solutions. This could have major implications for the long-term profitability of your current product range or the returns you can expect from capital investments with ten or 20 year lifetimes. Think carefully. Does this prospect not tilt the scales towards innovation?

Notes

1 Ditz, D., Ranganathan, J. and Banks, D. *Green Ledgers: Case Studies in Corporate Environmental Accounting.* Washington, DC: World Resources Institute, 1995.

2 Quoted in Tuppen, C. *Environmental Accounting in Industry: A Practical Review.* London: BT (British Telecommunications), 1996, p.71.

Chapter 10

The business precautionary principle

▶ ISN'T THERE PLENTY OF TIME ?

St. Augustine wanted to be made virtuous – but not just yet. So too many will approve of sustainability in principle while still preferring to avoid the costs and inconvenience of reconsidering their products and processes "just at the moment." Won't there be plenty of time to react to the alarm bells when they ring more persistently?

A chaotic world can change quickly

Not if the world is in fundamental disequilibrium. Chaos theory tells us that complex systems can switch from one state to another with great rapidity – and with inherent unpredictability. The deep movements of demographics, environmental stress and changing value creation described in Part 1 already create fissures and tensions in the landscapes of economic, political and social life. The world economy grows and yet unemployment increases in many countries. The rich grow richer and yet the poor grow poorer. Information is everywhere and yet only the IT privileged can use it. The young fight for resources and influence in a world ever more dominated by the old. The media and a growing planetary awareness unify every part of the world while competition, crime and loss of faith erode the sense of social solidarity.

History shows that customer concerns and markets can change rapidly. The American auto industry was complacent before the 1973 oil crisis: within several years Japanese producers had won unprecedented market share. The scare about "mad cow disease" (BSE) in the UK in early 1996 crippled the beef industry within days (see box). Similar shocks will recur as consumer values shift and the constraints of sustainability become tighter, and as innovators realize that consumers' concern is an unmet need. It is they who will change the rules of the game by finding new ways of creating value.

▶ DEALING WITH RISK

Many issues of sustainable development can appear threatening, especially those involving unsubstantiated risks to human health or ecosystems. Out come the reasonable demands to delay "until we have all the evidence," and to take action only when there is proof that benefits will exceed costs. These demands are too often counter-productive. It can make industry seem uncaringly simplistic and thereby cost it the support of public opinion and policy makers.

The precautionary principle

It also puts business at odds with trends in public policy. This has broadly adopted the "precautionary principle," or *Vorsorgeprinzip* in Germany, where the principle was invented. Principle 15 of the *Rio Declaration* states:

> In order to protect the environment, the precautionary approach shall be widely applied by States according to their capabilities. Where there are threats of serious or irreversible damage, lack of full scientific certainty shall not be used as a reason for postponing cost-effective measures to prevent environmental degradation.

● BSE: BUSINESS WINNERS AND LOSERS

The *Financial Times*'s Lex column is famed for its hard-headed appraisals of corporate prospects. When the news of a probable transfer of BSE to humans broke in March 1996 it lost no time in considering the business implications:

> The result is likely to be a switch to pork, poultry and fish. This will create winners as well as losers. Hillsdown is one: it looks smart, having sold its abattoir business. And although it has a small red meat processing operation, it is the UK's largest poultry operator. Turkey producer Bernard Mathews also looks attractive.
>
> The losers from the latest beef scare are not only beef producers and suppliers. Feed operators, for which the largest and most profitable part of the business is cattle feed, also stand to suffer. Increased demand for other types of feed would probably not compensate for the lost business. Those at risk include Dalgety and Harrisons & Crosfield.
>
> The list of losers would become longer still, however, if beef and dairy farmers' worst fears are realized, and the entire UK herd is slaughtered. This is a possibility because, although there is no evidence of any risk from milk, BSE is largely found among dairy cattle. Since the UK is 85 per cent self-sufficient in milk, this would mean importing vast quantities – a logistical nightmare since, although continental Europe has a milk surplus, it might have to be pasteurised in the UK. Given the already high price of British milk, the impact would be somewhat muted. But, Unigate and Northern Foods look vulnerable, even after recent rationalisation to cope with changes in the milk industry.[1]

The quote provides a striking example of how apparently secure businesses can suddenly be hit by a crisis of this kind. And how those who anticipate, whether by design or inadvertently, can benefit.

The Global Climate Change Treaty requires signatories to adopt this approach to global warming, and, as evidence of environmental degradation mounts, the principle will be applied in more and more areas.

In the USA, the President's Council on Sustainable Development, a group of 25 leaders from government, business, environmental, civil rights, labor and native Americans' organizations states its belief that . . .

> even in the face of scientific uncertainty, society should take reasonable actions to avert risks where the potential harm to human health or the environment is thought to be serious or unrepairable.[2]

It makes several policy recommendations in the areas of extended product responsibility, ecosystem integrity and better science for improved decision making.

The precautionary principle has a number of meanings but is generally interpreted as requiring prudence and minimizing of risks when there is scientific uncertainty about environmental problems. The bottom line implication is to invest in environmental actions even though the benefits are still uncertain.

A complex and uncertain world

The precautionary principle seems relevant because our world appears ever more complex and uncertain and the relationship between causes and effects ever more fuzzy. Brian Wynne identifies four descending states of knowledge:

- risk
- uncertainty
- ignorance
- indeterminacy (see box).

Major environmental problems such as global warming combine most or all of these. Even in this age of information we continue to deal with another state of knowledge – the secret. The information known to a minority is withheld or distorted. Access to complete information will remain an issue for environmental communicators as they want to build credibility and public trust.

● WHAT DON'T WE KNOW?

Brian Wynne makes a distinction between the following states:

- *Risk* – system behavior is basically known, and outcomes can be assigned a probabilistic value. The insurance business depends on such risk assessments to make money from writing policies.

- *Uncertainty* – important system parameters are known, but not the probability distributions. Scientists agree that greenhouse gases should warm, not cool, the atmosphere as they concentrate. Their climate models however calculate a wide variation for the extent, the probability and the timing of temperature change and the impact on sea levels.

- *Ignorance* – what is not known is not known.

- *Indeterminacy* – causal chains, networks or processes are open, and thus defy prediction.[3]

Unreliable science?

Wynne and other academics show that even scientists themselves do not always recognize the full extent of uncertainty, ignorance and indeterminacy. Science, like business, is the activity of real people with their biasses and their egos. It also has several characteristics that weaken its reliability:

- Scientific training and work are still organised in narrow disciplines that do not communicate effectively. Different disciplines can have very different approaches to the same environmental problem. This makes it difficult to do the multidisciplinary research needed to understand complex environmental issues.

- Science goes where the funding goes. Many department leaders need to market their services to round up their budgets and play skillfully on the scares of the day, the biasses of their funding partners and early releases to the media to fuel interest in their research.

The result? Different scientific evaluations of the trends and threats. The contrarians' school has responded to the alarmists; another proof that scientists have their bias.

Of course environmental problems need sound science to resolve them. But the "sound science" needed to deal with their systemic and social nature is still being forged and will need time – more time than the various stakeholders are willing to wait on certain issues.

Risk perceptions vary

Risk provides an example. Uncertainty, ignorance and indeterminacy are difficult enough to deal with. They make people anxious and insecure. But in some ways risk is worse. We are clear about a cause–effect link. But we can only estimate a probability of when the effect will strike: a one in a million chance that something causes cancer seems low to a scientist but very high if you have been exposed.

In fact scientists perceive risk very differently than the public:

- a high familiar risk (speeding, smoking) is often ignored or discounted

- a new risk (AIDS or BSE) draws more attention and public support than a chronic risk (tuberculosis, cholera, firearms)

- a familiar disease with a new uncertain cause gets the same prime attention (endocrine effects on breast cancer).

This is not pure irrationality. It mostly reflects personal "world views," experience and values.

Technocratic approaches do not work

The chemical, energy and other industries have learned this the hard way. They have had a technocratic approach which has focussed on "facts" rather than values and feelings, so, when criticized, they have been hurt and kept information to themselves so they will not be misunderstood.

It cannot work: a technocratic risk communication and management is doomed to failure and public antagonism. The company will be accused of being hard and secretive adding the burden to prove openness and honesty, and complicating the communication of risk even further.

You handle risk all the time

Take a step back and ask yourself what is really new about this risk and uncertainty question? You have to consider them all the time in your personal life: do you smoke? speed? indulge in sweets? Whatever the answer you should have thought about the risks and if they are worth the pleasure.

Risk: the essence of business

All business decisions are made under conditions of uncertainty. A new product launch is similar to atmospheric modeling. The overall direction of change seems clear – more greenhouse gases should warm rather than cool the atmosphere and competitors will respond with price cuts, new substitutes or counter advertising. But the extent, probability and timing of specific changes remain highly uncertain.

Companies know also that they cannot predict all accidents. But they can develop extensive safety data bases to understand how to prevent them and to continuously decrease occupational risk.

In fact business is mostly performing very well in evaluating and managing risks, and in taking due precautions against uncertainty. Engineering calculations, marketing strategies, accident and loss prevention, financial hedging, credit management, product liability and so on are all honed business techniques to face uncertainty and risk. They keep the complex economic machine alive and the consumer safe. A few exceptions that hit the media, court rooms and bankruptcy toll can only confirm the normal working of this complex web of decisions.

Be innovative, not defensive

So why does business paint itself into a corner when debating the precautionary principle? Why does it insist on a complete scientific understanding and a full cost benefit analysis as a requisite for environmental decisions? When it makes its own decisions without these? In all other categories?

The relative novelty of the issue and the potential costs are one explanation. But the costs of not doing it are also considerable. You are vulnerable to attack by those who have no trust in data, perceive the risk ominous and will accuse business of concealing the facts to gain time and save costs. (This has happened, of course.)

Even so, the innovative approach is to develop a precautionary philosophy in business. If you defend the status quo you become part of the problem. Look for the unmet needs being expressed in the public debates and innovate to meet them. You can build on existing practices of risk management and cost benefit analysis and develop some new techniques.

▶ MAKING BUSINESS DECISIONS UNDER UNCERTAINTY

If an event is uncertain you must rely on judgment, take a calculated risk and gamble. The central question is whether to wait or to act. When it comes to environmental issues many companies prefer to wait and see whether they are real before taking action.

Regulators and environmentalists must overcome this inertia. They must create sufficient costs to make waiting expensive so that acting is in a company's self-interest. The box outlines a probabilistic model to consider this decision.

● FINANCIAL ASPECTS OF DECISIONS UNDER UNCERTAINTY

When faced with uncertainty about any issue, companies have two options:

- *Do nothing or wait the problem out.* If the event happens indeed there can be a penalty for the negligence of timely action. You lose. Call L this loss. If the event never happens you saved yourself the money and trouble. Business continues as usual.

- *Act now and invest in preventive measures.* Call c the cost of taking action. If the event happens you are ready. You can benefit from early action over those who have done nothing. They may now spend a lot more under time pressure. Call g this gain. But if the forecast was wrong you invested for no advantage.

Figure 10.1 represents this balance of consequences. The financial equation is represented by a set of "Wait / Act" curves that reflect the cost of capital over various delay periods. You can use the curves for a financial evaluation of a precautionary measure. You must first assess the potential advantage g of taking this action and the potential penalty L for missing the chance. The cost c for taking this action can flip your cash impact from L to g. The curves therefore consider the ratio $(g+L)/c$ as a function of the probability of the event for various delay periods.

Assume the cash impact is 10 times the cost to act. For a probability of 1 in 10 you are better off to postpone your initiative. If you judge the probability to be 1 in 3 you gain by acting now even if you wait 10 years to reap your advantage. As the margin of error shrinks, the incentive to act grows exponentially. Likewise as the loss–gain exceeds 20 times the cost to act.

▶

● **FIGURE 10.1**
  Financial aspects of decisions under uncertainty

Financial balance of consequences

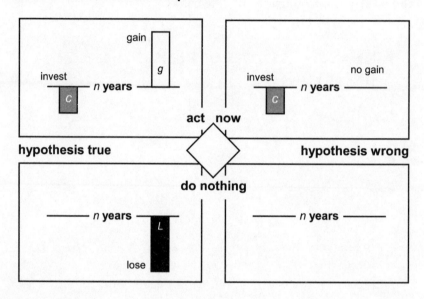

Wait/act curves   *for discount rate of 10%*

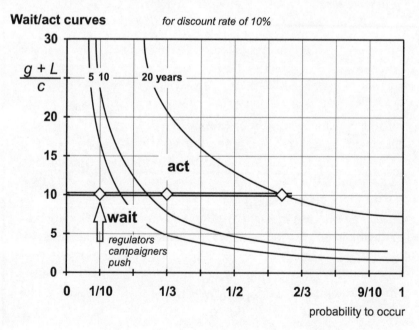

▶ The graph in Figure 10.1 is not an absolute decision tool but a way to put precaution into a financial perspective. Regulators use fines and other levies to push specific actors over the wait/act boundary. Regardless of the probability of the event they make sure that the penalty is significant and with short delay. Campaigners often use consumer pressure to threaten large, rapid business loss that jolts a company up the vertical axis into the reaction zone. From an ethical point of view you could as well reject the relevance of a discount factor that greatly minimizes the impact of future costs in today's decision.

Probabilities are difficult to assess. A probabilistic financial model is only useful to check the magnitude and sensitivity of the economic impacts. But there are other important reasons to take action despite the uncertainty. It could be the desire to preserve a good image or to maintain a record of continuous risk reduction or profound respect for Murphy's Law. If anything can go wrong, it eventually will.

But techniques alone will never be adequate. The essence of the precautionary principle in business is a vision of and a faith in a sustainable future. Enter the back casting and scenario planning approach described in Chapter 2. By identifying the end game you want to reach, you get a balanced view. You see where resistance to environmental pressures is merely delaying the inevitable. There will be other cases where those pressures are driven by short-term fallacy or considerations and should legitimately be resisted.

So the precautionary approach tells you constantly that things need to improve, that there is an opportunity to anticipate solutions. It also reminds you of the need for dialog with other social actors – to communicate risk (since there is no such thing as a risk-free option), to understand their concerns and to work together to resolve them.

But how can precaution be implemented? The next chapters will tell you.

Notes

1 "BSE," *Financial Times*, 23 March 1996.

2 The President's Council for Sustainable Development *Sustainable America*. Washington, DC: US Government Printing Office, 1996.

3 Wynne, B. "Uncertainty and Environmental Learning," *Global Environmental Change*, **2**, 1992, pp.111–127.

Part 3

HOW TO CHANGE?

In Chapter 11 we explore the business implications of sustainable development. There are many examples of companies responding to this challenge either as a result of their own initiative or as a result of national and international programs.

In Chapters 12 and 13 we present the most promising concepts to guide business. One is the concept of Cleaner Production developed by the United Nations Environmental Program. The other is "eco-efficiency" which has been defined by the World Business Council for Sustainable Development.

Changes will be helped by new tools such as environmental management systems and life cycle analysis. In Chapter 14 we describe their value but also argue that, by themselves, no existing tools will focus enough attention on opportunities for innovation.

By reading this section you will get:

- *an outline of the business implications of sustainable development;*

- *a briefing on the UN Cleaner Production Program;*

- *a briefing on the World Business Council for Sustainable Development and its concept of eco-efficiency;*

- *an understanding of the synergy and potential of eco-efficiency and cleaner production;*

- *an explanation of new tools such as environmental management systems and life cycle and analysis and insight into their usefulness.*

Chapter 11

Innovation for sustainability

We know. You may be frustrated at this point. We keep talking about sustainable development and you were looking for a book and material to turn broad geopolitical concepts into a practical business proposition.

First the concept. The central meaning of sustainable development is that present actions do not jeopardize the future.

It has always been a principle of good husbandry and the actual term originated in the forest industry over a century ago. But it reached global impact in the hands of the World Commission on Sustainable Development, usually referred to as the Brundtland Commission after its chair, Norwegian premier Gro Harlem Brundtland. The Commission's 1987 report calls for a "new era of environmentally sound sustainable development."

> *Humanity has the ability to make development sustainable – to ensure that it meets the needs of the present without compromising the ability of future generations to meet their own needs – Brundtland Commission.*

Most of the world's governments now accept its logic and are committed, at least on paper, to achieve it. *Agenda 21* describes a route towards it. But sustainability's very strength as a mobilizing idea – the broad nature of its message – is a handicap to its implementation. You are not alone if you do not fully understand it.

113

Few know precisely what it means at a practical, day to day, business level. We believe that you will once you have reached the end of this book.

You have a steer. The US National Wildlife Federation worked with companies, industry groupings and a business academic, Thomas Gladwin, to define the "sustainable corporation."[1]

▌ SUSTAINABILITY – THE THREE SECURITIES

Their report sees sustainable development in terms of "security" – a term which dictionaries define as being about reliability, dependability and freedom from anxiety, desperation and danger. It identifies three securities as being relevant to sustainable development:

- ecological security

- resource security

- socio-economic security (see Figure 11.1)

● FIGURE 11.1
The three securities of human activity

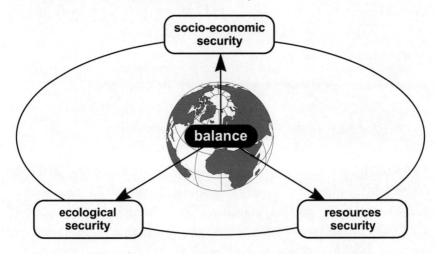

Ecological security

Ecological security means being able to rely on the continued functioning of natural systems. Paul and Ann Ehrlich have listed some of the ways in which these contribute to human well-being:

- the maintenance of a benign mix of gases in the atmosphere;
- moderation of the weather;
- regulation of the hydrologic cycle that provides fresh water in a manner that minimizes the occurrence of floods and droughts;
- the generation and preservation of the fertile soils that are essential for agriculture and forestry;
- the disposal of wastes and cycling of nutrients;
- control of the vast majority of agricultural pests and organisms that can cause disease;
- pollination of many crops;
- provision of forest products and food from the sea;
- and maintenance of nature's vast genetic library from which humanity has already drawn the very basis of civilization.[2]

All relate to the maintenance of a quality food chain and air and water to sustain our health. This is fundamental to the preservation of the life of humans and most species. Ecological security requires that these services are not jeopardized by the destruction or degradation of ecosystems, climatic cycles or other natural systems. Reduced biodiversity, global warming and stratospheric ozone depletion are just three environmental effects which could do this.

Resource security

Resource security is the confidence that the food, energy, raw material and other physical requirements of humanity will be available in required quantities at reasonable cost. Resource security is lost when we live from the planet's capital instead of from its dividends. This "mining" of resources deprives future generations of opportunities to make use of them as surely as shareholders would be deprived after several years of accumulated cash outflows and the company at the brink of bankruptcy.

The way to achieve resource security is to:

- use all resources with maximum efficiency, eg minimum wastage;

- minimize and wherever possible eliminate the use of non-renewable resources;

- maximize use of renewable ones;

- do not exceed the rate at which these resources can be regenerated.

● HOW BIG IS YOUR FOOTPRINT?

The Canadian academic William Rees uses the term "ecological footprint" to describe and measure a city's or country's use of distant land to provide its resources. Calculations by the International Institute for Environment and Economic Development (IIEED) demonstrate how large this is.[3] London requires a land area 120 times greater than its actual size to meet its needs. The UK as a whole uses in other countries:

- three times its own area of productive forest to provide wood products;

- the equivalent of a fifth of its own total cultivated land to grow its cotton needs.

Another study calculates that a Colombian prawn farm requires a land area between 35 and 190 times larger than its own acreage to support it.[4]

The footprint tool has its limits. But it graphically demonstrates the inequality of resource use. IIEED's conclusion from its work is that:

Much more can and needs to be done to assist developing countries establish the sustainable production and trading systems that allow both them and us to benefit from their scarce environmental resources.[5]

Socio-economic security

Socio-economic security is not a state where individuals are shielded from the normal ups and down of life. We all experience frustration, unrequited love, unrealized dreams and we all must die. But it is a state where people are not stunted by unemployment, high crime, excessive inequalities in income and wealth, illiteracy and serious threats to health before old age is reached. Losing this security usually results in runaway demography and environmental destruction. But by the same token, affluence can also result in a squandering and disproportionate usage of natural resources and space (see box on previous page).

Poverty is the greatest threat to socio-economic security. According to the World Bank, reducing it requires a dual strategy:

> The first element is to increase the productive use of the poor's most abundant asset, labour. It calls for policies that harness market incentives, social and political institutions, infrastructure, and technology to that end. The second is to provide basic social services to the poor. Primary health care, family planning, nutrition, and primary education are especially important. The two elements are mutually reinforcing; one without the other is not sufficient.[6]

Socio-economic security is critical to the achievement of the other securities.

Investment in human capital is also essential if technical and other means of using resources frugally are to be developed. And psychological theory suggests that basic human needs such as hunger and shelter must be met first. Only then will people begin to consider "higher" things such as harmony with nature or intergenerational equity.

Experience shows that literacy and expanding life chances – especially for women – are the key to reducing the population growth which is a major driver of resource use and environmental impact.

Several indexes of welfare try to measure socio-economic security. Their components include:

- income and wealth levels

- health and nutritional status

- educational levels

- access to resources

- distribution of income and wealth

- access to basic freedoms.

The calculation of such indexes demonstrates that there is no correlation between wealth and welfare.[7]

Socialism by another name?

Are sustainable development and socio-economic security socialism by another name? We think not. They certainly pose a challenge to the existing patterns of resource use, waste creation and wealth disparities. But sustainable development in itself has no bias towards or against free markets or private enterprise. Both are an important means to its achievement. Nor does sustainable development entail complete egalitarianism, but simply a world where everyone's basic needs are met and there are no gross inequalities. That is good for business because it is a world of consumers with disposable income.

Poor people are not good customers – Thomas Gladwin

Henry Ford realized the need to develop such a society when he paid high wages to his assembly workers. The difference in sustainable development is that their income will be spent on lighter, smaller, maybe virtual goods and enhanced services. Henry Ford's customers could have any color car as long as it was black. His ecological equivalent of the future will offer any kind of good or service as long as it is efficient, dematerialized and produces no wastes.

● BUSINESS BENEFITS OF SUSTAINABLE DEVELOPMENT

Ecological security

- enhances the productivity of natural resources that industry already exploits (eg, farmland, forests, fisheries, and recreational areas);
- ensures access to critical natural inputs used in production (eg, water);
- maintains genetic resources important to future progress in a range of industries (eg, pharmaceuticals, agriculture, energy, chemicals, construction, etc.);
- protects corporate assets from potential adverse impacts of climatic instability (eg, coastal flooding affecting real estate and production facilities);
- promotes growth in markets for environmentally benign technologies and services; and
- supports healthier customers, more productive workers, and lower medical, legal and insurance costs, as health risks and toxic liabilities diminish.

Resource security

- saves costs from energy and material efficiency;
- reduces dependence on unstable energy sources;
- stabilizes markets and prices for natural resources;
- spurs innovation and new product development;
- creates markets for resource-efficient technologies, products and services; and

▶

● brings competitive advantages from frugal use of raw materials.

Socio-economic security

● enlarges the pool of healthier and better educated workers and customers;

● opens large markets for products and services which meet basic material needs in environmentally sound and resource-efficient ways;

● reduces vulnerability to social breakdown, conflict, famine, plague or war; and

● in general, increases confidence in a stable future, something that is vital to a prosperous world economy.

▶ SUSTAINABILITY IS A BUSINESS LANGUAGE

The triple balance of securities translates into business language (see Figure 11.2). Resource security means providing resource-efficient *goods and services*.

Socio-economic security also translates into basic marketing philosophy – providing products and services which can be consumed by all and improve their *quality of life*.

Ecological security translates into the concept of *environmental care*. This is already part of the mainstream for many corporations.

The sustainable corporation must provide resource-efficient goods and services with minimal environmental impact and maximum value to customers' quality of life

● **FIGURE 11.2**
The three securities of eco-efficiency

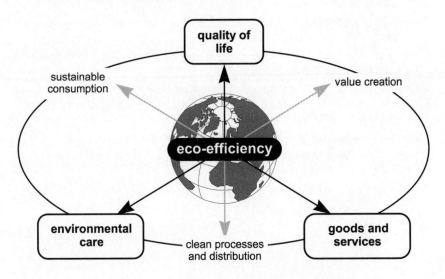

These three securities create three particular imperatives:

● the reconciliation of environmental care and quality of life by developing *sustainable consumption* patterns;

● the building of greater environmental care into goods and services through *clean processes and distribution*;

● *value creation* through goods and services which provide quality of life.

121

Notes

1 Gladwin T. *Building the Sustainable Corporation*. Washington, DC: US National Wildlife Federation, 1992.

2 Ehrlich P. and Ehrlich A. *Healing the Planet*. Reading, Mass.: Addison-Wesley, 1991, p.3.

3 International Institute for Environment and Development *Citizen Action to Lighten Britain's Ecological Footprints*. London, 1995.

4 Larsson, J., Folke, C. and Kaustky, N. *Ecological Limitations and Appropriation of Ecosystem Support by Shrimp Farming in Colombia*. Stockholm: Beijer International Institute of Ecological Economics, 1994.

5 International Institute for Environment and Development *op cit.*, p.6.

6 World Bank *World Development Report 1990: Poverty*. Oxford: Oxford University Press, 1990. Cited in Gladwin *op cit*.

7 Van Dieren, W. (ed.) *Taking Nature Into Account*. New York: Springer Verlag, 1995.

Chapter 12

Cleaner production goes global

Convinced that sustainable development is a serious business development concept? And that you can still innovate, grow your business and make money? We hope so. After a hundred pages of why, are you ready for some how? How can you get assistance to achieve eco-innovation? The United Nations Environmental Programme (UNEP) should be your first port of call.

▶ UNEP'S INDUSTRY AND ENVIRONMENT PROGRAMME

The Left Bank in Paris used to spread political revolution around the world. Now the same area is exporting business revolution. The message is Cleaner Production. Its theme is opportunities for industry and primary producers to gain financial rewards from environmental improvements. Its origin is UNEP's Industry and Environment unit.

From its offices on Quai André-Citroën, the unit has worked with more than 100 organizations to implement Cleaner Production initiatives in over 60 countries. Thousands of companies take part in its demonstration projects and discover win-win business and environmental opportunities. Many more people make use of its data base, the International Cleaner Production Information Clearing-house (ICPIC). Perhaps more importantly, a resource of trained and aware managers and professionals is being created for the future.

Wanted: a new term

The Cleaner Production program began in 1989. At that time, says its director Jacqueline Aloisi de Larderel:

> There was no term to describe the fundamental change we wanted to achieve. Waste minimization, pollution prevention, low waste technology – none of these communicated our idea. We wanted something which went beyond technical aspects and industrial processes to encompass broader issues like management and government policy.
>
> After a lot of debate we decided on Cleaner Production. It recognizes that we have to produce, but says we must do it differently. It suggests that the solution is prevention, not end of pipe. It indicates that achieving it is a step by step process. And it's clear that governments and consumers contribute to it as well as industry.

Defining cleaner production

This holistic perspective comes through in UNEP's practical definition:

> Cleaner Production is the continuous application of an integrated preventative environmental strategy to processes and products to reduce risks to humans and the environment.
>
> For production processes, cleaner production includes conserving raw materials and energy, eliminating toxic raw materials, and reducing the quantity and quality of all emissions and wastes before they leave a process.
>
> For products, the strategy focusses on reducing impacts along the entire life cycle of the product, from raw material extraction to the ultimate disposal of the product.[1]

▶ ACHIEVING CLEANER PRODUCTION

How can cleaner production be achieved? In many ways, but three are especially important:

- changing attitudes

- applying know-how

- improving technology.

Not just a technical activity

UNEP's experience is that Cleaner Production is never just a technical activity. Increasing people's awareness of environmental problems and their relationship to them is vital, which makes it easier to implement technical solutions as the need is more obvious. And it often identifies simple "good housekeeping" opportunities which need no major change or investment.

> *Involving staff of the Beijing Chemical Works in a Cleaner Production Audit immediately generated ideas which cost $1200 to implement – and had a payback of 15 days.*

How did the Beijing Chemical Works get these spectacular results? Because it applied the right know-how, as a later case study shows. Not just about the environment but also about the day to day operation of the factory and how this could be changed.

Quick paybacks from four techniques

But, of course, technology can be helpful. Beijing Chemical Works is following up its initial successes with more expensive options involving new equipment. UNEP identifies four effective ways of doing this:

- change process or manufacturing technology

- change input materials

- change the final product

- reuse materials on site, preferably within the process.

It also has many examples of the financial benefits they create:

- Improved process control at an Indonesian cement company has saved $350,000 per annum, with a payback of under one year.

- Recycling chromium at a Greek tannery has reduced emissions of this toxic metal and saved $43,000 a year – payback period eleven months.

- A Tunisian battery manufacturer is saving over $2 million over a two year period for an investment of under $400,000.

▶ CLEANER PRODUCTION HELPS DEVELOPING COUNTRIES

It is no accident that all these examples are from developing countries. UNEP works in all parts of the world but places great emphasis on the developing world and Eastern European and other countries undergoing economic transition. Firstly because industrialized countries have more internal resources to work on Cleaner Production. Secondly because of the rapid economic growth of many developing countries. If Cleaner Production can influence the design of the new equipment and processes which such growth requires they can avoid many future environmental problems. In UNEP's words, developing countries can . . .

> seize the opportunity to invest relatively cheaply in Cleaner Production now rather than pay heavily later for clean-up operations, as the industrialized nations have had to do. Doing so will also provide developing countries with a competitive edge over those firms long since established and now encumbered with expensive end-of-pipe control technologies.[2]

● CLEANER PRODUCTION IN CHINA

China's population growth and economic dynamism make Cleaner Production vital. The Chinese Academy of Sciences warns that environmental stresses will be unbearable unless improvements are made.

UNEP Industry and Environment's involvement with China began in 1993. It was asked to advise the country's National Environmental Protection Agency (NEPA) on a cleaner production initiative, financed by the World Bank. The initiative involved:

- awareness raising seminars for policy makers and industrialists

- training of Chinese experts

- a Chinese language Cleaner Production Audit manual

- 30 company demonstration projects.

The latter included that at the Beijing Chemical Works.

A second stage is now underway. Additional activities in this include:

- industry-specific Chinese language audit materials

- Chinese language videos and training materials

- extension of seminars and demonstration projects to more regions and city areas

- a policy study to identify government actions to further encourage Cleaner Production.

UNEP's program in China demonstrates the scale of the challenges and opportunities – and what can be done in practice (see box). It has proved an inspiration to Jacqueline Aloisi de Larderel:

> I've been amazed at the response we've had in China. The Chinese want growth, but realize it can't be at any cost. Many officials now see Cleaner Production as the best means of development, which will make their industries leading edge in future. And the practical initiatives show that the message is being heard in industry. It's very rewarding.

Jacqueline Aloisi de Larderel's vision

Such positive messages are important at a time when recession has reduced environmental commitment in the industrialized world. Jacqueline Aloisi de Larderel is widely admired for the energy and vision with which she has overcome such obstacles and brought Cleaner Production into the mainstream in every continent. Now she wants to realize her long-term vision, which is making sustainability integral to every business or political decision. For her:

> Innovation is driven by the dreams of men and women. For centuries we dreamt of flying. Leonardo and others tried to achieve it but failed. But eventually we succeeded, and now it's routine. Environment must be part of the dreams we have today. Otherwise we'll wake into a nightmare.

Notes

1 "What is Cleaner Production?" *UNEP Industry and Environment*, special issue on Cleaner Production, Oct–Dec 1994, p.4.

2 United National Environment Program, Industry and Environment *Government Strategies and Policies for Cleaner Production*, Paris, 1994.

Chapter 13

The challenge of eco-efficiency

▶ WORLD BUSINESS COUNCIL FOR SUSTAINABLE DEVELOPMENT

Leading international companies such as BP, 3M and Sony need ideas about, and assistance, with sustainable business development just as much as do smaller businesses. To get them they work with the World Business Council for Sustainable Development (WBCSD). This Geneva-based organization is a coalition of 120 companies from 33 countries and has nine regional and national centers in Asia, Eastern Europe and Latin America. The box overleaf provides details of one of these in Colombia.

WBCSD was born in 1995 and unites two separate organizations. One was the World Industry Council for the Environment (WICE), an affiliate of the International Chamber of Commerce. The other was the Business Council for Sustainable Development (BCSD).

WBCSD's work is based on the concept of eco-efficiency, which it originated.

> *Eco-efficiency – "the delivery of competitively priced goods and services that satisfy human needs and bring quality of life while progressively reducing ecological impacts and resource intensity, through the life cycle, to a level at least in line with the earth's estimated carrying capacity."*

● ECO-EFFICIENCY IN COLOMBIA

The Colombian Business Council for Sustainable Development (CECODES) was founded in 1993. Its director, Maria Emilia Correa, feels that eco-efficiency in Latin America is rather different to eco-efficiency in Europe and America:

> Our main exports are agricultural products, which usually compete in highly unstable markets which offer low prices. Many people believe that social and environmental investments are luxuries our countries can't afford until we get richer. We have to offer an alternative view which can be applied in agriculture and stresses social equity as much as economic efficiency and environmental improvement.

She points to CECODES' collaboration with the Colombian sugar producers' association, Asocana, as a successful implementation of this alternative view. Asocana has encouraged its members to reuse and recycle wastes and reduce water consumption. As a result water consumption per tonne of sugar has fallen by 34% since 1990. It has also communicated the benefits of investing in employee training and the development of their communities.

A simpler definition of eco-efficiency is "producing more with less." Its content is very similar to UNEP's Cleaner Production concept but places more emphasis on creating additional value for customers through environmental actions.

Does this seem to be a truism? To many companies it still is not, and it was to even fewer when BCSD and WICE began their work six years ago. If you accept that environment and competitive advantage are compatible you have probably been influenced by their ideas somewhere along the line. We certainly have.

▶ FROM EITHER:OR TO SUSTAINABILITY AND DEVELOPMENT

Remember that the 1970s was the era of Limits to Growth. Many assumed that environmental and resource constraints would block further increases in production and wealth. Only in the 1980s did the logic of either:or change to one of sustainability and development.

At the policy level the change was associated with the name of Norwegian premier Gro Harlem Brundtland, who chaired a commission on sustainable development. At the level of business it owed much to the work of an industrialist, Stephan Schmidheiny, and his associate, Frank Bosshardt (see box overleaf). They worked with colleagues such as Maurice Strong and Hugh Faulkner to establish BCSD in 1991 and to flesh out the ideas of eco-efficiency into a practical approach for industry.

Their ideas reached the public domain in Stephan Schmidheiny's book, *Changing Course*. Published just before the 1992 Rio summit, it still is a core text on business and environment.

● A WORD IS BORN

How are new words invented? Lexicographers search the printed media for their first publication. They seldom identify the moment of their birth. But the origin of the term "eco-efficiency" can be dated to a single day in 1990. The proud parent was Frank Bosshardt, a senior executive in Stephan Schmidheiny's Anova holding company. This is his story:

> As Stephan (Schmidheiny) became more involved with environmental issues in the build up to Rio he felt we needed a catchword to sum up the business implications. Sustainable development is very much a macro concept, it's difficult to apply at company level. It was obvious we had to get a micro equivalent which showed how companies could contribute.
>
> So at one of the early BCSD meetings I proposed a competition to find a word. We had about 50 entries, of which I put in three or four. One of mine was eco-efficiency. At that time I wasn't sure it was the best. I got my secretary to make all the entries anonymous and then sent them to Stephen. After a couple of days I called and said what should we do? Have another meeting, set up a jury? He said, no. It's obvious there's only one proposal that's valuable. I asked which one and was amazed when he said it's eco-efficiency.

WBCSD's director-general Jan-Olaf Willums thinks he knows how Bosshardt came to the term:

> It's because he's an engineer. You're trained to think about efficiency and improvement. I'm an engineer too. Even when I wash the dishes I'm thinking about how to make it more efficient. And Frank's in business, where efficiency's about the most used word there is. So it was natural for him to bring the word into the environmental area.

Four success factors

Since then WBCSD and its predecessors have run three international workshops. The result? A refined concept of what eco-efficiency is and what it is not. Shared experience of implementation. Four success factors have been identified:

1 *An emphasis on customer service.* By focussing on what services to provide, not just what products to supply, companies open up opportunities to deliver less eco-intensive, higher value applications.

2 *An emphasis on quality of life.* Companies' performance and success will be judged increasingly on how their products or services meet real needs, not perceived wants.

3 *A life cycle view.* Companies will add value from their activities by monitoring and assessing their impact at every stage. A life cycle approach can lead to decisions to redesign processes and products to minimize impact, maximize efficiency and measure the value added.

4 *The eco-capacity imperative.* Eco-efficiency's "bottom line" is to enable business to add ever more value within the realities of the earth's carrying capacity (for example, its ability to absorb more wastes, maintain bio diversity etc.), through a continuous process of improvement, reflecting the philosophy "we can continually do more with less."[1]

▶ INTEGRATING SUSTAINABLE DEVELOPMENT AND BUSINESS

What is the value of the eco-efficiency approach? It is integration of sustainable development with business considerations, with a long term vision of how both can be achieved, allowing short term conflicts between them to be seen as temporary problems rather than fundamental constraints. It acknowledges too that even altruistic businesses have to satisfy their customers and be sufficiently profitable to invest and to meet their cost of capital. In this perspective environmental achievement and business success go hand in hand. If the former does not lead to the latter then markets will be dominated by the poor environmental performers.

But business does not operate in a vacuum. Its actions are influenced by what WBCSD calls framework conditions. This includes government policies and the effects of the financial system. WBCSD believes that these generally impede rather than encourage eco-efficiency.

WBCSD also wants more market-based regulation to drive up the costs of environmental "bads." However it wants the change to be revenue neutral, so that raised taxes or levies in one area are offset by cuts elsewhere.

The prices of goods and services must increasingly recognise and reflect the environmental costs of their production, use, recycling and disposal – Changing Course.

Above all WBCSD believes that the financial markets must become more aware of the benefits of eco-efficiency. They will then penalize poor performers by imposing credit conditions or will sell their shares and bonds to invest in good performers. This is yet another reason to reappraise the relative costs and benefits of incremental rather than radical responses to the issues of sustainable development.

Notes

1 World Business Council for Sustainable Development *Eco-efficient Leadership – for Improved Economic and Environmental Performance*. Geneva, 1995, p.8.

Chapter 14

Current tools for change and their limitations

Eco-efficiency and cleaner production are closely interlocked concepts. Achieving them is being made easier by innovations in environmental management. Two important mechanisms are:

- the rapid delineation and standardization of environmental management systems (EMS)

- life cycle assessment (LCA).

▶ ENVIRONMENTAL MANAGEMENT SYSTEMS

Many companies now have an environmental management system. There are also three well known standards for them:

- British Standard 7750 (BS7750)

- the draft ISO (International Standards Organization) 14000

- the European Eco-Audit and Management Scheme (EMAS).

These differ in their precise requirements but all require applicants to define a proactive policy, and to systematically consider their environmental impacts, then take action to manage those which are significant.

Positive features ...

Environmental management systems have many positive features: they ensure consistent standards across an organization; they assign responsibility for implementation; they ask you to think deeply about your significant environmental impacts. So they are an essential underpinning for eco-efficiency. The quality principles on which they are based also translate well into environmental terms, as our final section discusses.

But do these systems foster environmental innovation? EMAS is site based and therefore has no influence over corporate activities such as R&D or product development. ISO14000 and BS7750 are already criticized for allowing companies complete freedom to define their significant issues and improvement targets, a freedom which is more likely to result in incremental than radical change. And none of the standards asks companies to move beyond ecology and resources and consider issues of socio-economic security.

... But unlikely to stimulate breakthrough innovations

In practice too, environmental management systems are the province of environmental managers (see Figure 14.1). They are not always well integrated with the mainstream of the business and so cannot always influence innovation processes.

Above all, standards are "me-too" instruments, that is, potentially achievable by a majority, with some stretch, but their bias is towards incremental improvement.

> *Environmental management systems are unlikely to drive the breakthrough innovations we need for sustainable development.*

● FIGURE 14.1
Environmental management and improvement systems

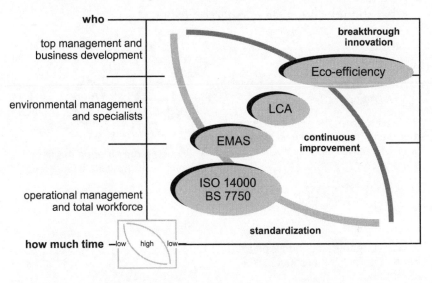

▶ LIFE CYCLE ASSESSMENT (LCA)

If environmental management systems are naturally conservative then LCA is inherently radical. It asks you to extend your horizons from your immediate business to consider where your raw materials come from and the disposal of your products, and the links between them (see Figure 14.2), with the implication that you bear some responsibility for any upstream or downstream impacts.

This challenging technique involves the collection and analysis of input and output for all stages of the product life cycle. It therefore provides a holistic picture of a product's environmental footprint and allows the most significant environmental impacts to be identified, both overall and for each stage.

The box gives more details of the four LCA steps:

● initiation

● inventory analysis

● impact assessment

● interpretation.

137

● FIGURE 14.2
What should a life cycle perspective include?

3 Which downstream operations and distribution lie between your company's operation and the enduser?

4 Which function does the final product perform while it lasts with the consumer?

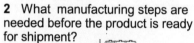

2 What manufacturing steps are needed before the product is ready for shipment?

5 What are the revalorization options that can be considered at the end of the product's service life?

your company

1 What upstream operations (extraction, culture, separation, etc) are necessary to provide raw materials to the first major manufacturing unit?

6 What are the disposal options of the ultimate waste streams?

● STAGES OF LIFE CYCLE ASSESSMENT

David Russell, Dow's life cycle specialist, has summarized the four main stages of an LCA study in this way.[1]

Initiation

The first step is initiation, a step where a clear goal and scope need to be defined. These will have a significant influence on the duration and costs of the study. The initiation step begins by recording the *purpose* of the study. This should be clearly understood and stated in terms of what decisions will be based on the findings, what information is required, at what level of detail and for what purpose.

Next, the *scope* of the study is defined. This includes a description of the system and its boundaries, the data requirements, the assumptions made, and any limitations. It is important to define the *functional unit*. This is derived from the function service that the system performs. In comparative studies it is essential that systems are compared on the basis of equivalent function.

Many LCAs have erred when they tried to compare products that did not fit similar service requirements. Comparing steel and aluminium only makes sense once their usage has been defined, like delivering a 33 cl serving of beer. Others have limited their system boundaries to the extent of data already available and run into similar problems of reliability and credibility.

The initiation phase is completed by a *data–quality assessment*, which describes the type and quality of data that will be needed to meet the study purpose.

Inventory

The life-cycle inventory (LCI) phase is fundamental. It provides a comprehensive view of the material, energy and pollutant flows across the *system boundary* and its reliability will affect the complete study. It needs to aim at reproducibility and needs to be extensively documented to allow review and updating. Here the "Code of Practice" produced by the Society for Toxicology and Chemistry (SETAC) can guide the LCA practitioner in the key decisions of boundary definition, energy accounting and allocation rules in complex material flows.[2] ▶

▶ The system boundary must be defined, not only in terms of its function, but also in relation to factors such as geography and time frame. Then the data for each subsystem must be collected. It is important to check the mass and energy balance of each subsystem before the calculation of the overall system inventory is made. LCA often requires exchanges of data sets between suppliers, customers, consultants, and even public authorities.

Impact

The impact assessment phase characterizes the effects of the environmental burdens identified in the inventory on resource conservation and on pollution. This is likely to be a combination of technical, quantitative and qualitative processes. It should be based on facts and circumstances and not on assumption. While the impacts of the use of raw materials and fossil fuels on the world's nonrenewable reserves can be fairly well characterized, it is important to note that many of the flows of materials, and pollutants described by the inventory phase will have context specific impacts that cannot be generalized. One ecosystem may be particularly sensitive to additional salinity while another may be at the limit of absorbing more solid waste. The process of impact assessment is not straight forward because an LCA data set does not provide data on exposure. The presence of a toxic substance does not assume a risk. One must consider the dose response curve and not take account of substances which are below the no effect level. Clearly, the stage of impact assessment is in its infancy and still requires significant methodology development. The Society for the Promotion of LCA Development (SPOLD) will have an important role to play here.

Interpretation

After having examined the system one is rewarded by new insights and improvement opportunities. The broad view provided by LCA will reveal strengths and weaknesses in comparison to competing or potential substitution services.

As much an improvement process as a scientific technique

David Russell, Dow's life cycle specialist, believes that LCA is not just a scientific technique but . . .

> an environmental improvement process that takes us outside our factory fence, our home or our business to look at the driving forces behind the products and services that society uses. It requires us to answer the question, "What is it that a particular product or service is ultimately meant to achieve?" We call this the defined function.
>
> Once you've decided this, you identify all the activities which contribute to this function. Setting the right boundaries for this is crucial. When you've gathered the data you can identify the key environmental improvements. Investments, regulations and economic instruments can then be directed at the areas of greatest benefit. LCA can therefore lead to real business improvement, reducing environmental impacts and risks while optimising costs.

LCA provides many benefits

Good LCAs deliver additional benefits. They can:

- clarify environmental controversies

- reveal upstream or downstream impacts of a product or service which would otherwise remain hidden

- generate new ideas for providing the same function with reduced environmental impact.

> *LCA shows that recycling is not always environmentally beneficial.*

Recycling is a case in point. A few years ago everyone was espousing it. Doubters often kept quiet. But numerous LCAs show that it is not a panacea. Often the energy and other inputs needed to recycle more than the fraction that is easy to collect and clean outweigh any benefit. Sometimes equipment is recycled into

141

raw materials when reuse or remanufacture would make better environmental and business sense.

Revealing spurious green claims

LCAs can also undercut spurious green claims. A manufacturer advertized a new product as cadmium-free. A competitor commissioned an LCA that showed that the cadmium-plated product is more electrically efficient. Fossil fuel power stations actually emit cadmium. The extra electricity consumption of the cadmium-free product therefore caused continuous cadmium emissions at the power plant. The calculations showed these to be far greater than cadmium escaping from the plating process of the electrically efficient product.

Definitions and assumptions are crucial

But there are problems with LCAs:

- The margins of accuracy are often loose enough to let some bias their assumptions to prove that a particular product is environmentally acceptable.

- Environmental effects are often context specific. A product using hydro-generated power in Norway has very different impacts than one using electricity from a brown coal station in the former East Germany. As a result it is difficult to provide standardized data which can be plugged into an analysis.

- LCAs often make different assumptions about system boundaries and relevant data. Some, for example, include all air and water inputs to the system, others exclude some or all of them.

- LCAs provide no data on exposure. They will tabulate a hazardous input or output. This will not mean that there is exposure and a defined risk.

The eco-compass – making LCA useful for business

These problems would matter less if LCA results were easily assimilable by managers and other lay audiences. But they are not. They usually have pages of detail and executive summaries covering tens of different environmental issues with no easy way of discovering the significance of the findings and their sensitivity to the underlying assumptions.

David Russell spends much of his time grappling with such issues and helping resolve them through involvement with SPOLD (the Society for the Promotion of LCA Development). He sees a need for new techniques to communicate LCA data and integrate them into business decision processes. His dream is a multilevel information source that . . .

> distils all the key environmental points into a few numbers for busy executives. But those who want more information can drill down to find the detailed data and assumptions that lie behind the numbers.

He has worked with Dow colleagues and visiting researchers and student assignees to develop one such technique, the eco-compass. We believe that it:

- condenses environmental data into a simple model which summarizes strategic issues, trade-offs and improvement opportunities for lay audiences

- does not over simplify and remains connected with the detailed analysis

- can be reliably applied to a variety of business circumstances.

The next section describes it in greater detail while Part 5 gives examples of its use.

Notes

1 Russell, D. *What is Life-Cycle Assessment, and What is So Special About it?* Brussels: Society for the Promotion of LCA Development, 1993.

2 Society for Toxicology and Chemistry (SETAC) *Guidelines for Life-Cycle Assessment: A Code of Practice*. Brussels, 1993.

Part 4

THE ECO-COMPASS

In Chapters 15 to 21 we describe the six dimensions of the eco-compass – material utilization, energy, environmental toxicity and quality, revalorization, resources and service extension. We provide information on scoring, and case studies of companies which have achieved exemplary progress on one or more of these dimensions.

In this section you will get:

- *a detailed explanation of the six dimensions of the eco-compass;*

- *practical advice on how to assess and score for each dimension;*

- *case histories of companies which have achieved eco-efficiency and made significant progress on one or more dimensions.*

Case objectives and limitations

This section contains 16 case studies of companies. All contain seven sections:

1 Background.

2 Details of product or process innovation.

3 Description of drivers (vision, commercial imperatives and/or regulation).

4 Contribution to sustainable development.

5 Business benefits.

6 Future challenges.

7 Learning either by the organization or drawn out by us.

Each also has a summary graphic (see Figure 15.1). This describes the key points of the case and provides relevant data on some or all of the six dimensions. It also scores the performance of the dimension on a scale of 0–5. The next chapter provides detailed information on the basis of this scoring. A general point is that a product or process is always scored relative to a base case.

We stress that this scoring is a device to illustrate how the eco-compass works. Generally we do not have the data to undertake a rigorous scoring. Two exceptions where we have tried to do this are Azurel and Sony, (see Figures 21.1 and 16.4 respectively).

The summary graphics are partial views only in the cases where we describe process rather than product improvements. IBM, for example, has made many product improvements which are not reflected in the compass score. The graphics may also be unfair to some large companies. Relatively small improvements score poorly on the compass. But if they reach millions of customers they can create more environmental benefit than substantial improvements which score highly but reach only a few.

A final point is that the cases rely on information provided by the companies. We validate this wherever possible and always try to examine it objectively. But it retains an element of subjectivity which you should bear in mind. Every case also focuses on individual products or processes rather than a company's overall environmental performance or degree of social responsibility. We do not try to assess either of these. Rather we have three specific aims:

- to show that eco-efficiency is possible in a wide range of countries, industries and sizes of companies;

- to provide a feel for its consequences and the way it has been achieved;

- to draw out learning points for you the reader.

● **FIGURE 15.1**
  Case study synopsis

The case studies show how companies innovate in one or several dimensions of the eco-compass to achieve eco-efficiency. Each case starts with this layout. It represents a short synopsis of the major improvements and the score. It is an indicative score on a side of 0-5 (as explained in Chapter 15). The score is relative to a base case - an alternative product or a previous generation.

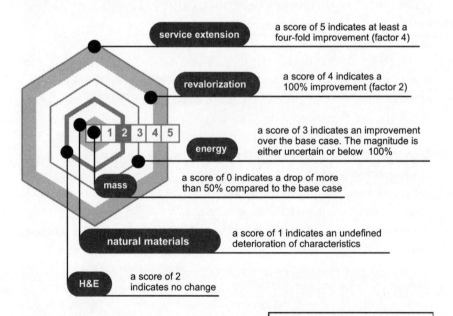

service extension — a score of 5 indicates at least a four-fold improvement (factor 4)

revalorization — a score of 4 indicates a 100% improvement (factor 2)

energy — a score of 3 indicates an improvement over the base case. The magnitude is either uncertain or below 100%

mass — a score of 0 indicates a drop of more than 50% compared to the base case

natural materials — a score of 1 indicates an undefined deterioration of characteristics

H&E — a score of 2 indicates no change

contact
company's contact person for further information where available

Chapter 15

Using the eco-compass

The previous chapter emphasized that life cycle assessment (LCA) is a very useful tool for gathering and analyzing environmental data. By calculating the inputs and outputs of each stage we gain a full picture of a product's total environmental impact (see Figure 15.2). But the final assessment is usually too complex and detailed to make sense to most business decision makers. We need a means of weighing the inputs and outputs to clarify important issues and make comparisons between options.

▶ A TOOL FOR IMPROVEMENT AND INNOVATION

At Dow we have developed an eco-compass to overcome these disadvantages (see Figure 15.3). We use it to identify and evaluate improvement projects and as a creative method to envision a sustainable future and back cast from it. We can then identify the necessary innovations which will move us towards sustainability.

● FIGURE 15.2

A complete life cycle perspective to evaluate inputs and outputs

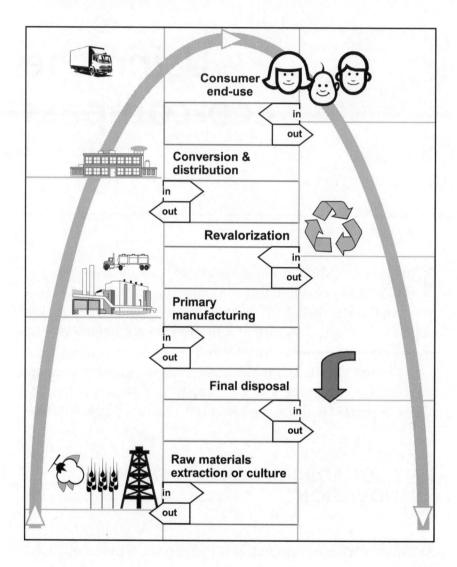

Six dimensions ...

The eco-compass has six poles or dimensions, which are intended to encompass all significant environmental issues. Two are largely environmental:

● **FIGURE 15.3**
The basic eco-compass

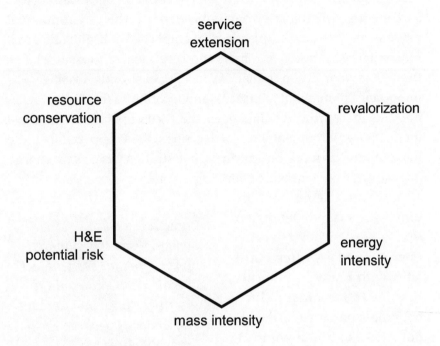

● health and environmental potential risk

● resource conservation.

Four are of business as well as environmental significance:

● energy intensity

● materials intensity

● revalorization (remanufacturing, reuse and recycling)

● service extension.

The latter measures the ability to deliver greater service from given inputs, for example by improving durability.

... Cover the main environmental concerns

The dimensions correspond to the concerns of significant actors and theorists in the environmental debate. The environmental movement, for example, places great emphasis on health and environmental risks, resource conservation and closing substance loops through revalorization (remanufacturing, reuse and recycling). The importance of material intensity – and techniques for conceptualizing and measuring it – has been the focus for one of the most innovative environmental research centres, the Wuppertal Institute in Germany. Its work builds on earlier studies which saw energy intensity as a core measure of environmental performance.

However, none of the dimensions is independent of the others. They overlap. Energy intensity often correlates with material intensity. Revalorization often reduces both these parameters, though not always. When someone drives ten miles to recycle a few bottles or newspapers they consume more energy and materials than they save.

> *Considering all six dimensions of the compass makes sure that every aspect of ecological and resources security is taken into account. The tradeoffs between them are highlighted too.*

A comparative tool ...

The eco-compass is not for stand alone use but can also be used for comparison, including:

- comparing one existing product with another, or
- comparing a current product with new development options.

When making comparisons it is always important to compare like with like. If widget factory A produces twice as much waste as widget factory B it appears to be "dirtier." But if A produces four times the number of widgets of B its waste generation per widget is only 50% of B's. It is really the less wasteful factory.

● FIGURE 15.4

The eco-compass – a new approach to breakthrough innovation

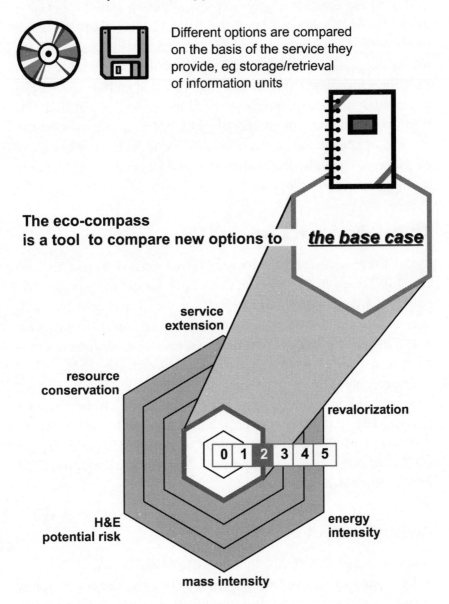

Different options are compared
on the basis of the service they
provide, eg storage/retrieval
of information units

The eco-compass
is a tool to compare new options to *the base case*

service
extension

resource
conservation

revalorization

| 0 | 1 | 2 | 3 | 4 | 5 |

H&E
potential risk

energy
intensity

mass intensity

... Based on the functional unit

Eco-compass data are always expressed per specified functional unit. The unit is always taken from the customer or consumer phase of the life cycle and is a measure of the delivery of a service to a customer. For paint this is coverage of surface, the functional unit therefore being the area covered by a specified amount of paint, such as square meters covered per kilogram applied. For building insulation materials the functional unit might be the thermal insulation value of a kilogram or one centimeter thickness of material. For archiving systems it could be the capacity of information storage per kilogram of support material.

There's always a base case

One of the products or activities to be compared is chosen as the base case (see Figure 15.4). This could be a book for archive storage. The base case always scores a 2 in each dimension. The alternative product or activity is then given a score relative to this base case on a scale of 0–5 in each dimension. The precise score depends upon the percentage increase or decrease in performance (see Figure 15.5).

The scoring is more logarithmic than linear. The cutoffs for each score are chosen to match some key concepts in the environmental debate. The distance between a 2 and a 5 is a "factor of four" improvement. Ernst von Weizsacker, Amory Lovins and Hunter Lovins among others say that this is the bare minimum required for sustainable development.[1]

A visual output

A screening of the life cycle data of the base case and the new option leads to a score for each dimension. The output of this is six scores and a "map" of the environmental attributes of both the base case and the comparison product or activity (see Figure 15.6). The closer the new options contour gets to the outer limit of the

● FIGURE 15.5

Evaluation grid to compare a new option against a base case

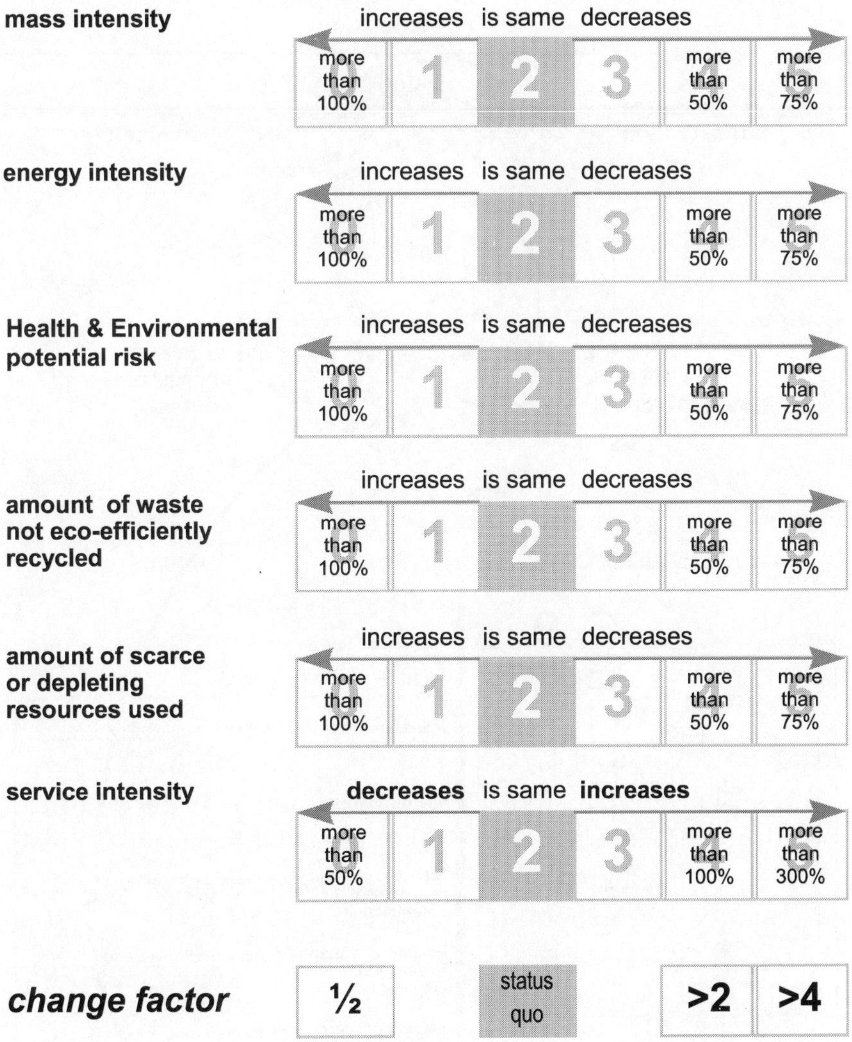

mass intensity

increases is same decreases

| more than 100% | 1 | 2 | 3 | more than 50% | more than 75% |

energy intensity

increases is same decreases

| more than 100% | 1 | 2 | 3 | more than 50% | more than 75% |

Health & Environmental potential risk

increases is same decreases

| more than 100% | 1 | 2 | 3 | more than 50% | more than 75% |

amount of waste not eco-efficiently recycled

increases is same decreases

| more than 100% | 1 | 2 | 3 | more than 50% | more than 75% |

amount of scarce or depleting resources used

increases is same decreases

| more than 100% | 1 | 2 | 3 | more than 50% | more than 75% |

service intensity

decreases is same **increases**

| more than 50% | 1 | 2 | 3 | more than 100% | more than 300% |

change factor   ½   status quo   >2 >4

● FIGURE 15.6

An overview of the life cycle stages helps to score every dimension of a new option

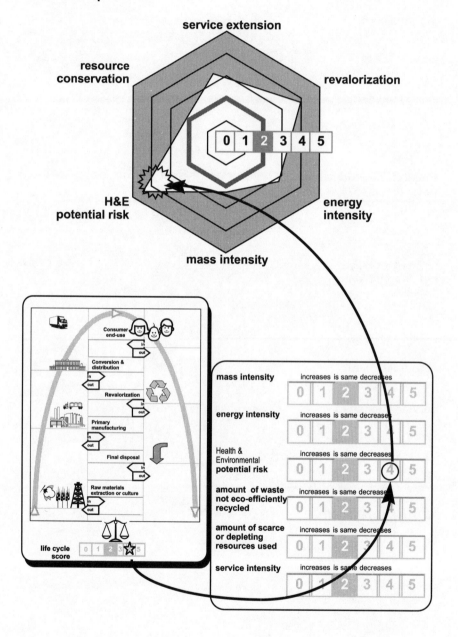

hexagon the better. Gross differences are immediately visible. The aggregate scores can be supplemented by individual scores for specific stages of the life cycle. The stages at which the main positive or negative impacts occur become equally visible.

David Russell feels that this visual quality makes:

> the compass into a very good communication tool. It highlights major differences between alternatives. If the alternatives include a current product and its possible future development you get a very immediate picture of improvement opportunities. Of course, the compass data is generated by LCA and those who want to go back to the detail can. The compass allows you to move between these different levels of detail very easily.

The Azurel and Sony case studies in the following chapters have a summary eco-compass. Chapter 22 provides illustrations of how the compass was used to help a particular Dow decision.

Following chapters explore in detail each of the six compass dimensions. To illustrate the scoring principles of the compass we use a real case. This is Swissair's Papyron incinerator project. (The text box overleaf provides details of this.) A box at the end of each chapter then scores the project on the dimension under discussion.

● SWISSAIR'S PAPYRON SCHEME

Papyron is a product of the drive and vision of Ueli Gautschi, Swissair's energy manager. He is also responsible for waste, and long dreamed of recovering the energy content of the airline's wastes.

His dream is now reality in the form of Papyron, a new incinerator at Swissair's Zurich headquarters. It burns nonrecycleable waste wood, cardboard and paper from the offices, Swissair planes and other sources. The energy released heats the headquarters and nearby apartments and a hotel. Some is also used to generate electricity and cool computer equipment. The new incinerator replaces two existing oil-fired boilers.

The Papyron plant is a new design which is very energy efficient. Two thirds of the energy content of the wastes is recovered as useful heat.

Papyron is a profitable investment for Swissair. It gives a return on investment (ROI) of around 24% per annum. The figure below shows that it also produces great environmental benefit compared with the base case of oil-fired heating. In following chapters we show how we generate these scores for each of the dimensions. All data are related to a functional unit. This is the provision of heating and cooling services to Swissair headquarters, the apartments and the hotel for one year.

Papyron eco-compass

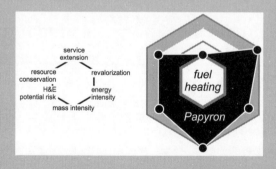

Notes

1 von Weizsacker, E., Lovins A. and Lovins, H. *Faktor Vier*. München: Droemer Knaur, 1995.

Chapter 16

Material intensity

◗ EIGHTY TONS OF MATERIAL PER PERSON

The world needs materials – and ever more of them. While "natural" man or woman could sustain themselves on a yearly intake of six tons of air and food, their modern equivalents among the most affluent billion consume an additional 80 to 90 tons of materials.[1] A recent study of the material budget of Germans established that they consume a yearly average of 76 tonnes of solid materials per capita and 60 tonnes of domestic water to enjoy their standard of living (see Figure 16.1).[2] Only a small fraction of this contributes to an extension of infrastructure. The rest results in sewage, atmospheric load and solid waste.

Materials production and processing has many environmental effects

The production and processing of the materials needed by modern man has many environmental effects. It:

- consumes large amounts of fuels and creates significant pollution;
- destroys or degrades habitat and biodiversity;
- causes loss of top soil and vegetation cover;
- disturbs drainage and runoff patterns;
- affects humidity and climatic patterns;
- contaminates water with trace materials.

All materials have a hidden rucksack

Many of these effects are hidden. Like the hitchhiker who appears to have little luggage, but pulls heavy baggage from behind a wall when a car stops, all raw materials carry a hidden "rucksack." This is the additional weight of materials displaced or consumed during their production and distribution, such as:

- masses that are moved in order to win raw materials – overburden in mining, erosion in agriculture, excavation in construction, etc;

- fuels, water and air consumed in heating, cooling and moving;

- equipment and materials (eg, concrete) required to extract and process them.

● FIGURE 16.1

The average material budget of Germans in the 1990s

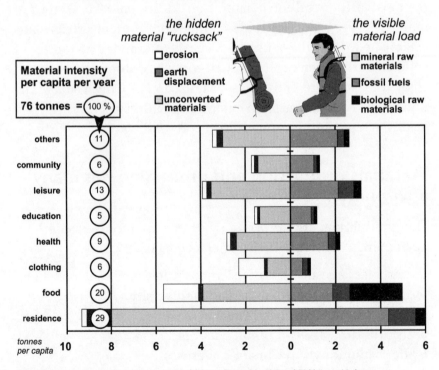

Source Behrensmeier and Bringezu in *Zukunftfähiges Deutschland*, Basel Birkhäuser Verlag
Wuppertal Institut, 1996

This displacement or consumption creates further environmental effects, which form part of the environmental cost of using the original raw material.

The rucksack concept was developed by Friedrich Schmidt-Bleek and co-workers at the Wuppertal Institute in Germany. They believe that material consumption is a key aspect of sustain-

● **FIGURE 16.2**

World mineral production and associated rucksacks

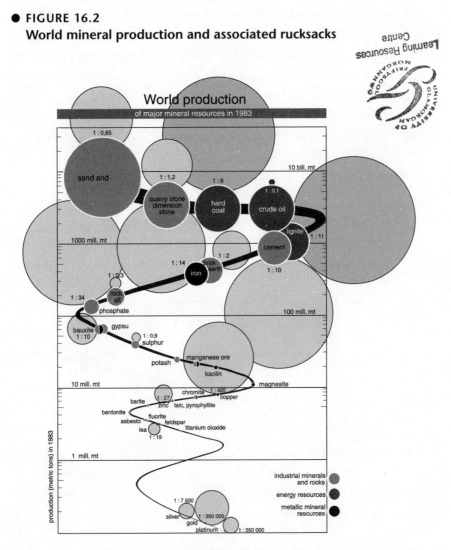

Source:Lüttig/merian/IEA Coal Research/ US-DOE: Ruckeacks: Schütz, Liedtke Wupperial Institut
UM –201e

able development and needs to be carefully measured and apply this by calculating the rucksacks of many everyday materials and products (see Figure 16.2).

Dematerialization is critical

The aim of eco-efficiency is to dematerialize, that is reduce the mass burdens of product or service chains. The key measure for this compass dimension is therefore the material intensity per unit of service (MIPS).

Friends of the Earth provide an example of three products with very different MIPS.[3] They all provide the same service; that of cutting a piece of adhesive tape (see Figure 16.3). Their size, weight and energy and material intensities are totally different. But the light, simple, metal clip on the left does the job as well as the monster on the right.

● FIGURE 16.3
Three ways of providing a service – cutting adhesive tape

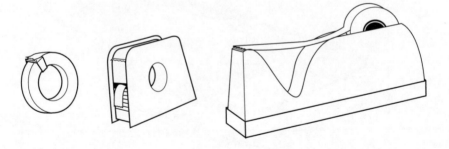

The Dow Elanco case provides an example of a service – termite control – being delivered with a material intensity less than 10% of similar but conventional treatments. The Procter & Gamble and Sony cases are less dramatic but also demonstrate how mass can be removed from product chains.

● SCORING PAPYRON'S MATERIAL INTENSITY

There are two main items of mass in the life cycles of Papyron and the base case of oil-fired heating. One is heating oil which was the main fuel in the base case and which is also used on an occasional basis in Papyron. The other element is the materials involved in generating the electricity used for powering equipment and other purposes in both schemes. The "rucksacks" – the materials used to produce the heating oil and generate and deliver the electricity – of both must also be taken into account.

One dilemma is whether to include the water passing through the hydro schemes which provide much of Switzerland's electricity. We exclude it on the grounds that Swiss hydro does not affect water's physical properties or location.

The base case of oil-fired heating per year uses a total mass over the life cycle (including rucksack) of 2612 tons per year. Papyron's corresponding material requirements are 654 tons annually. Papyron's mass intensity is therefore decreased by around 75% compared to the base case. This "factor four" improvement in environmental performance gets a score of 5.

MATERIAL INTENSITY (tons per annum)

	Base case	Papyron
Heating oil	747	146
Heating oil rucksack	1192	234
Materials for electricity used	267	108
Materials to produce and deliver electricity	406	166
	2612	654

❯ NIGHTMARE ON TERMITE STREET

DowElanco

> A new technology to control termites is more effective than most other methods. It is also less toxic, less odorous and requires substantially fewer material inputs.

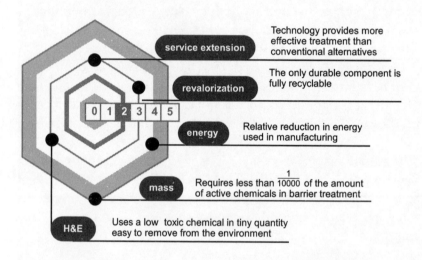

Technology provides more effective treatment than conventional alternatives

service extension

The only durable component is fully recyclable

revalorization

Relative reduction in energy used in manufacturing

energy

Requires less than $\frac{1}{10000}$ of the amount of active chemicals in barrier treatment

mass

Uses a low toxic chemical in tiny quantity easy to remove from the environment

H&E

Contact:

Customer Information Service,
Dow Elanco, 9330 Zionsville Road,
Indianapolis, Indiana 46268
USA

1 Termites chew up dollars

A deadly battle is being fought on the quiet campuses of American universities. Soldiers and workers are dying at Clemson University's Calhoun Mansion, a National Historic Landmark, and Auburn University's Extension Hall. The buildings have three things in common: historic significance, beauty and termite infestation – a characteristic they share with several million other buildings in the southern USA and hundreds of millions worldwide.

The small insects have much in common with ants. They are social insects with soldiers, workers and queens. But one difference is the termites' taste for wood, an expensive taste, which creates an estimated $1.5 billion of damage annually in the USA alone. Once established, termites are difficult to eradicate. The only effective weapon currently available to property owners is chemical barriers containing powerful insecticides.

> *Termites cause $1.5 billion of damage to buildings in the USA alone.*

Chemical barriers

However, it is very difficult to apply barriers uniformly over large areas, and termites are adept at finding the slightest chink and wriggling through it. The insecticides are contained in organic solvents whose evaporation makes conditions unpleasant for workers and residents. They may biodegrade slowly so that barriers seldom last for more than 10–20 years. And, although years of use have proven them to be safe, there is always a risk with powerful chemicals that future research will reveal health or ecological dangers.

> *Chemical barriers to prevent termite infestation have environmental, safety and cost disadvantages.*

DowElanco

DowElanco, a joint venture between Dow Chemicals and Ely Lilly, is the market leader in termite treatment. In the late 1980s, its termiticide product development manager, Sterett Robertson, initiated an

R&D program the aim of which was to identify more effective means of protecting structures whilst being environmentally sound. In doing this he had one unique advantage: a period as the owner of one of the pest control businesses which actually apply DowElanco's products. This practical experience taught him that the need was not just for a new chemical but a complete system to apply it.

2 How to kill termites

In addition to barrier type treatments, other methods can kill termite directly. One option is to inject insecticides into the timber. But this seldom achieves 100% coverage and is very expensive. Another option is to release naturally occurring or genetically engineered organisms which are lethal to termites. But the insects are constantly surrounded by parasites and pathogens in their natural environment and adapt to them quickly.

The third option is to feed the termites with poisonous or otherwise harmful material contained in bait which to be effective must be slow acting. If it kills too quickly remaining termites recognize the threat and avoid the bait. There are a few slow acting toxins which are currently being tested. In collaboration with Dr Nan-Yao Su of the University of Florida, DowElanco is working on another slow acting mechanism – insect growth regulators which kill by disrupting the insect's growth processes.

> *Insect growth regulators kill by disrupting termite's growth processes.*

Disrupting growth mechanisms

Laboratory and field tests show that one growth regulator, hexaflumuron, is particularly effective. It is of low toxicity and kills a wide range of termites because it operates as a chitin synthesis inhibitor. The effect is to disrupt the moulting process so that old exoskeletons (shells) are not properly shed and the termites become trapped in shells which are too small and eventually die from suffocation, starvation or other causes. The analogy is of human adults suddenly having to eat and breathe while wearing childhood clothes that are too strong to ease the pressure by ripping.

Sentricon™ Colony Elimination System

By itself hexaflumuron cannot kill termites. There has to be a mechanism to get it into a nest. DowElanco's concept is a hexaflumuron-laced cellulosic bait which is tasty for termites. The bait containment must restrict access by humans or animals and be durable in all soil and weather conditions, while also being easy and cheap to manufacture and install.

The answer is the Sentricon™ Colony Elimination System. Stage one of the system involves a monitoring device to see if termites are present. If they are, stage two follows. The system has a hollow plastic housing like a giant rawlplug with small holes for termites to pass through. The solid, wood-like, bait – marketed as Recruit™ – fits into the hollow space. The housing pushes into the ground and awaits the first termite visitors.

● FIGURE 16.4
The Sentricon™ Colony Elimination System for termite control uses one ten thousandth of the amount of active chemicals present in standard termite barriers.

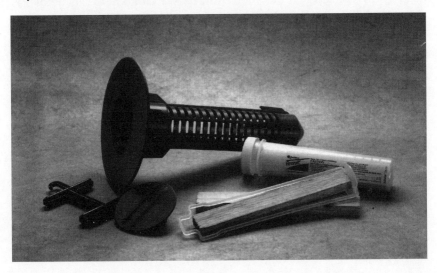

> *The Sentricon™ Colony Elimination System gets bait to termites while protecting animals and humans.*

According to Sterett Robertson, Sentricon™ required . . .

> a complete rethink of our approach to termite control. It requires extensive knowledge of termite biology and behavior, something which wasn't critical with the liquid termiticides.

Tests at Auburn and Clemson Universities and other locations demonstrated the system's effectiveness against all damaging termite species in the USA. As a result, Sentricon™ won Dow's annual R&D award in 1993 and its "environmental care" award in 1996. It was also the first product to receive accelerated approval under the US Environmental Protection Agency's Reduced Risk Pesticide initiative. Sentricon™ is now being marketed in the USA and, says Sterett Robertson, "is generating outstanding customer interest and acceptance."

3 Developing a more effective product

Existing termite treatments are imperfect so DowElanco's main motivation was to develop a more effective product. Environment is an important constraint in developing termiticides and some have been phased out because of it. DowElanco also has a corporate commitment to develop environmentally sustainable products. However there are no major environmental controversies, nor impending legislation, about existing termite treatments. Commercial rather than environmental requirements were the primary driver in the development of Sentricon™.

4 Reduced toxicity and material requirements

The Colony Elimination System uses only one ten thousandth of the amount of active chemicals in termite barriers. Hexaflumuron is also of low toxicity. The most vulnerable species are crustaceans but DowElanco believes that the combination of hexaflumuron's low solubility and the application method minimizes any risk to them.

The overall Colony Elimination System has only a tenth of the material requirement of barrier treatments. It therefore eliminates much of the energy, pollution and other impacts associated with their production.

5 Replacing DowElanco's existing products

Sentricon™ now has a 3–4% share of the US market. DowElanco expects that its advantages will eventually create a 50% share. It will gradually replace many of DowElanco's existing products as well as those of competitors. It hopes for similar success outside the USA.

6 Educating the market

Sentricon™ is a new concept for pest control companies and their customers. DowElanco has to educate them in its benefits and use if the product is to become the market leader.

7 Developing systems, not products

The Colony Elimination System demonstrates how new product development is as much about integrating different actors as developing a technology. Sterett Robertson's background as a pest controller helped to achieve this. According to Jean-Louis Leca, DowElanco's European product development manager, "we've learnt that our business is developing systems. It means we have to work together with pest controllers, house owners and others. That's the best way to find solutions to customers' problems and minimize any environmental impacts."

> *"We have to work together with pest controllers, house owners and others ... to find solutions to customers' problems and minimize any environmental impacts."*

▶ MORE FROM LESS AT PROCTER & GAMBLE (P&G)

Procter & Gamble

Compact washing products such as P& G's Ultra brand require less raw materials, packaging and energy to wash as effectively as bulkier equivalents. Consumers find them more convenient and they are cheaper for manufacturers to produce and retailers to handle.

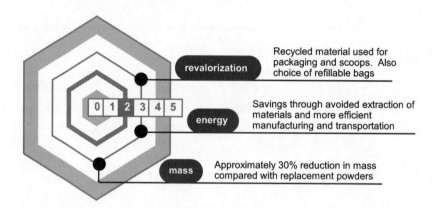

revalorization
Recycled material used for packaging and scoops. Also choice of refillable bags

0 1 2 3 4 5

energy
Savings through avoided extraction of materials and more efficient manufacturing and transportation

mass
Approximately 30% reduction in mass compared with replacement powders

Contact:

Dr Deborah D. Anderson, The Procter & Gamble Company, Two Procter & Gamble Plaza, Cincinnati, Ohio 45202, USA

1 P&G's achievements – marketing and environment

Remember those packets of washing powder you needed biceps like Arnold Schwarzenegger's to lift? Now they are almost museum items, consigned to history by the introduction of much denser "compact" or "ultra" washing powders only half a cup of which is needed for the average wash compared with a whole cup of their low density predecessors.

> Compact washing powders use only half a cup per washload, compared with a whole cup for lower density powders.

The result? Happier consumers, retailers with extra shelf space and manufacturers with lower materials and packaging costs. And the environment benefits because 30% less materials and packaging, and reduced amounts of energy are needed to provide a washing machine load of clean clothes.

Environmental improvements

P&G is the market leader in compacts. It is also seen as an environmental leader by many other companies. Its environmental achievements include:

- packaging savings over the period 1985–95 almost equivalent to the 1.2 million tonnes of packaging material used in 1995;

- a halving of energy used and waste generated per unit of production over the same period;

- a similar reduction in total waste disposed (solid waste, air emissions, wastewater effluent) since 1991.

Linking quality and environment

P&G has also been a pioneer in applying quality principles to environmental management. One aspect of this is an annual environmental audit and rating of its plants. Established operations are expected to have a minimum score of 80%. Newly acquired plants typically score around 25% and require a number of years of effort and investment to achieve the 80% level.

These and other achievements have led to a number of environmental awards, including the World Environment Center's Gold Medal for International Corporate Environmental Achievement in 1992. Recognition has also come in more utilitarian ways. P&G calculates that its annual insurance costs and uninsured losses are $113 million lower than comparable corporations. It attributes part of this saving to its good environmental record and effective auditing and management systems.

> *Good environmental performance is one reason why P&G's insurance costs and uninsured losses are $113 million lower than comparable corporations*

2 Consumers prefer compacts

The appearance of washing powders changed little between the 1950s and 1980s. They were of low density, were used in high volume doses and came in bulky packages which dominated store shelves. This changed when a new manufacturing process made denser granules possible and made easier the use of special ingredients. Some new materials, principally enzymes, were added to improve performance but a greater mass was taken out. The result? Compact washing powders, sold in smaller packages and used in lower dosages.

Compact detergents were first marketed successfully by Kao in Japan. P&G entered other markets quickly. It was the first company to launch a compact washing powder in the USA, Ultra Tide, and is now the world's largest producer. Its compact range, branded as Ultra, currently includes ten different kinds of washing and cleaning products.

Marketing skills

P&G responded to changing consumer demands. According to Deborah Anderson, P&G's chief environmental officer, consumers were saying "they wanted to use less powder in a wash, they didn't like carrying home huge volumes of grocery, they wanted less packaging waste and they wanted corporations to use less ingredients in their products."

Even so, achieving compact's high market share did require P&G's legendary marketing skills – and learning from previous mistakes – to change consumer attitudes and behavior. Some of its previous concentrated products had not sold well because customers had not appreciated the benefits. The solution? Better product information to communicate the advantages. Many purchasers continued to use the same dosage per wash. Not surprizingly they were disappointed about value for money. P&G dealt with this by using totally different packaging and including a special measuring scoop.

3 Meeting new customer needs

Compacts are the result of commercial responses to changing consumer needs. However their introduction was helped by environmental concern about packaging and waste.

4 Materials, packaging and energy reductions

The environmental benefits of compacts are considerable. According to a life cycle inventory conducted by Franklin Associates they include considerable savings of materials and energy and avoidance of waste at many stages of the product chain. Indeed P&G calculates that in the USA alone its Ultra brands have saved 304 million pounds of packaging between 1992 and 1995. Part of this is due to the refillable bags it introduced in 1993. The bulk of compact packaging is also made from recycled materials.

In addition compacts benefit from general improvements to P&G's manufacturing processes and product quality. There is less generation of waste and toxic emissions at P&G plants and all detergent performance is continually upgraded to increase the durability of clothing. Examples include color protectors, dye–transfer inhibitors and stain removers.

● **FIGURE 16.5**
Life cycle analysis data on compact washing powders, such as this popular P&G brand, shows that these formulations yield considerable material and energy savings.

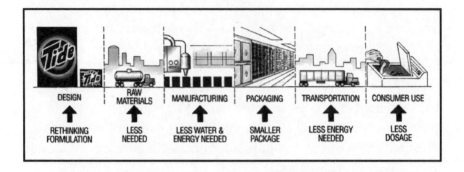

DESIGN	RAW MATERIALS	MANUFACTURING	PACKAGING	TRANSPORTATION	CONSUMER USE
RETHINKING FORMULATION	LESS NEEDED	LESS WATER & ENERGY NEEDED	SMALLER PACKAGE	LESS ENERGY NEEDED	LESS DOSAGE

P&G calculates that Ultra compacts have saved 304 million pounds of packaging material.

5 New markets, cost savings in production and distribution

Consumers have indicated their satisfaction with the lighter, more easily stored and more effective compacts by voting with their washing machines. Compact powders now have almost 60% of the total US laundry market, with much of the remainder being in the form of similarly concentrated liquid detergents. P&G has gained from lower costs for energy, raw materials, packaging and transporting products. Retailers appreciate not only the additional shelf space but also reduced costs for distribution and storage – savings estimated at 65¢ per case of Ultras.

6 Introducing a dry process

Additional environmental benefits are coming. P&G is rolling out, worldwide, a new "dry" manufacturing process to replace the existing "wet" one for making powders. This has no need to evaporate water, and so is more energy efficient while simultaneously generating less waste. It also gives greater flexibility for product formulation and the ability to use a wider range of ingredients. The result should be a further increase in the performance: weight ratio of the powders.

7 Changing consumers

Deborah Anderson believes that "consumers have made it clear that environmental benefits are important – but poor performance and low value are not acceptable, even for 'environmentally friendly' products."

Of course not everyone sees P&G or other multinationals making cleaning products as being friends of the environment. Many Greens question the need for the products they produce and believe that some of the ingredients are harmful to human health and ecosystems. However, Celeste Kuta, responsible for Laundry and Cleaning Product Safety at P&G, believes that . . .

> cleaning products provide many benefits which improve quality of life and human health. These include reducing the time and effort spent on cleaning, extending the useful lives of clothes and linens, and contributing to personal hygiene and good housecleaning. The regular use of soaps and detergents has been a primary contributor to advances in human health and well-being over the last century and a half. Consumers value these benefits but also want products that are safe for their families and the environment. P&G extensively evaluates its cleaning products to ensure that they are safe for consumers under normal use and foreseeable misuse. It also ensures that they will be extensively removed in wastewater treatment through biodegradation and other processes, and that low levels of ingredients which are released in the environment will not be harmful to organisms.

Is switching to compact detergents one of the quickest and most effective ways to help the planet?

Compact powders achieve eco-efficiency by simultaneously delivering greater convenience and performance to customers, profitability to suppliers and a steep environmental improvement on the bulkier products they have replaced. Indeed, a leading figure in the US Green consumer movement, Joel Makower, considers a switch to compact cleaning products as being one of the quickest and most effective ways that an American can help the planet.

▶ VIEWING THE FUTURE THROUGH THE GREEN TV

Sony

Sony Europe's green TV is lighter, less energy intensive and creates less health and environmental risk than previous models. It also has better picture quality and is cheaper to produce than its predecessor.

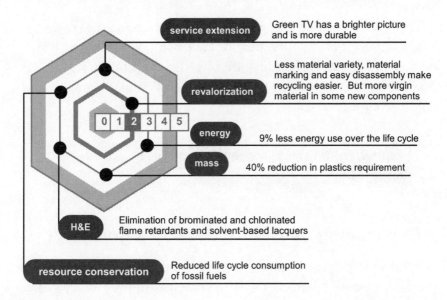

service extension — Green TV has a brighter picture and is more durable

revalorization — Less material variety, material marking and easy disassembly make recycling easier. But more virgin material in some new components

energy — 9% less energy use over the life cycle

mass — 40% reduction in plastics requirement

H&E — Elimination of brominated and chlorinated flame retardants and solvent-based lacquers

resource conservation — Reduced life cycle consumption of fossil fuels

Contact:
Sony Deutschland GmbH,
Environmental Center Europe,
Stuttgarterstrasse 106,
D-70736 Fellbach, Germany

1 Public concern triggers action

What lies behind the television screens that most of us watch each day? Few Germans stopped to think until 1989 when the news magazine *Stern* ran a story about the toxic materials inside their televisions.

Not all *Stern's* facts were correct. But the article, and public reaction to it, influenced TV manufacturers. Their environmental agenda was already growing. The public and political desire for recycling included electronic waste products. Dr Lutz Gunther Scheidt was departmental head of mechanical development at Sony Europe's R & D centre in Fellbach, Germany. He and his colleagues agreed that TV design must take environmental factors into account. Since then he has been responsible for greening the manufacture and design of TV sets.

The initiative builds on a tradition of environmental concern. The Fellbach R&D facility and TV factory alone has ten full-time or part-time environmental staff. It is also the first European TV plant to be accredited under the European Eco-management and Audit scheme (EMAS).

> *Fellbach is the first European TV plant to be accredited under EMAS.*

2 Overcoming barriers to develop a green TV

Scheidt's long term objective was to redesign completely existing products to make a green TV. His short–medium-term objectives were to make incremental improvements to existing designs, either by incorporating aspects of the green TV or in other ways. This sometimes meant compromise in order to achieve progress. An example is short-term replacement of the most controversial materials, brominated fire retardants, with chlorinated substitutes even though it was clear that the latter are only marginally less controversial.

Creativity, hard work and persistence

Change is never easy. Not everyone in Sony gave environment a high weighting especially when Scheidt's suggestions meant phasing out familiar materials and processes and substantial retooling and other costs. Considerable creativity and hard work has been necessary from the development team and from suppliers. Scheidt recalls his stress when new parts were often not 100% complete a short time before production started. "There was real time pressure and I had some sleepless nights!"

He also took heart from external reactions and trends. The Dutch and German consumer testing institutes now include environment in their evaluation of TV sets and regulations about electronic waste have become ever more likely in Germany and the European Union. Competitors and makers of similar products or components now pay great attention to Sony's eco-efficiency initiatives.

1995 – green TV launched and wins Sony environmental award

Interest rose after the launch in 1992 of a first generation ecological TV (C-Mark 2/3). But the R & D effort has only come to full fruition with a second generation model. This is the C-Mark O Series or "green TV," introduced in 1995. The TV is lighter and more easily recycled than its predecessor and Scheidt believes that it represents the current "state of the art" for environmental performance.

> *The C-Mark O Series – "state of the art" for TV environmental performance?*

In the early 1990s Sony set up an international Environmental Award scheme to reward environmental achievement in its subsidiaries or sites. In June 1995 the Fellbach mechanical engineering department received the Award's Grand Prize for the development of the green TV.

3 Regulatory threats and a vision of eco-efficiency

The green TV originated from public controversy about toxic materials in televisions. This created two drivers: a growing possibility of regulatory constraints on materials and end-of-life disposal; and

● FIGURE 16.6
Sony's "green" TV provides a clearer picture, leaves a lighter ecological footprint and is less expensive to manufacture than its predecessor.

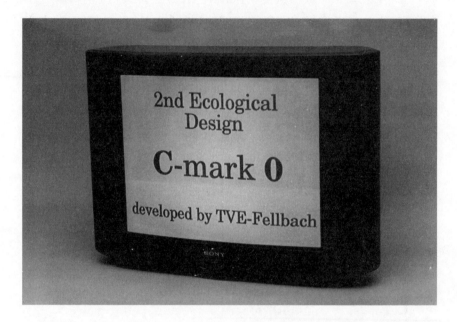

a vision in Scheidt and his colleagues that there are better environmental solutions which can also create business benefits.

4 Scoring the green TV on the eco-compass

Figure 16.7 provides a radar for the green TV (C-Mark O series) and the base case of the previous C-Mark 2/3 model. Both cases assume a 12 year lifetime with an average five hours viewing daily (and 19 hours in standby mode). We are grateful to Sony for providing the data. The judgments are our own.

Dematerialization

The green TV uses 14% less material compared with the base case. This scores 3 on the eco-compass. Lighter materials substitute for heavier ones. There is 40% less mass of plastic components, resulting from a new air moulding technique and the previously

● FIGURE 16.7
Sony green TV eco-compass

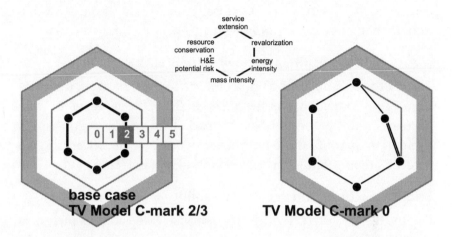

separate speaker grills now form part of a single unit. As a result the front TV cabinet weighs 23% less than in previous designs.

More recycleable ... but more inputs of virgin material

Recycling is made easier by material marking, by reduced material variety – 95% of the plastics used now derive from a single base polymer – and by making sets easier to disassemble. In addition the chassis frame now uses 100% recycled materials. However the air moulding technique in combination with integrated speaker grilles operates to fine tolerances and requires virgin material. For this reason we score the green TV at 3, i.e. modest improvement over the base case.

A net reduction in energy ...

These changes reduce the life cycle energy required to manufacture the TV and the materials within it. And energy consumption in stand by mode now requires 4.5W compared to the previous 10W. The set's better picture quality partially offsets this saving, however there is a reduction of around 9% over the life cycle, so this merits a 3 on the eco-compass.

... Means resource conservation

The reduced energy intensity and use of plastics means that, in most countries, the O-series uses less fossil fuel. This is a nonrenewable resource and therefore an improvement. We score this as a 3.

... And reduced health and environmental risk

The energy and material savings means there are fewer emissions from their production over the life cycle. The O-series assembly line also uses water-based lacquers instead of solvent-based ones. It is difficult to quantify these but they probably are significant. So we give a score of 3 for health and environmental risk reduction.

Brighter pictures and greater durability

Finally, the O-series provides some service extension. Its picture is brighter. This too merits a 3. By basing the calculations on a 12 year life we exclude another potential benefit of the green TV. The greater simplicity and strength of materials and components could make it more durable.

The overall picture from the eco-compass is that the green TV scores a 3 on all dimensions. It is a significant improvement over existing models. But, as Scheidt acknowledges below, there is plenty of scope for further development.

> *The eco-compass verdict – significant improvements but scope for further development.*

5 Reduced costs and potential marketing advantage

The green TV has already made business sense for Sony. The initial development tooling costs have been quickly offset by reductions in materials and assembly costs. Disassembly and recycling will also be more cost-effective when the TVs reach the end of their lives.

The environmental improvements do not yet feature in Sony Europe's marketing. The company is aware of suspicion among environmentalists and the general public about environmental claims by large manufacturers. It prefers to test its innovations thoroughly before going public and to include them in all of its range. But Scheidt is confident that "when the time is right, the TV's environmental attributes will prove to be a valuable marketing point."

6 Green product check sheets ... and new product concepts

One challenge for Sony is to introduce the green TV innovations into all its TV designs, both in Europe and worldwide, as well as greening all its product development processes. To assist this there is now a corporate-wide Green Product Check Sheet. All new products get a score and evaluation for nine criteria:

- use of hazardous substances
- disassembly time
- material labeling and marking
- recyclability
- use of recycled materials
- material intensity
- product life
- energy consumption
- packaging.

A third challenge is public education about the environmental aspects of TVs and other electronic equipment. While many retailers are aware and concerned, some customers are not. There is little understanding that bigger screens, better sound and other improvements in functionality usually require more energy.

From evolution to revolution in product design

Scheidt's personal challenge is to move towards "factor four" or greater improvements:

It's nice to have small improvements. But to make substantial progress we need a revolution in product concepts. We have to combine TVs, computers and stereos into a common multimedia platform. Then we'll need less material and have more scope for modular construction.

> *"To make substantial progress we need a revolution in product concepts."*

7 Need for a long-term perspective

Scheidt believes that the key to the development of green TV is a belief – shared by himself and key senior managers – that environment is a long-term issue requiring long-term action. He comments:

When I began with the environmental idea people often smiled at me. And there were frustrations as we went along. Not everything worked first time. And when people are under pressure it's easy to go back to the old ways that worked well. In such moments you need to have management standing behind you and setting targets. And you must keep motivated by thinking that you're not doing it for yourself but for your descendants.

Notes

1 Brunner, P. and Baccini, P. "Regional Material Management and Environmental Protection," *Waste Management and Research*, **10**, 1992, pp.203-212.

2 Behrensmeier, X. and Bringezu, S. in *Zukuntftfähiges Deutschland*, Basel: Birkhäuser Verlag/Wuppertal Institute, 1996.

3 Friends of the Earth Europe *Towards Sustainable Europe*. Brussels, 1995, p.218.

Chapter 17

Energy

▶ ENERGY – THE UNIVERSAL CURRENCY

Vaclav Smil has expressed the energy question perfectly:

> Energy is the only universal currency. It must be transformed to get anything done. Manifestations of these transformations in the physical universe range from rotating galaxies to the erosive forces of tiny raindrops. Life on earth, the only known life in the universe, would be impossible without the photosynthetic conversion of solar energy into plant biomass. Humans depend on this transformation for their survival and on many more energy flows for their civilized existence.[1]

Enormous environmental impact

Energy is consumed during all stages of the life cycle of products and services. Its production and consumption create enormous pollution and waste materials, also generate most man-made emissions of carbon dioxide and when derived from fossil fuels it depletes nonrenewable resources.

Rising demand offsets efficiency and maintains fossil fuel dependence

Most technologies and products become more energy efficient with time. Today's most efficient lamps use less than 100 times the electricity of Edison's bulb to provide equivalent illumination. But population and economic growth and rising standards of living mean that overall energy consumption constantly increases (see Figure 17.1 and Chapter 1).

What remains unchanged is the world's dependence on fossil fuels. Nuclear power has not lived up to its promise and is now declining. Nor have renewables yet taken off but their time may still come.

Improvements are possible

Can the inexorable growth of energy demand be reversed or even slowed up? As Chapter 1 showed, many of our energy-using industrial and consumer processes are a long way from their theoretical efficiency. Simply incorporating current best practice into new designs can yield substantial savings and new technologies and systems promise much greater efficiencies. The *ComfoHOME* case shows how buildings can be redesigned for sustainable levels of energy consumption.

In the nearer term Audi's aluminium bodied A8 car is 40% lighter than a steel equivalent. A 10% weight reduction creates a 6–7% fall in fuel consumption. If this is applied to all models there should be substantial energy savings. And the innovation is already stimulating steel companies to develop lighter products for auto use. Similarly, the RTT case demonstrates the scope for improvements in the energy efficiency of freight transport.

Government policies can also make a difference. Stringent regulations in countries like Sweden and Switzerland greatly reduce building energy needs. Japan's strong energy conservation program drastically cut that country's consumption in the decade after the oil crisis (although some of the ground has been lost since).

● **FIGURE 17.1**
   World energy

Energy demand in the world

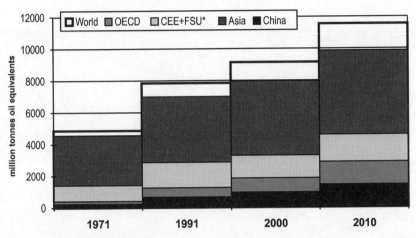

* Central and Eastern Europe and the former Soviet Union

OECD demand by sector

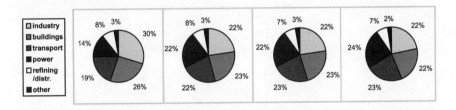

World CO$_2$ will grow 50%

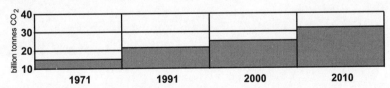

Source: World Energy Outlook, International Energy Agency, 1994, Paris

Scoring the energy dimension involves a similar process to materials. Calculate the total energy inputs over the whole life cycle then convert this into energy intensity per unit of service (EIPS). The box does this for Papyron.

● PAPYRON'S ENERGY SCORING

As with mass, heating oil and electricity are the main energy variables for both Papyron and the base case. Papyron's total energy usage over the year is 27590GJ. The base case has a total energy usage of 87337GJ.

Papyron's energy usage is 68% less than the base case. This is almost but not quite a "factor four" improvement. It narrowly misses a score of 5 and receives a 4 on this dimension.

ENERGY INTENSITY (GJ per annum)

	Base case	Papyron
Heating oil	31608	6192
Energy rucksack of heating oil	5729	1034
Electricity used	19800	8064
Energy rucksack of electricity used	30200	12300
	87337	27590

▶ LIVING IN GREEN COMFORT AT ComfoHOME®

comfoHOME®

Innovative house design with sustainable energy consumption and enhanced comfort for residents. Marketed on the basis of improved functionality rather than environmental performance.

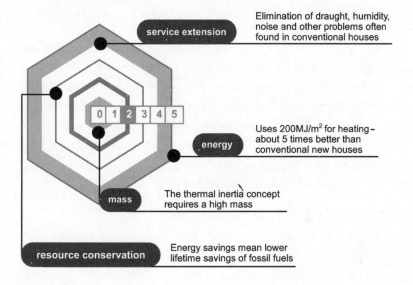

service extension — Elimination of draught, humidity, noise and other problems often found in conventional houses

energy — Uses 200MJ/m² for heating – about 5 times better than conventional new houses

mass — The thermal inertia concept requires a high mass

resource conservation — Energy savings mean lower lifetime savings of fossil fuels

Contact:

Ruedi Kriesi
Meierhofrain 42
CH-Wädenswil, Switzerland

1 Sustainable lifestyles need sustainable buildings

What is a sustainable level of energy consumption? A German parliamentary environmental commission estimates a level of one tonne of carbon dioxide per person per year. The current European level is over *seven* tonnes.

> *A sustainable level of consumption is one which generates one tonne of carbon dioxide per annum – compared to the current seven tonnes.*

The Zürich government wants to foster lifestyles that generate this sustainable amount of carbon dioxide. Abstract calculation is also a practical challenge for Swiss engineer, Dr Ruedi Kriesi, who has designed a house whose energy consumption is compatible with the target. Now he wants to market it throughout Europe. But his long-term ambitions reach beyond a mere continent: he sees the design, and the innovative technologies it uses, as being perfect for extreme environments such as the polar regions.

A career in building energy management

Kriesi's career spans both private industry and Swiss public administration including stints in the building trade and his current position as head of the Zürich State Office of Energy Management. In the late 1980s he worked with a consortium of federal and state governments, an architect and private interests to build four zero energy and six low energy houses in Wädenswil, a town on Lake Zürich. One of these is now his own home.

2 Houses with minimum energy and maximum comfort

The Wädenswil development taught Kriesi that the move from very low to zero energy is one of diminishing returns. He decided to calculate the sustainable level of energy consumption for a new house and design to this specification. His figures – which are accepted by the Swiss government – indicate this level is around 200 MJ per square metre, which compares with the current Swiss average of 800 MJ for an existing house and 550 MJ for a new one.

Kriesi invented a term to describe his objective: MINERGY, which he defined as a product that provides full functionality with an energy consumption compatible with sustainable development.

High insulation ...

Kriesi has used his Wädenswil experience to design a new house which uses only 200 MJ per square metre, ie, a sustainable level of consumption. The design uses no radically new technology. But it is innovative in the way it integrates and uses existing ones. High insulation values for walls, floors and roofs are achieved generally by high mass materials and in particular by extensive use of extruded polystyrene foam. Triple glazing gives a similarly high value for windows. The large mass also acts as a slow heat store which buffers external temperature variations.

... Air management

Fresh air enters the house through pipes embedded in the soil. The inlets are some distance from the structure so air preheats in winter and cools in summer. When necessary a heat exchanger warms it further. The exchanger captures energy from exhausted air. These measures alone reduce space heating needs by 70% compared with a conventional house. A ventilator circulates air gently within the building so that no discomfort is caused to occupants. This prevents build up of humidity, odors or carbon dioxide in individual rooms.

A MINERGY home conserves the waste heat from sunlight, lighting and home appliances. The low additional heating requirement gives MINERGY houses much greater flexibility in energy sourcing than conventional ones. They can, for example, operate on solar heat for much of the year even in northern countries. Ambient heat piped from external sources such as ground water is another possibility.

Greater comfort ...

The MINERGY house has other benefits in addition to energy efficiency. It is easier to create stable temperatures than in conventional houses, which often fluctuate between too hot and too cold. There are no draughts and no cold spots on external walls or other surfaces. This, plus the constant air circulation, eliminates any possibility of damp and mould. The circulation also prevents stuffiness so that windows do not need to be left open.

MINERGY homes are quiet because their high mass and triple glazed windows greatly reduce noise penetration and are bright during the day because their triple glazing permits big windows without heat loss.

... A higher purchase price

But the MINERGY home costs around 10% more than conventional alternatives. How can this price barrier be overcome? A collaboration with a strategic consultant, Heinz Uebersax, gave a solution. Uebersax has a deep concern about global warming and other environmental problems. He also feels that most potential buyers will not pay a premium for environmental performance. Those who will are often confused about what is and what is not environmentally beneficial. His conclusion? "Don't try to sell low energy houses on ecological arguments. Stress their improved comfort."

Uebersax's search for a means of improving both comfort levels and environmental performance ended when he learnt of Kriesi's design. Now the challenge is marketing the concept, using the brand name *ComfoHOME®*. And providing standardized "software" (designs and advice) and "hardware" (special components and materials) to architects and builders wanting to build low energy houses.

3 The objective – sustainable, comfortable homes

ComfoHOME® is the culmination of two paths. One is the almost 20 years of analysis of, and practical experimentation in, building energy management by Ruedi Kriesi. The other is Heinz Uebersax's experience of industrial production and marketing. Both are motivated by strong ecological convictions and a personal objective of designing sustainable but comfortable homes. Until now profit has been more a constraint to be satisfied than a purpose in its own right.

● FIGURE 17.2
ComfoHOMES® are designed with "MINERGY" in mind. The builder defines the term as "full functionality and energy consumption levels compatible with sustainable development."

4 Energy savings means less environmental impact

The MINERGY house has minimal direct energy consumption. It avoids most of the environmental impacts of winning, processing, transporting and burning the fuels used to heat conventional homes. The energy savings also outweigh the extra energy used in creating the MINERGY house's additional materials requirement. Kriesi calculates that a *ComfoHOME®*'s energy balance becomes positive after only two years.

> **A MINERGY *house avoids most of the environmental impacts associated with space and water heating of conventional homes.***

The large mass of a MINERGY house gives it a poor material intensity score when compared with conventional non-Swiss alternatives. But there is no disadvantage in Switzerland because all homes must have nuclear shelters and so are concrete-intensive. However, with the exception of some plastics, most materials are renewable or so abundant as to be virtually so.

5 A viable business?

ComfoHOME® is only just established but initial demand suggests that it can become a viable business.

6 Pay now, save later and be comfortable

ComfoHOME®'s ultimate challenge is persuading house buyers to pay a premium in exchange for increased comfort, low energy bills and a better environmental conscience. One target market is public housing agencies or other organizations with a strong environmental commitment. Another is up-market residences where exclusivity and high performance are important and the customers relatively price insensitive.

In the medium term *ComfoHOME®* will establish franchisees to offer a similar support and distribution services in other countries. It sees particularly big opportunities in tropical areas, where MINERGY homes should provide cost-effective cooling. In the long term it envisages large markets for MINERGY mobile dwellings as well as buildings which adapt the technology to extreme environments.

7 Improved quality is the selling point

The Wädenswil development and the ComfoHOME® design demonstrate that sustainable technology is available. They also show that while there are many obstacles, there are also opportunities. Unlike the car industry which has only a few models, housing is flexible. You can change one house or one street at a time.

But Kriesi and Uebersax have also learned that you cannot market houses primarily on their environmental or energy saving properties. Kriesi believes – and Uebersax concurs – that "they have to be sold on their improved quality. That's a message which customers will listen to. They like having quiet, bright rooms. And they do not miss draughts and condensation. The people who live in the Wädenswil houses are generally very positive. Most could not imagine going back to an ordinary house."

> *Owners of MINERGY homes "couldn't imagine going back to an ordinary house."*

▶ ROAD MEETS RAIL AT RTT

RTT

RTT is a Dutch freight operator committed to intermodal (road and rail) transport and using satellite communications to increase truck utilization. These cut costs and safety risks and reduce air pollution and noise.

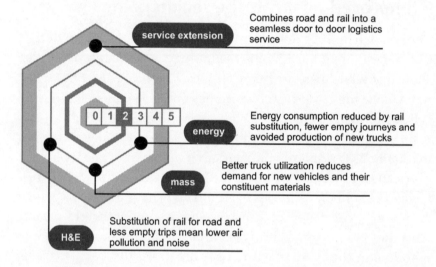

service extension — Combines road and rail into a seamless door to door logistics service

energy — Energy consumption reduced by rail substitution, fewer empty journeys and avoided production of new trucks

mass — Better truck utilization reduces demand for new vehicles and their constituent materials

H&E — Substitution of rail for road and less empty trips mean lower air pollution and noise

Contact:

Dick Perridon, RTT Rotterdamse Tank Transport BV, Oude Maasweg 50, 3197 KJ Botlek RT, The Netherlands

1 Environment already influences RTT's freight business

Trucks and satellites inhabit different worlds. One is heavy and earth bound, the other ethereal. But Dutch freight operator RTT is linking them together. The result? Better service and lower costs for customers. And reduced air pollution and noise through cutting journeys made by empty trucks.

RTT is one of Europe's biggest land transporters of bulk liquids and dry products such as chemicals. Most of these are shipped between the port of Rotterdam, where RTT is based, and sites in western and southern Europe.

RTT is owned by a German company, Hoyer, and there are subsidiaries in every major European country together forming Europe's largest transporter of bulk goods: over 4000 containers and 1000 road tankers.

RTT must take account of several environmental issues. Its truck purchasing is influenced by regulations on noise and emissions of nitrogen oxides and other substances. It has recently installed a "state of the art" water treatment plant at its Rotterdam depot, which has one of the largest vehicle and tank cleaning units in Europe. It is also a prime target of the Dutch government's policy of switching freight from road to rail wherever possible.

> *The Dutch government wants more freight to go by rail.*

2 RTT favours rail and increases vehicle utilization

RTT is achieving eco-efficiency in two ways: greater use of rail for long distance freight transport; continuous satellite tracking of its vehicles so that they are utilized more effectively thus reducing the number of empty journeys.

Rail is generally cheaper than road over long distances and is therefore preferred by RTT. When good connexions exist, RTT ships goods to a rail terminal for onward transport by train. Local Hoyer subsidiaries then collect the goods at the destination and deliver to the final customer. This way RTT can remain in overall control of the logistical chain and provide the same level of service as if driving the whole distance itself.

Most of RTT's new investment is going into new containers for intermodal (road and rail) transport. It also has a stake in a Dutch intermodal company, which transfers freight from trucks to trains and *vice versa*. Several other Hoyer subsidiaries have made similar investments in their own countries.

Road transport's environmental costs cause switch to rail

RTT benefits from the Netherlands' position as the transport hub of western Europe. But the economic gains have environmental costs in the form of air and noise pollution from the millions of trucks which use its highways. So the Dutch government is now determined to switch freight from road to rail.

RTT believes that, over time, similar policies will be adopted in other European countries which will lead to increased taxes on trucks and their fuels. Long distance road transport could almost disappear. Only freight operators which are effective at intermodal transport, and are highly efficient truckers, are likely to survive.

> *Higher taxes on road transport mean that freight operators must be effective at intermodal transport and highly efficient truckers.*

New rail freight routes need support

RTT is confident it already meets both these criteria and that it can improve further. It is giving more long-term commitments to use new international rail freight routes. These are usually loss making in their first years and pre-commitments from customers are important. They not only make operators confident that investments will pay off but also make it easier to obtain the government subsidies which are available for new routes.

Satellite tracking reduces empty journeys

A major determinant of truck efficiency is their utilization. Trucks making empty journeys to or from pickups or dropoffs burn fuel and money for no useful purpose. In the early 1990s RTT decided to reduce such empty loading by introducing a real time satellite communication system for its vehicles. The precise location of every one can now be plotted and the nearest empty and suitable truck dispatched to pick up new loads. At present dispatching is done manually but a computer program is being developed to make it automatic. The project has been costly in both hardware and software but should make commercially acceptable returns.

3 RTT's primary drivers are good service and low costs ...

Freight transport is highly competitive. Good service and low costs are therefore essential. The main aim of RTT's initiatives is to maintain and improve these commercial attributes. However its willingness to invest is influenced by the long-term direction established by the environmental policies and legislation of the Dutch government. According to RTT's managing director, Wout van Neuren, "we saw that environment was increasing costs. We started an internal discussion on how we could respond and stay competitive. The satellite project was one outcome."

4 ... But intermodality and fuller trucks are environmentally beneficial

Substitution of rail for road transport of freight generally reduces air pollution and means that fewer people are affected by noise. Fewer empty journeys means that fuel consumption and air pollution is reduced. Avoiding one empty trip of 1000 kilometers means a fuel saving of 320 liters. The higher utilization of trucks also means that a smaller number is needed to transport a given amount of freight. Hence the energy, materials and health and environment risk impacts of manufacturing the additional trucks are avoided.

> *Empty journeys burn fuel and create pollution for no useful purpose.*

5 Cost savings now and a platform for the future

Greater use of rail for long distance transport already reduces RTT's costs. Its experience with intermodality puts it in a strong position if it is required or strongly encouraged by future governments. The improved truck utilization which the satellite system makes possible also reduces the costs of empty journeys and means that fewer new vehicles are required. RTT's competitive advantage will become even greater if there are new environment-based taxes on road transport.

6 Intermodality requires integration

RTT is the leading Hoyer company for the satellite system. The intention now is to introduce it in all Hoyer's European sub-

● FIGURE 17.3
Through the application of modern communications technologies RTT has improved the eo-efficiency of its fleet and reduced its operation costs.

sidiaries, as well as to extend its use within RTT, meaning a given load can be picked up by the nearest truck, irrespective of its nationality. The organizational challenge of doing this may well be greater than any technical ones.

Another obstacle remains the fragmentation of the European rail network into national monopolies whose operations are not fully integrated. Transfrontier traffic is difficult to track and negotiate on competitive terms. This is why rail often loses out *vis à vis* road haulage of freight. A unified rail freight market and integrated management of railcar movements would cut the cost of logistics and encourage a switch from road to rail.

In any event, the growth of intermodality will require even closer cooperation between RTT and train and terminal operators. Currently RTT has no desire to become directly involved in these areas. But the need for a fully integrated service could eventually require it.

> *"... the discussion has to be about what future we want and what future the market wants. And we're sure the market will be more influenced by environmental factors."*

7 What future do you believe in?

Wout van Neuren is convinced that long-term projects such as the satellite one should not be solely determined by conventional payback calculations. "Of course these should be done wherever possible. But if we want to remain in business as a logistical supplier, we have to invest in the future even though we do not know the precise returns. There are risks. But most of the discussion has to be about what future we want and what future the market wants. And we're sure that the market will be more influenced by environmental factors."

Notes

1 Smil, V. *Energy in World History*. Boulder, CO: Westview, 1994, p.1.

Chapter 18

Health and environmental risk

In nature nothing gets lost. All systems conserve mass element by element. As carbon, sulphur, chlorine and other atoms get involved at one end of the chain they will continue to move through in various forms. Sometimes high initial concentrations are diluted by natural mechanisms. But those same mechanisms can also increase concentrations at other points. It was initially thought that environmental releases of DDT were harmless because they were diluted by air and water. Now we know that, because of their high solubility in fat, they accumulate in the parts of food chains where fat is stored, such as breast milk and blubber

Toxicologists think two things are important. First to identify and assess the generic ways in which a product or process can create health and environmental risk. Second to consider the relative importance of different risks on a case-by-case basis (see Figure 18.1). There is not always going to be consensus on this question. The best you can do is to choose in good faith and make the assumptions behind your choice transparent.

You can also do your best to eliminate completely any potentially hazardous substances from your products and processes. Our Beijing Chemical Works, Hofpfisterei and IBM cases demonstrate the scope for this in three different industries and countries.

● ASSESSING RISKS

There are many potentially risky substances that can be released in many ways during the life cycle of a product that includes them. Simple methods for dealing with such complexity are very difficult to find. Risks to human health from toxic, carcinogenic or other harmful substances can be managed by taking the following steps:

- Measure relevant quantities, whether emitted to air, soil and water, contained in products and wastes or formed from precursor substances in the environment. Modern detection techniques and equipment allow substances to be detected at very low concentrations.

- Assess their persistency in the environment.

- Model their actual dispersion within the environment and the extent of their bioaccumulation.

- Calculate dose–effect relationships.

- Integrate previous steps into a risk and impact characterization.

- Risk management to guard against hazardous substances which may cause harm.

In order to score the health and environmental risk reduction potential of a new option we recommend an evaluation of six generic risks to human health and six environmental risks. The box on page 206 provides details of them.

● FIGURE 18.1

The DOSE effect of toxins and risk management steps

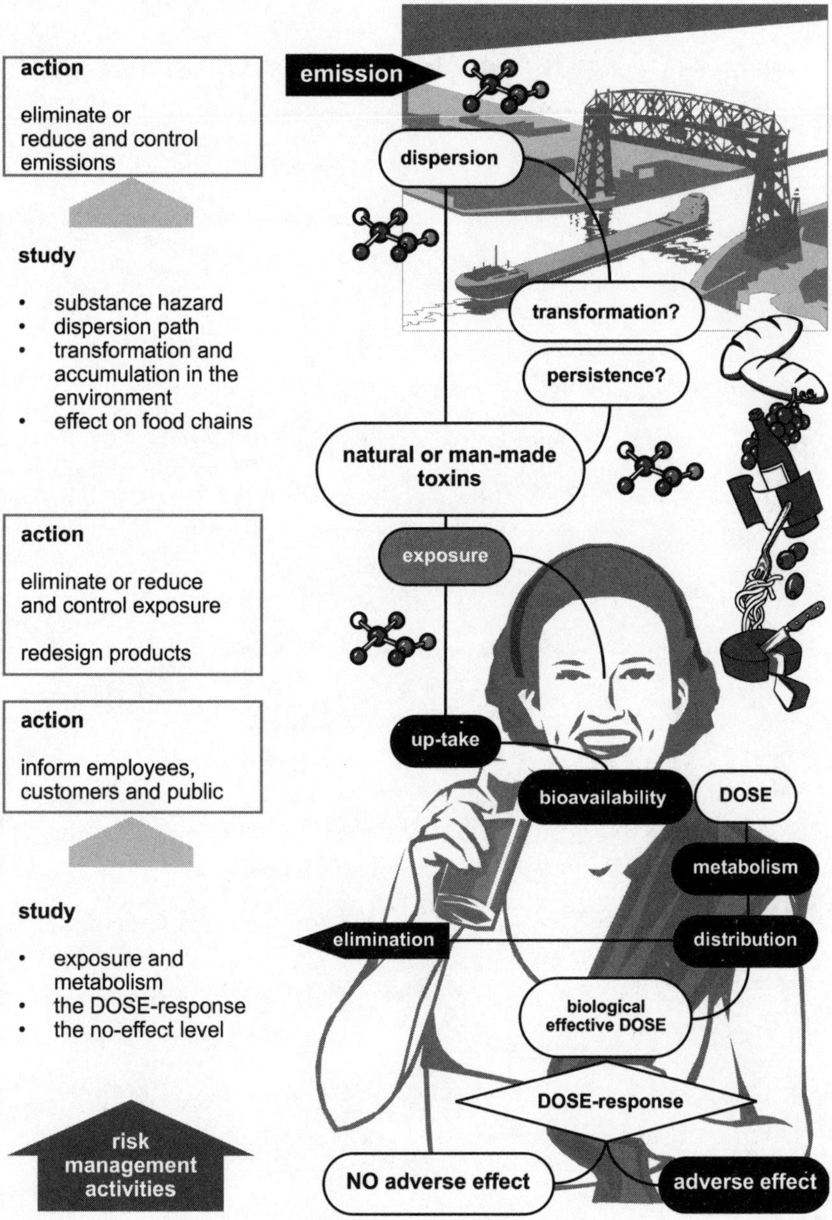

action

eliminate or reduce and control emissions

study

- substance hazard
- dispersion path
- transformation and accumulation in the environment
- effect on food chains

action

eliminate or reduce and control exposure

redesign products

action

inform employees, customers and public

study

- exposure and metabolism
- the DOSE-response
- the no-effect level

risk management activities

emission

dispersion

transformation?

persistence?

natural or man-made toxins

exposure

up-take

bioavailability

DOSE

metabolism

elimination

distribution

biological effective DOSE

DOSE-response

NO adverse effect

adverse effect

● TYPES OF HEALTH AND ENVIRONMENTAL RISK

The six risks to human health are:

- *acute human toxicity* (AHT), that is, short-term effects caused by direct exposure to a substance;

- long-term *carcinogenic, teratogenic and mutagenic* (CTM) effects;

- the potential dangers of *persistent toxins that bioaccumulate* (PTB);

- *emissions to the atmosphere of organic substances* (EAOS). These can result in formation of photochemical smog and consequent breathing difficulties, irritation and other effects;

- the potential for creating *allergies and irritations* (A&I);

- *accident risk*, influenced by such properties as the flammability of materials and the potential for explosions.

We also use six indicators for environmental risks:

- *terrestrial ecotoxicity* (ECT) to assess the health of flora and fauna;

- *aquatic ecotoxicity* (ECA) to assess effects on aquatic flora and fauna;

- the *acidification potential* (AP) to assess the amount of acid deposition on soil and water which could be created (calculated relative to 1 kilogram of sulphur dioxide);

- the *nutrification potential* (NP) to assess the effects of any nutrients generated on biological oxygen demand (BOD) of watercourses (calculated relative to 1 kilogram of phosphate (PO_4));

- the *global warming potential* (GWP) of any releases of greenhouse gases (calculated relative to 1 kilogram of carbon dioxide);

- the *ozone depletion potential* (ODP) of any releases of ozone depleting substances such as CFCs (calculated relative to 1 kilogram of CFC-11).

These indicators also differ in scale:

- two (global warming potential and ozone depletion potential) are essentially global;

- three (emissions to the atmosphere of organic substances, acidification potential and nutrification potential) are regional and local;

- the remainder are primarily local.

At Dow we use a decision tree to score each of these parameters individually. We then add the scores to give the total score for the dimension. Always remember that the final output of the compass is not scientifically accurate but best judgement.

● HEALTH AND ENVIRONMENTAL RISKS OF PAPYRON

Papyron's reduction in energy and material intensity via the oil-fired base case means a corresponding fall of 68–75% in health and environmental risks. The only other potential risk is that of dioxin or other emissions from the waste incineration. As Papyron uses state of the art combustion and monitoring equipment, this risk seems low. Papyron therefore receives a score of 4, corresponding to a 50–75% reduction in health and environmental risk.

THE EAST IS GREEN – BEIJING CHEMICAL FACTORY NO. 3

Beijing Chemical Factory No.3

A UNEP supported Cleaner Production initiative has halved COD discharges, reduced consumption of raw materials and energy and improved product yield. First stage measures had a payback of 15 days.

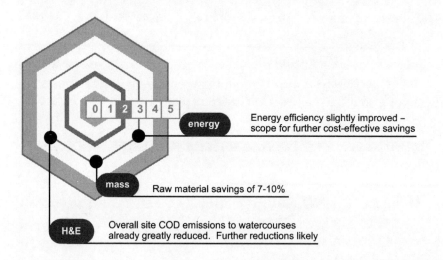

0 1 2 3 4 5

energy — Energy efficiency slightly improved – scope for further cost-effective savings

mass — Raw material savings of 7-10%

H&E — Overall site COD emissions to watercourses already greatly reduced. Further reductions likely

Contact:

Liang Bo Quing, Wang Hong and Zheng Maokun, Beijing Chemical Factory No. 3, Beijing 100078, P.R. China

1 China – a key to sustainable development

China's population growth and economic dynamism make it critical to sustainable development. If the country takes environment seriously then sustainability might be achieved. If it doesn't . . .

For this reason the Cleaner Production program of the United Nations Environmental Program (UNEP) has worked with China's National Environmental Protection Agency (NEPA) to establish training programs and 18 demonstration projects in Chinese companies. The ultimate goal is to introduce cleaner production to 5000 companies – including China's top 100 polluters – by 1998.

> *Cleaner Production will be introduced in 5000 Chinese companies – including the top 100 polluters – by 1998.*

BCF3 ... a factory in transition

Several demonstration projects have been in the chemical sector, where UNEP has collaborated with the Ministry for the Chemical Industry. One of the most successful, and one which still continues, has been at Beijing Chemical Factory No. 3 (BCF3). Owned by the Beijing Chemical Industries Corporation the factory is one of the main Chinese producers of additives for polymer products such as paints and plastics.

Despite an expanding market, BCF3 was in trouble in the early 1990s. Its production costs were rising due to obsolete equipment and inefficient use of raw materials. The factory also discharged organic pollutants to the air and the Liang Shuihe river system. Its waste water discharges amounted to 7600 tons daily, making it the third largest water polluter in the Beijing region. All life in the plant's region of the river had been killed by it.

Workers and residents were becoming unhappy about these impacts. The emissions were also incurring heavy charges from the Beijing Environmental Protection Bureau. In 1993 BCF3 was told, after discussions between its parent company and environmental agencies, to substantially reduce the chemical oxygen demand (COD) of its discharges. But doing this by installing waste water treatment would be expensive and could possibly tip the enterprise into bankruptcy.

● FIGURE 18.2
Working in conjunction with UNEP's Cleaner Production initative, Beijing Chemical Factory No. 3 dramatically reduced discharges and raw material consumption.

2 Reducing toxic emissions and wastes

After attending a UNEP/NEPA seminar, BCF3 initiated a cleaner production audit in 1993. The team was led by the factory's chief engineer, Madame Zheng Maokun, and brought together eight people from different sections of the plant. The audit soon established that the factory's penta-erythritol (PE) plant generated more than 40% of the COD in the discharges. This became the focus of further work, with a target of reducing these discharges by at least half.

> *A cross-functional team set a target of cutting the COD by at least half.*

Mass balance identifies twenty options

The team first conducted a mass balance of the plant to quantify the source and extent of waste generation. It then identified 20 cleaner production options. Nine of these had minimal cost and were introduced immediately or within a maximum of six months. They included:

- training of staff

- more frequent and thorough maintenance inspections

- improved process control

- collection of waste materials

- packaging raw materials in larger containers.

Four others could reduce COD further and create higher yields and reductions in energy and raw material consumption. One of these options, to recover aldehyde as a raw material, was approved at a cost of 1.5 million yuan ($125,000).

One good audit leads to another

The success of the PE initiative led to a subsequent audit of the site's butyl acetate plant. On this occasion BCF3 was assisted by the Norwegian Society of Chartered Engineers. The plant was chosen for the high COD of its effluent and its excessive consumption of expensive raw materials. Usage of two of these, acetic acid and butyl alcohol, had risen by 11% and 8% respectively per ton of output since the early 1990s. The increased costs were jeopardizing the product's and the plant's financial viability.

A similar cross-functional team to that established for the PE set itself three ambitious challenges: to reduce raw material usage to the best historic levels; to cut COD of discharges by 85%; and to substantially reduce consumption of energy and water.

> **Three ambitious targets – reduce raw material consumption to best historic levels, cut COD of discharges by 85% and improve energy and water utilization.**

As with the PE audit a number of low-cost measures were identified and rapidly implemented. These have reduced consumption of acetic acid by 8% and that of butyl alcohol by 5% – saving money although still above the best-ever level. COD emissions have also been cut but again by less than had been hoped. Four measures have been identified to cut COD discharges to 90% of their early 1990s level but these require capital investment.

3 From compliance to cleaner production

The BCF3 actions were initially driven by compliance, albeit with parent company demands rather than environmental regulation directly. As initial experience has demonstrated how cleaner production can reduce costs and improve quality, commercial drivers have become more important. Officials at NEPA and other agencies also have a vision of cleaner production as a pathway to sustainability for Chinese companies and have been important in ensuring the success of both the BCF3 project and others.

4 Restoring river life

The project has more than halved the COD of discharges from BCF3 into a sensitive river system. This has benefited both public and ecological health. Effluents with a high COD deplete the oxygen available to aquatic life. The result can be the death of fishes and plants, breakdown of food chains and loss of biodiversity. Raw material requirements have been cut by up to 10%, with a consequent reduction in the material and energy requirements of their production. Energy consumption in BCF3's own processes have also been reduced.

5 Lower costs, higher quality

The low-cost measures identified by the PE audit cost under $1200 to implement and created immediate annual savings of $30,000 – a payback period of 15 days. The main benefits are increased yield (up by a quarter) and reduced consumption of water. The higher cost projects have payback periods of between 1 and 4 years. As well as direct savings the cleaner production measures have allowed PE product quality to be improved, to the point where it can now be sold as the highest grade. The result is higher revenues.

> *The initial cleaner production measures had a payback of 15 days.*

The first stage of the butyl acetate project has also given good, if less spectacular, results. The initial measures cost $20,000 and created annual savings of $55,000 – a payback period of five months.

One additional benefit of both schemes is a reduction in the capital and operating cost of the wastewater treatment plant which BCF3 is planning to build.

6 Resource constraints

Further investments of around 4 million yuan ($330,000) could reduce the COD of discharges from the butyl acetate plant to around 8% of their level prior to the cleaner production initiative, and greatly cut energy and water consumption. The payback periods for the investments range from one to four years. However, BCF3 has not felt able to afford this investment because of competitive market conditions and the need for investment in other areas of production. Finding the resources to maintain progress remains a challenge. Nonetheless an agreement to conduct further cleaner production audits was made with the Asian Development Bank in 1995.

BCF3 is also being used as an example to encourage other Chinese companies to adopt cleaner production and representatives of the company speak regularly at workshops organized by the Ministry of Chemical Industry and the National Environmental Protection Agency.

7 Increased enthusiasm and self-confidence

The PE project taught BCF3 the value of staff involvement and techniques such as mass balances as a driver of cleaner production. These lessons made it easier to accomplish the second, butyl acetate, project. A BCF3 report on its experience speaks of a "magical change" at the plant which has made all staff aware of the opportunities for eco-efficient production. It also reflects on the lessons of implementation. Echoing Western studies, it states that "the thinking and manner of top management in factories are the first most important factor in taking action." The second most important factor, it states, "is that all sections, technicians, engineers and workers in the factory should be involved in the actions. If every company, and every individual, pays more attention to eco-efficient production tremendous changes will take place."

Liang Boqing of the Ministry of Chemical Industry's Environmental Protection Institute also feels that the BCF3 project has increased Chinese self-confidence that they can deal with environmental problems. "It shows that implementing cleaner production doesn't only mean importing processes and equipment from abroad. We can look for opportunities and make improvements ourselves."

"If every company, and every individual, pays more attention to eco-efficient production tremendous changes will take place."

▶ HOFPFISTEREI'S ECO-EFFICIENCY COMES FROM TRADITIONAL BAVARIAN VALUES

Hofpfisterei

A family-owned Bavarian bakery has converted all its bread and roll production to use organic materials and traditional baking methods over a 15 year period. The result is substantially increased turnover and a loyal customer base for Hofpfisterei and stable and growing markets for Bavarian organic farmers.

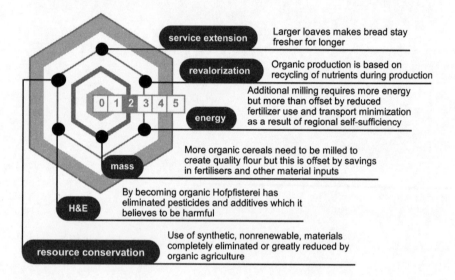

service extension	Larger loaves makes bread stay fresher for longer
revalorization	Organic production is based on recycling of nutrients during production
energy	Additional milling requires more energy but more than offset by reduced fertilizer use and transport minimization as a result of regional self-sufficiency
mass	More organic cereals need to be milled to create quality flour but this is offset by savings in fertilisers and other material inputs
H&E	By becoming organic Hofpfisterei has eliminated pesticides and additives which it believes to be harmful
resource conservation	Use of synthetic, nonrenewable, materials completely eliminated or greatly reduced by organic agriculture

Contact:
Ludwig Stocker, Hofpfisteri GmbH,
Kreittmayrstrasse 5,
80019 Munich, Germany

1 Six centuries of traditional baking

Who best represents "traditional Bavarian values?" The Catholic Church? The Munich brewers and their beer halls? Perhaps, but neither has built an environmental policy around itself. That distinction belongs to the Hofpfisterei, a family-owned Bavarian bakery which was founded in 1331.

During the 1970s the Stocker family grew increasingly dissatisfied with the way they made bread and the quality of the final product. They had remained closer to traditional baking methods than other bakers but felt that the cereals they used were produced with too many fertilizers and pesticides, and that the standardized baking methods which had been introduced during the twentieth century involved the use of too many additives. The result for them was tasteless, artificial bread which was a far cry from the appetizing and regionally distinctive loaves of the past.

Market research showed that many Hofpfisterei customers shared their concern. So in 1981, as part of its 650th birthday celebrations, the company took advertisements in the main Bavarian newspapers announcing its intention of reintroducing traditional breads based on organic ingredients and inviting potential suppliers to contact them.

Traditional Bavarian values – the path to sustainability?

2 Switching to organic bread

The ad did not result in a high response. But it did allow Hofpfisterei to identify four farmers who could supply it with organic wheat flour. As a result the company was able to convert two existing wholemeal loaves into organic products in 1982. In a pattern which has since become familiar, sales initially fell due to the higher price but were gradually recouped as new customers valued the purity and taste of the new loaves.

Impact of Chernobyl

Hofpfisterei's strategy received a further boost from the Chernobyl accident of 1986. This created a high level of radioactive contamination in Bavaria and focussed attention on the benefits of organic production. Within a few days of the accident, Hofpfisterei managed to buy up nine months' supply of flour enabling it to avoid the worst of the contamination for most of its breads.

Ironically, the bakery's one real problem was with organic flour, for its supplier's land was heavily contaminated and alternative, uncontaminated stocks were not available. It therefore warned customers about the risks by publishing the contamination level of each of its breads on a daily basis. For the first few weeks after the accident, its organic loaves had a contamination level of 40 to 50 becquerels. Although still a long way below dangerous levels, this compares to only three or four in ordinary bread.

According to Friedbert Forster, marketing director at Hofpfisterei, "secretly everyone believed that sales of organic bread would fall so much that it wouldn't be worth producing it any more. But they only fell by 10–15%. When we checked out why, we found that the customers so valued the overall idea of organic bread that they were prepared to put up with short-term contamination. So we said, if these people think this way maybe there's a bigger group who feel the same."

> **Organic bread creates loyal customers.**

Nitrates – the final straw

The feeling that Hofpfisterei could move to completely organic production and still run a successful business was confirmed by a 1987 report on water pollution. It said that around 10% of Bavaria's drinking water sources would have to be discontinued because of nitrate contamination, which was mainly caused by agriculture.

As a major purchaser of Bavarian cereals Hofpfisterei felt some responsibility for causing the problem – and finding the solution. So in 1988 it took the decision to make all of its products organic by the mid 1990s. It also determined that, to reduce transport costs and to support the local economy, it would purchase at least

80% of its cereal requirements from Bavaria. Hofpfisterei would like to achieve 100% but it needs some flexibility in sourcing to maintain quality.

The first challenge – expanding supply

One immediate challenge was to expand the supply of Bavarian organic cereals. Hofpfisterei worked in collaboration with the German organic farming association, Naturlandverband, to develop new suppliers and check that their farming was genuinely organic. In order to guarantee that organic and nonorganic cereals could not be mixed together during milling the company purchased a stake in a flour mill and used it to process all its raw materials.

The second challenge – maintaining markets

A second challenge was maintaining the market for its products, despite the 10–20% average increase in price caused by the lower yields of organic agriculture. There was also a slight fall in the quality of its wheaten breads due to a reduced protein content. Organic flour is generally lower in protein than others, in part because protein levels are boosted by heavy use of artificial fertilizer during critical periods of cereal development.

These challenges have been overcome. By 1991 all Hofpfisterei's wholemeal breads were organic, by 1993 all bread had been converted and by 1994 all rolls. The company has also introduced a new product line, the slow baked heavy loaf that benefits consumers by remaining fresher for longer.

All breads and rolls were fully organic by 1994.

3 An ecological commitment

Hofpfisterei has been driven by the ecological commitment of its family owners and the staff. This has strengthened rather than weakened over time. Although they always believed the move would be commercially viable few others would have persevered for the 10–15 years it has taken to produce fully organic bread and rolls – particularly as there have been no legislative requirements to change.

4 No additives in the food chain

From its customers' point of view, the main environmental benefit of Hofpfisterei's activities is that it removes potentially harmful substances such as nitrogen, pesticides and additives from the product chain. As an LCA has confirmed, the overall energy and material requirements of the chain have also diminished, largely due to the ending of artificial fertilizer use. However this has been partially offset by greater wear and energy consumption in the milling process. This is due to the greater bulk of organic cereal which must be milled *vis-à-vis* nonorganic to achieve the same amount of flour.

5 Existing customers maintained, new ones found

Hofpfisterei's turnover rose from 65 million DM in 1990 to 90 million DM in 1995 – an increase well above that achieved by other bakery groups. This was a result of volume growth as well as increased prices. (Its loaves are generally 10–15% more expensive than nonorganic equivalents.) It also retained much of its old customer base. Friedbert Forster estimates that about a quarter of those existing customers positively welcomed the change and most of the rest grumbled about the price increases but remained loyal because of the bread's purity and taste. Forster believes that this customer loyalty – and the long-term stability it provides for the company – is the real business benefit from Hofpfisterei's actions.

> *Going organic has increased turnover by 40%.*

6 Make pastry organic ... and make organic bread mainstream

Hofpfisterei still has one nonorganic product line, which is pastry. So far organic flour has not been of high enough quality to produce this but work continues to try to achieve it. The company is also collaborating with others to develop a modern version of the "altdeutschen Steinbackofen" (old German stone oven). The brief is to maintain the special character of bread made in the oven but to increase its energy efficiency, which currently is poor. Finally, Hofpfisterei hopes to extend the benefits of its bread from those willing (and able) to pay a premium to the mainstream market by developing a low priced organic loaf for large scale baking. This will increase its capacity utilization and lower average production costs.

7 Changes take time but support comes

Hofpfisterei's experience shows that it takes time for customers to change their expectations and behavior – but that they do so eventually. It also shows that emotion and quality are important product attributes, especially in food.

Friedbert Forster thinks that other food and drink companies could follow Hofpfisterei's example – but only if the top managers are firm believers in organic products. "What you can't do", he says, "is show someone a balance sheet at the start of the journey. It's a gradual process, which needs vision and a willingness to experiment." The other keys, he believes, are "being consistent and making customers and employees aware of what you're doing. Even though we only started with little experiments, they soon realised that we were changing for the long-term and gave us their support."

> *"What you can't do is show someone a balance sheet at the start of the journey. It's a gradual process, which needs vision and a willingness to experiment."*

▶ BIG BLUE GOES GREEN – TOXICS REDUCTION AT IBM

IBM

> Semiconductors now require much less material and energy for a given output. This case focusses on the elimination or reduced use of many toxic or environmentally harmful chemicals in manufacturing, creating cost savings and improved product quality.

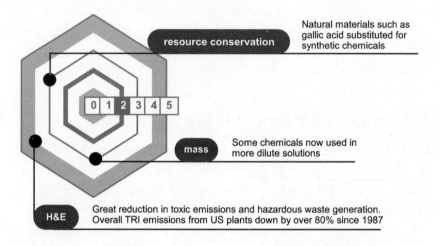

Natural materials such as gallic acid substituted for synthetic chemicals

resource conservation

Some chemicals now used in more dilute solutions

mass

Great reduction in toxic emissions and hazardous waste generation. Overall TRI emissions from US plants down by over 80% since 1987

H&E

Contact:
Edan Dionne, IBM Corporation, Route 100, Somers, New York 10589, USA

1 Computers and the environment

The statistics are familiar but still amazing. The average computer is now a hundred million times faster than just two decades ago, but has shrunk in size from a room-filling monster to a neat desk-top appliance. The new generation of 256MB chips squeeze almost 500 million transistors on to a chip little larger than those which contained a mere thousand in the 1960s.

Without any environmental intention, individual computers, and most IT products, therefore have materials requirements and energy consumption which are many orders of magnitude less per unit of service. Indeed, they are sufficient to meet the "factor of ten" criterion discussed in Chapter 3. Of course, the growth of IT production has meant that the industry's absolute consumption of materials, and users' consumption of energy, has increased but the achievement is nonetheless striking.

> *Computers have achieved "factor of ten" improvements in materials and energy consumption per unit of service.*

IBM's environmental programs

In addition to these "incidental" gains, computer manufacturers have also achieved environmental improvements by design. This is certainly true of IBM, which established an environmental policy in 1971. Its environmental programs have since helped to:

- greatly reduce emissions of toxic chemicals and hazardous waste generation (see below);

- cut carbon dioxide emissions from energy use from 7.7 million tons in 1990 to 5.5 million in 1995 (of which around half was attributable to energy efficiency measures);

- establish an Engineering Center for Environmentally Conscious Products with a brief of ensuring that all IBM products are designed for high environmental performance during their life and easy disassembly and revalorization at the end of it.

The latter objective is met by the new System/390 mainframe computers. These are air-cooled and use advanced electronics.

They reduce power and cooling requirements by 90% compared with older, water-cooled machines.

> *IBM has an Engineering Centre for Environmentally Conscious Products.*

2 Eliminating toxics and solvents

This case examines IBM's activities in one particular area – that of "clean" semiconductor manufacturing processes. Making such "chips" is a complex and exacting multistage process which uses many speciality chemicals. Chemicals are used to etch away sections of the silicon substrate, to add materials to it and to clean away dirt and debris. Cleaning is especially important as even a speck of dust can disable a chip. As a result, the semiconductor industry has been one of the largest users of organic solvents such as CFCs, perchloroethylene and glycol ethers. Many of the solvents and other chemicals used are toxic and/or contributors to local air pollution and/or contributors to atmospheric ozone depletion.

IBM took a number of initiatives in the 1980s, such as committing to phase out CFCs by 1993 and methyl chloroform by 1995 from its manufacturing processes. Both were achieved by 1993. It also updated its environmental policy. One explicit aim in the 1990 update was to . . .

> use development and manufacturing processes that do not adversely affect the environment, including developing and improving operations and technologies to minimize waste, prevent air, water and other pollution, minimize health and safety risks, and dispose of waste safely and responsibly.

Voluntary toxics reduction program

In 1991 it also joined the US Environmental Protection Agency's "33/50" voluntary toxics reduction program. Its goal was to reduce emissions of 17 specified chemicals by 33% by the end of

1992 and 50% by the end of 1995, from a 1988 base. Although IBM's early efforts meant that it had actually accomplished both goals at the time it joined, it continued its program and by 1995 it had reduced emissions of the 17 chemicals by 80% and achieved similar or greater reductions in many others. A number of chemicals were also completely eliminated from its processes.

Achievements at IBM's Burlington plant ...

One particularly successful site was at Burlington, Vermont, which manufactures memory and logic chips. One key process in such plants is removal of "photoresist," the film which covers specific sections of chips from etching. In collaboration with IBM's R&D department, the site developed a method of using harmless ionized gases to do this as a substitute for organic solvents such as n-butyl acetate.

> *IBM's Burlington plant has substituted harmless gases for organic solvents and reduced concentrations of other harmful chemicals.*

The same partners also collaborated to improve the "Huang Clean Process," an industry standard procedure to clean wafers using reactive and hazardous chemicals such as hydrogen peroxides and ammonium hydroxide. They managed to achieve comparable levels of cleaning performance from more dilute solutions of the chemicals. These solutions also increased the process yield. IBM has since shared this innovation with other semiconductor manufacturers.

... Are matched at Austin

IBM's Austin site uses hydrochloric acid for cleaning circuit boards. Experiments showed that acceptable surface preparation could be accomplished with only a tenth of the quantity of acid used previously. According to an environmental engineer

● **FIGURE 18.3**

IBM's semiconductor productivity has increased dramatically in recent years and the amount of hazardous wastes it produces has headed in the opposite direction.

involved with the project, Gayle Woodside, "it shows that waste minimization, by way of chemical source reduction, can reduce expenses as well as reduce waste."

Little acorns grow into natural etchants

One of IBM's overall aims is to use as far as possible wholly biodegradable materials preferably of natural origin. It has achieved this in micromachining of silicon structures, which was previously done with toxic and hazardous chemicals such as ethylenediamine and pyrocatechol. A new process has been developed which uses gallic acid extracted from oak tree galls. This is nontoxic and therefore safer and also increases yields and reduces disposal costs by $115,000 per annum. IBM has patented the invention and now receives further income from royalties.

IBM's new hi-tech ingredient – oak tree galls.

3 Proactivity reinforced by legislation

IBM's initial impetus came from US legislation on, and political debate about, emissions of toxic chemicals. Its initiatives have since been reinforced by the progressive tightening of regulations and pressure for voluntary action. However, IBM was as receptive as it has always been environmentally proactive. It sees computers and information technology as being able to substitute for physical activities in order to reduce environmental impacts, and help long-term sales. The toxics reduction program has also achieved more immediate cost savings but these have never been the main driver of IBM's environmental actions.

4 Deep cuts in toxic emissions

IBM has improved on most if not all dimensions of the eco-compass but this case focusses on environmental toxicity and quality. Overall the company has reduced its worldwide generation of hazardous waste from over 240 million US tons in 1987 to under 100 million in 1994. Over the same period it has reduced emissions and external transfers of the 300 or so toxic chemicals it is required to report under US Toxic Release Inventory (TRI) legislation. Emissions of TRI chemicals from its US plants fell from 11 million pounds in 1987 to under 2 million in 1994. These achievements have taken place even though the overall volume of production has remained constant or increased and the performance of the products has increased exponentially.

IBM has reduced its US TRI emissions by over 80% since 1987.

IBM's Burlington site reduced its TRI releases from 36 tons in 1991 to only 5 tons in 1994. Its hazardous waste generation declined from 6407 to 1642 tons over the same period. Increases in production and other changes meant that the real achievement was even greater than these figures suggest. According to site calculations, both TRI emissions and hazardous waste generation would have risen by 50% rather than fallen if no environmental initiatives had been taken.

5 Environment sense makes business sense

According to engineer Edan Dionne, a program manager with IBM's corporate environmental organization, IBM has found that "what makes environmental sense also makes business sense. Environmental initiatives have made our processes more cost-effective, cut waste generation and made for better resource conservation." The change to the Huang process alone created an additional $5.2 million of revenues from yield improvements. Chemical use is also down 48% and reduced cycle time saves three million gallons of water a year. These and other improvements mean cost savings of over $1 million over a three year period.

6 Beyond low hanging fruits

According to Edan Dionne IBM "wants to carry on addressing environmental issues proactively and maintain its leadership position. The challenge we face is that we've picked the 'low hanging fruits.' Opportunities are becoming harder to identify, but we'll keep on trying."

7 Toxic reduction can create business benefits

IBM's experience shows that proactivity pays and that eliminating hazardous, corrosive liquids in finishing operations brings safety, lower capital and maintenance costs and reduced waste. It also demonstrates that milder technologies can produce equivalent results to harsh ones.

Chapter 19

Revalorization

When we recycle or reuse we mimic natural systems. Nature abhors waste so all dead organic material is decomposed. The nutrients are then available for living organisms to make use of. Would you like to ride a roller coaster of joy and despair? Cut down a tropical rainforest and grow crops. The first year they will be abundant. But then yields will decline and within a few years the land will be useless. The reason? Many tropical soils are infertile. Tropical luxuriance occurs because all nutrients are quickly recycled before they can be leached away. The forest canopy also protects the soil from heavy rainfall. Growing crops block these mechanisms. Nutrients vanish in the runoff, the soil compacts and the land will only grow scrub for decades, if not forever.

▶ INDUSTRIAL ECOLOGY MIMICS NATURE

Can we mimic nature and make our wastes into raw materials? An "industrial ecology" of this kind is the dream of many environmentalists. A remarkable scheme at Kalundborg, Denmark, has made it happen on a small scale (see box). While many companies have created integrated recycling loops on their own sites, Kalundborg goes a step further by integrating material flows between different producers. Cooperative action at the regional scale presents many more opportunities for revalorization.

● INDUSTRIAL ECOLOGY IN DENMARK

Over a 30 year period an industrial estate at Kalundborg has been steadily closing the loops for energy and materials. Five plants have worked with the local authority to make use of each other's products and waste streams. The resulting energy and water savings are worth $12–15 million dollars a year.[1]

Statoil's oil refinery provides gas to an electric power plant and Gyproc, a plasterboard manufacturer. It also creates sulfur which forms the raw material for sulfuric acid production. The power plant's flue gas desulfurization equipment creates a gypsum waste. This forms Gyproc's raw material. The steam which exists from the power plant's turbines provides heating for Novo Nordisk's pharmaceutical plant and the city's district heating scheme. Its warmed cooling water is ideal for fish farming.

● FIGURE 19.1
Kalundborg

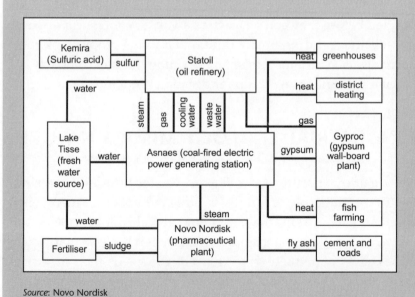

Source: Novo Nordisk

Kalundborg is one example of recycling, another is our 3M case study. But revalorization also encompasses reuse and remanufacturing. When these are feasible, they are usually the best environmental and business options. The Rank Xerox case demonstrates their value. The company reuses components that are still functional and remanufactures the casings of end of life copiers. This avoids a large proportion of the energy and raw materials needed to make them from new – and gives big cost savings.

> **When feasible, reuse and remanufacturing are usually the best revalorization options.**

▶ COSTS AND BENEFITS NEED TO BE CALCULATED

Experience shows that there are many opportunities to revalorize. Considering "end of life" during the design stage makes it easier to take advantage of these. But it is important to prove rather than assume that revalorization is beneficial. The amount of energy, material and pollution involved in the collection, preparation and processing of end of life products and recyclates can be considerable, and may negate any environmental benefits from reduced use of virgin materials.

IS INCINERATION A GOOD THING?

Does incineration count as revalorization? Waste materials can have a high energy content so it seems sensible to utilize this. Numerous cities and factories now do so. But many environmentalists have doubts, worrying that incineration is an easy option, that it distracts attention from the sometimes harder but often more valuable options of reuse, remanufacture and recycling, or, even worse, that it accepts the existence of waste and prevents consideration of waste minimization options. Some environmentalists are also worried about incineration's potential for dioxin creation. Several studies demonstrate that modern incineration equipment actually destroys dioxins and emits significantly less than it gets in the feed.[2] Energy recovery from waste is therefore a beneficial revalorization option as it substitutes primary fuels and all their rucksacks.

Our eco-compass calculations do count energy recovery from waste as revalorization. That is the case with our example, Papyron.

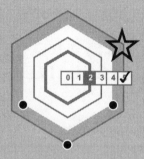

● **PAPYRON AND REVALORIZATION**

Almost all of Papyron's fuel is waste which would otherwise be landfilled. The oil-fired base case uses no recycled inputs. Papyron therefore decreases the amount of nonrecycled waste by 100% compared to the base case. This is the maximum reduction possible and therefore scores as a 5.

▶ CLOSING THE LOOP FOR CAR COOLANT

Dow Coolant

Dow operates a recycling scheme in Germany for used auto coolant. The scheme is well established but less successful than hoped because anticipated legislation to make recycling mandatory has not been introduced.

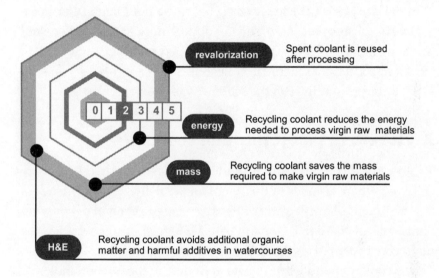

revalorization	Spent coolant is reused after processing
0 1 2 3 4 5	
energy	Recycling coolant reduces the energy needed to process virgin raw materials
mass	Recycling coolant saves the mass required to make virgin raw materials
H&E	Recycling coolant avoids additional organic matter and harmful additives in watercourses

Contact:
Dow Deutschland,
Stefan Lind,
Am Kronberger, Hang 4,
D-65824, Schwalbach, Germany

1 Money down the drain

Every year in Germany some 100,000 tonnes of spent auto coolant is flushed down the drain, around 90% of the amount sold. Disposal in this way is illegal. The main active ingredient monoethyleneglycol (MEG), is biodegradable but mildly toxic as are some of the additives. The new MEG which has to be manufactured to replace spent coolant also consumes large amounts of energy. This could be avoided by revalorization.

> **Every year in Germany 100,000 tonnes of used auto coolant is flushed drown the drain.**

In the late 1980s vehicle recycling became a hot issue in Germany. A Dow associate, Safechem, saw an opportunity to develop coolant recycling based on systems it had developed for other chemicals. In 1993 it introduced a scheme to collect used coolant from garages for a small charge and in 1995 the scheme was taken over by Dow.

2 Closing the loop through recycling

To store used coolant Dow provides garages with drums that are collected when supplies of fresh coolant are delivered and then sent to a treatment plant. Treatment has two stages: removal of contaminants, and distillation to separate the MEG from water, which is the main constituent of coolant. The "as new" MEG is then shipped to Dow's coolant manufacturing site at Botlek, in the Netherlands.

Dow has agreements with several car companies, including BMW, Peugeot and Rover, to recycle coolant from their dealers, who provide most of the coolant returned for recycling.

Volumes are disappointing

The original hope was that coolant recycling would be very profitable. But volumes so far are below forecast levels because dumping used coolant down the drain remains the most "hassle free" way of dealing with it for garages. Many car manufacturers encourage their dealers to join the scheme but cannot force them to do so, and for those who do wish to recycle there is the alternative option of doing it through waste oil collectors. Competition

● FIGURE 19.2

Automotive coolant was, and in most cases still is, literally flushed down the drain. Dow collects and recycles the spent fluid from BMW and Peugeot in Germany.

from this source has meant that Dow now charges only half the price it originally hoped for.

Dow's costs are also relatively high because it has an exceptionally secure and reliable return loop which is under its complete control. Small waste oil collectors have been known to tip coolant down the drain when it cannot be sold.

Cost reductions

The reliability of the loop will be a significant competitive advantage as coolant recycling grows in scale so Dow is unwilling to compromise it. However, it has found ways of reducing costs in order to make the process more economical. It now takes drums to a depot, where they are emptied into tankers for onward transport to the treatment plant, and uses recyclable plastic drums rather than metal ones, thereby increasing their durability. From 1996 these will be sent to a more cost-effective new treatment plant nearer to Dow's Botlek site. CCR, the company which collects the drums along with other waste products from the garages, is now becoming more involved in marketing the service.

3 The missing driver – legislation

Coolant recycling was introduced in the belief that legislation and public pressure would force garages to undertake it. The scheme also formed part of Dow's long-term strategy of building businesses around solutions to environmental problems. The failure of legislation or public pressure to materialize means that the scheme is of marginal economic benefit, a situation that will not change until legislation is enacted.

> *The absence of legislation means the scheme is of marginal economic benefit.*

4 Recycling saves resources, avoids pollution

The main environmental benefits of recycling coolant are the avoided energy and material inputs which are required to manufacture a new product. Another benefit is avoiding the additional biological oxygen demand (BOD) and additives which coolant introduces to watercourses.

5 Break even but no profit

Coolant recycling breaks even at present. It should become slightly more profitable in coming years through reducing costs and increasing volume.

The scheme is beneficial for Dow's general image in Germany and has established the company as one of the most environmentally aware suppliers to the car industry. This reputation has been helpful in winning business, both for the supplies of coolant for newly manufactured vehicles and for other products.

6 Legislation needed for further progress

The environmental challenge for Dow is to increase coolant recyling rates. The business challenge is to gain more competitive benefit from it. Higher recycling rates will help by reducing the raw material costs of coolant manufacture. However, little is likely to happen without legislation to make recycling mandatory and although Germany is planning to ban coolant incineration, this will have only a modest effect on recycling rates.

7 Look ahead ... and have patience

The coolant recycling project manager Stefan Lind learnt that recycling will not happen if there are no economic or political drivers. Many people and companies believe in it as a principle but are unwilling to do it voluntarily if it involves extra work and cost. But Lind remains "100% sure that after the year 2000 everybody will recycle coolant. You have to have an ecological vision and look to the next ten years or more." He points to another Dow recycling scheme for metal cleaning solvents which required large initial investment but was similarly slow to take off.

> Today we have a market share of 70%. There are no alternatives coming from competitors, who reacted too late because they didn't realise the direction developments were going. The same will happen with coolant.

> *"You have to have an ecological vision and look to the next ten years or more."*

▶ NEW FROM OLD AT RANK XEROX

Rank Xerox

New revenues and cost savings from remanufacturing, or reusing and recycling materials and components from old copiers. Innovative Design for Environment (DFE) approaches will create further business and environmental benefits in future.

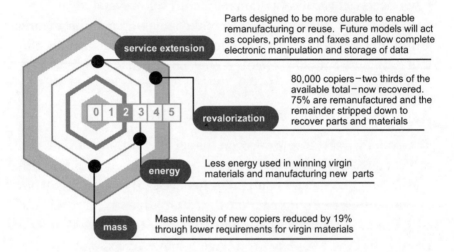

service extension — Parts designed to be more durable to enable remanufacturing or reuse. Future models will act as copiers, printers and faxes and allow complete electronic manipulation and storage of data

revalorization — 80,000 copiers—two thirds of the available total—now recovered. 75% are remanufactured and the remainder stripped down to recover parts and materials

energy — Less energy used in winning virgin materials and manufacturing new parts

mass — Mass intensity of new copiers reduced by 19% through lower requirements for virgin materials

Contact:

Dr Irina Maslennikova, Rank Xerox, Parkway, Marlow, Bucks SL7 1YL UK

1 Environmental leadership at Rank Xerox

Would you buy a used copier from this company? Over 60,000 customers of Rank Xerox, the Xerox Corporation's European affiliate, have already said yes and demand for its remanufactured copiers now exceeds supply by 50%.

Customers benefit from the lower cost of a remanufactured machine compared to a new one, while still enjoying the same Rank Xerox Total Satisfaction Guarantee. The environment benefits from the reduced energy consumption and emissions which results from reusing rather than making new components and using raw materials. And Rank Xerox saves money because reuse is cheaper.

Environmental and quality awards

This "triple win" is part of a long-standing commitment by both Rank Xerox and Xerox to demonstrate environmental leadership. Both have won a number of environmental awards, including the World Environment Center's Gold Medal for International Corporate Achievement which Xerox received in 1993. Rank Xerox was also the first winner of the prestigious European Quality Award (modelled on the US Baldrige prizes) in 1992. One criterion for this award is that applicants recognize and achieve excellence in managing their "impact on society," a category which includes environmental management.

> *Rank Xerox and Xerox have won many awards for quality and environmental performance.*

Success in both quality and environment is no coincidence for Rank Xerox sees them as closely connected. Waste in particular is a quality issue, indicating a failure to "get it right first time" so that all materials are either utilized in products or recycled. The company now summarizes its corporate environmental goal as "Waste Free Products from Waste Free Facilities."

Waste free facilities ...

Each factory is assessed on nine elements of waste management. If it reaches a set performance level, it becomes a "Waste Free Factory." The 1994 assessment was that its plants collectively were 60% of the way towards "best practice" performance. This reflected a number of achievements, including a halving of land-fill between 1992 and 1995, but indicates too that there is scope for further improvement.

... Making waste free products

The waste free products initiative also has a number of elements, including:

- introducing returnable and reusable packaging;

- making equipment more energy efficient;

- utilizing post-consumer waste in copier paper and consumables;

- making supplies more ecologically acceptable;

- increasing "asset recovery," that is, the remanufacturing, reuse and recycling of the 80,000 end of life copiers it takes back each year.

> *Rank Xerox is remanufacturing, reusing or recycling the 80,000 copiers it takes back each year.*

2 Reusing and remanufacturing copiers

Historically, Xerox and Rank Xerox rented rather than sold copiers and so have always had a product takeback operation. Although there was some recovery of valuable spares and materials, markets for them were limited. Most of the mass was sent to either landfill or, when toxic, safe disposal. However, these options became both more controversial and more costly during the 1980s and when, at the same time, the original Xerox patents expired, it meant that cost reduction was vital to compete with Japanese entrants.

Asset recovery

The solution? The establishment in 1987 of an Asset Management Center at Venray, in the Netherlands. Its mission? To maximize the

● **FIGURE 19.3**
Demand for Rank Xerox's recycled copiers outstrips supply by about 50%

financial return from the assets which were being returned to Rank Xerox, and to minimize the company's environmental impacts by developing the "3Rs" – reduce, reuse and recycle. From the start, the Center operated on a break even basis. It buys used machines from Rank Xerox operating companies and gains revenues by selling recovered machines, parts and materials back to them.

The Center began operations with ten staff but asset recovery now employs 400 both at Venray and satellite operations at other Rank Xerox manufacturing sites and has an annual turnover of almost $200 million.

Venray staff divide incoming copiers into four categories, in descending order of preference:

● *Excellent condition* – a small number of machines, typically used for demonstrations, which are simply cleaned.

- *Suitable for remanufacturing* – good quality returns which can be made as new with replacement of some components and repainting.

- *Suitable for disassembly* – returns which can be stripped down and most components reused after treatment.

- *Suitable for recovery* – returns from which recyclable materials such as aluminium, glass and metal are recovered with the residue being landfilled. This category includes the 3000 plus non-Xerox machines which are taken back annually when replaced by Rank Xerox products.

Of the 80,000 copiers returned, three quarters are remanufactured and a quarter dissassembled for reuse or recovery.

Rank Xerox has a corporate strategy target of zero landfill. It is currently focusing on ways of dealing with currently nonusable wastes such as foams, seals, painted plastics, toners and PVC power cords.

Several packaging initiatives are also in place. One of these substitutes reusable and highly flexible "tote" containers for wooden pallets in transporting new copiers to customers and returning end of life models to Venray. Rank Xerox's corporate environmental specialist, Irena Maslennikova, says that:

> The totes have given us a closed packaging loop. We've invested $4.1 million in buying new totes but we estimated that we'll save more than this amount each year.

Design for environment

In the longer term the best way to deal with troublesome wastes is to design them out of products. Design for environment (DFE) can also make remanufacturing, reuse and recycling easier by introducing end of life considerations at a product's conception. Rank Xerox's DFE approach has eight dimensions:

- *Life cycle assessment* – each new product must have an environmental plan which identifies impacts and ways of ameliorating them for all stages of its life cycle.

- *Reduced material mix* – designs must use as few materials as possible chosen from the company's Material Environmental Index of durable and nontoxic substances.

- *Design for commonality* – so that parts can fit a wide range of machines.

- *Durability* – ensuring minimal wear of parts and materials so that reuse is possible.

- *Disassembly* – ensuring quick strip down and minimal damage to components by minimizing different kinds of materials, avoiding nonseparable parts and materials and maximizing use of snap fastenings.

- *Recyclability* – marking of materials, for example by using the International Plastic Marking System, so that they can be easily identified and sorted during disassembly.

- *Environmental, health and safety standards* – ensuring that copiers at least meet and whenever possible exceed national and international standards.

- *Customer environmental requirements* – developing products which are nonhazardous and minimize energy use and materials consumption (for example, by making two-sided copying easier).

The first product to undergo DFE was toner cartridges. These now use six kinds of plastic, compared to the 17 previously used.

3 A business driver

Rank Xerox's primary driver has always been commercial. However, the possibility of takeback legislation, and the company's desire to minimize adverse impacts on society as part of its quality philosophy, now provide additional impetus.

4 Landfill, material and energy savings

The asset recovery program reduces the amount of landfill by over 7000 tonnes a year. This alone saves over $200,000. There are also considerable material, energy and other savings from the avoided manufacture of new components. Rank Xerox estimates that remanufactured copiers require 19% less mass of raw materials than new ones.

> *Asset recovery has reduced landfill by over 7000 tonnes a year.*

5 New markets and reduced purchases

While Rank Xerox welcomes the environmental benefits from asset recovery it makes it clear that this has to be run as a commercial operation. One source of revenue is the sale of the 60,000 remanufactured copiers, and there is the potential to sell more as demand now exceeds supply. Some of these sales cannibalize Rank Xerox's existing products but others substitute for lower cost copiers from competitors.

Asset recovery also avoided $80 million of raw material and component purchases in 1995. Component procurement costs too are reduced by the longer and more intensive service life of components.

> *Rank Xerox avoided $80 million of raw material and component purchases in 1995 as a result of asset recovery.*

Electronic document management cuts costs and wastes

In the longer run Rank Xerox also sees synergies between the waste free office and its strategy of becoming a supplier of document management services rather than equipment. According to Irina Maslennikova:

Our objective is to move to electronic transmission, storage and manipulation of documents. We're shifting to digital, multifunctional products. These combine the features of copiers, printers, faxes and other equipment and provide a complete capability to keep and deal with data electronically. Eliminating paper in this way is good for office costs and good for the environment.

6 Increasing return rates

Two thirds of the 120,000 copiers which every year reach the end of their useful lives with Rank Xerox's customers are presently returned for asset recovery. The rest are either sold on the second hand market or disposed of by customers. Increasing the volume of returns will reduce the unit costs of recovery operations and realize the environmental benefits of recovery and landfill reduction. Publicity campaigns in the Netherlands and elsewhere have pushed the return rate up towards 75% – as well as increasing customer awareness of the benefits of remanufactured products, and highlighting Rank Xerox's positive environmental actions. These campaigns will be extended to most countries in future with the ultimate target being 90% of all copiers returned.

> *The ultimate target – 90% of copiers returned for remanufacturing and reuse.*

The final challenge for Rank Xerox is to maintain the momentum of its 3R initiatives. Progress is not always easy, for more durable products and components often have a higher initial cost, and customer perceptions can be slow to change. Even now, and despite the European Commission's commitment to product take-back and recycling, remanufactured products are excluded from the invitations to tender of some public authorities.

7 A long-term process

Rank Xerox has learned that it pays to move up the waste mini-mization hierarchy. Reuse makes more money than recycling and remanufacturing creates the greatest value of all.

But making remanufacturing and reuse economically viable requires a long-term commitment to building markets and closing the loop between end of life and initial design. Customers may be suspicious about the quality of remanufactured goods, but they will eventually respond. Then everyone – customers, vendors and the environment – can be a winner.

Educating customers

Hugh Smith, Rank Xerox's manufacturing and supply chain envi-ronmental manager, summarizes the company's experience in this way:

> Remanufacturing involves us in supplying solutions and a service. It is a slow process convincing people but our long-term vision, for business and environmental reasons, is to establish the concept of remanufactured products being top quality. If sustainable develop-ment is rigorously applied to business, there is no alternative. We are in a pioneering stage, trying to lead demand by educating customers.

> *"If sustainable development is rigorously applied to business, there is no alternative."*

▶ PLASTIC PADS PAY AT 3M

3M

> 3M's new scouring pads are made from recycled plastic and outperform traditional steel wool scourers. They gained a 15% market share only three years after their launch.

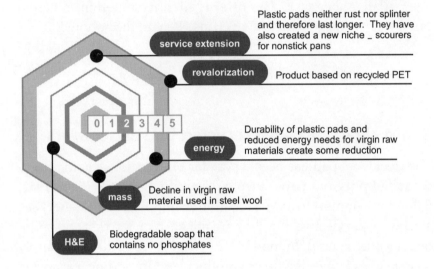

service extension — Plastic pads neither rust nor splinter and therefore last longer. They have also created a new niche – scourers for nonstick pans

revalorization — Product based on recycled PET

energy — Durability of plastic pads and reduced energy needs for virgin raw materials create some reduction

mass — Decline in virgin raw material used in steel wool

H&E — Biodegradable soap that contains no phosphates

Contact:
Alan Aspengren,
3M Center,
St Paul, MN 55144-1000, USA

1 3M's Environmental leadership

Clean your dishes with recycled plastic. That is the message of 3M's Scotch-Brite™ *Never Rust* and *Never Scratch* scouring pads. Plastic from end-of-life PET bottles is their main raw material, and its properties have allowed 3M to win 10–15% of the US soap pad market in little over three years.

3M is and always has been an environmental leader. Its "3P" (pollution prevention pays) program is world famous. 3M calculates that it has saved over $600 million since 3P was initiated in the 1970s, energy consumption has been reduced by half and emissions to air cut by one third per unit produced. The company is also a leader in eco-efficiency and has an eco-efficiency manager, Alan Aspengren. His brief is identifying environmental performance improvements which also benefit the bottom line.

> *3M now has an eco-efficiency manager.*

2 3M cleans up with recycled plastic scourers

The steel wool pad has been a popular product for cleaning heavily soiled pots and pans since the introduction of *Brillo* in 1917. Sales now amount to over $100 million annually. Consumers see steel wool as effective, but they are not keen on the rust and splinters it leaves behind. In the 1980s 3M saw an opportunity to apply its abrasives know-how to the product, and by adding a scouring pad to its range of cleaning products it became the only manufacturer to cover all product categories.

Plastic outperforms steel wool

The development brief was for a base material which could be impregnated with soap and have abrasives bonded to it. After four years of R&D it found the right base, polyethylene terephthalate (PET), from recycled plastic bottles. These can be processed into a tough fiber material which looks and feels like steel wool but outperforms it on several fronts: it keeps its shape, instead of becoming a compressed, hard to hold mess; it creates fewer splinters and so is kind to hands; and it rinses clean after each use. Overall, tests show that *Never Rust* out-cleans traditional steel wool pads three to one, based on surface area cleaned.

The *Never Rust* pad incorporates other technological break-throughs. High scouring power comes from some of 3M's advanced adhesives and abrasives. A specially formulated soap releases suds consistently without leaving a greasy residue. It also contains no phosphates. In addition, a super-concentrated formula delivers more suds and greater cleaning power for longer than steel wool pads.

The originality of 3M's work is such that it holds patents on both the product and its manufacturing processes.

Darrell Gacom, 3M's Home Care Business Unit manager sums up the *Never Rust* experience: "We're not pretending that this is the answer to the country's solid waste problems. But we think it's important to take every step possible to protect the environment. In this case, we developed a product that works better, eliminates rust and provides a new end use for recycled plastic. That's the kind of innovation upon which 3M has built its entire business."

> *"We developed a product that works better, eliminates rust and provides a new end use for recycled plastic."*

Never Scratch is perfect for nonstick cookware

In 1994 3M added Scotch-Brite™ *Never Scratch* pads to its range. The product is targeted at nonstick cookware, which accounts for 73% of all cookware sales today. Lacking alternatives, half of these buyers have been using steel wool pads to clean their purchases, knowing that the pads will scratch the non-stick surface.

3M makes *Never Scratch* pads from the same recycled PET fibres as *Never Rust*; they never scratch because they contain softer abrasives.

3 3M leverages its core competencies ...

Plastic scouring pads are an example of 3M using its core material competencies to respond to consumer needs and create new markets. So the primary driver is commercial. But 3M's environmental vision focussed it on using recycled rather than virgin materials in a way which other companies might not have done.

● **FIGURE 19.4**

3M boasts its own eco-efficiency department and has been a leader in developing environmentally improved products such as Scotch-Brite pads™. These cleaning pads are made from recycled plastic.

4 ... Creates environmental benefits

Using recycled PET reduces the need for virgin raw materials, the greater durability of pads cuts the energy and materials requirements of manufacturing and the soap used in the pads is readily biodegradable and free of phosphates.

5 ... And wins market share

In three years, 3M has gained 10–15% of the total market for soap pads and is now the market leader in nonscratch pads. The extension of its range helps sell other products as many retailers favour suppliers with a wide product range since it simplifies paperwork and offers more opportunity for volume discounts. Customer demand for *Never Rust* and *Never Scratch* means that most retailers stock them – and so are more inclined to sell other Scotch-Brite™ lines.

> After only three years 3M already has 15% of the scourer market.

6 Customer habits change slowly

3M's immediate challenge is to win further market share from steel wool pads. 3M marketing manager, Tom Paul, acknowledges the strength of competing brands. "They've been around for 80 years and customer awareness is high. So we have to persuade people who haven't tried our products that they can clean just as well. And avoid the rust and splinters they dislike about steel wool."

In the longer run 3M aims to develop more products using recycled materials.

7 Positive coverage for recycled materials

3M's success with plastic scourers is built on an intimate knowledge of customers, solid technical and marketing competencies and an environmental vision. The combination of the three has created consumer value and turned a problematic and costly waste into a useful feedstock.

One surprise for Tom Paul is the publicity generated by 3M's initiative. "One of the things we didn't predict was how much positive coverage we'd get for using recycled material. CNN, the CBS morning news, the *New York Times*, *Washington Post*, *Fortune* magazine ... the list goes on and on. It shows that people are paying attention to companies showing environmental responsibility."

> "People are paying attention to companies showing environmental responsibility."

Notes

1 National Technology and Science Council *Technology for a Sustainable Future*. Washington, DC: US Government Printing Office 1994, p.55.

2 Mark, F. *Energy Recovery Through Co-Combustion of Mixed Plastics Waste and Municipal Solid Waste*. Brussels: Association of Plastics Manufacturers in Europe, 1994.

Chapter 20

Resource conservation

The energy intensity and material intensity dimensions of the eco-compass measure the quantity used per unit of service. They are not in general concerned with the source of the energy or materials. But the source is important. Fossil fuels are nonrenewable. Their production and use has major environmental impacts. Solar energy is renewable and, in principle (if not always in practice), has lesser impacts. Similarly with materials: some are renewable or so abundant that they will never run out, others are geologically scarce and may eventually be depleted.

The resource conservation dimension focusses on the nature and renewability of the energy and materials needed for a product or process. It also considers the general impact of the specific resource needs. The effect on biodiversity is particularly important. A crop monoculture may be growable year after year, and is therefore renewable. But if it reduces habitat for species in danger of extinction it is not sustainable.

▶ BIOLOGICAL RESOURCES

How much of our current agricultural, fishing and forestry production is truly sustainable? We do not know. But environmentalists like Lester Brown make powerful arguments that much is not (see

Chapter 4). The implication? Change many current practices to achieve sustainability. One means of doing this is through certification schemes. The box describes pioneering examples for timber and marine resources. The B&Q case that follows shows how business can use them.

● CERTIFYING SUSTAINABLE PRODUCTION

How can a consumer or commercial buyer be confident that their purchases are sustainably produced? They pass through many hands on the journey from original production to point of sale. And, if their source is another country or continent, there are linguistic and cultural barriers to obtaining answers.

These difficulties are particularly acute for timber. Imports come from relatively small producers in a variety of countries. Yet more and more users want reassurance that their wood does not involve the destruction of forests and biodiversity.

The Forest Stewardship Council provides this reassurance. Set up in 1993 by a coalition of World Wide Fund for Nature (WWF), other environmental groups, international agencies and business, the Council's assessors certify that timber is sustainably produced. Twenty one forests covering 3.8 million hectares are now fully certified. They will soon be joined by the 8 million hectares owned by members of the Swedish Forest Industries Association. Their customers want to know that timber purchases are neither from "old growth" forests (which have never been cut down) or "clear cutting" of replanted forests. According to Association head, Jan Remrod:

> There is a gap between what is happening in our forests and what people think is happening. People do not really believe us when we say we have abandoned destructive techniques.[1]

Certification provides evidence of this.

The Forest Stewardship Council now has a clone, the Marine Stewardship Council. Established in 1996 by WWF and Unilever, the world's leading fish processor, the Council will certify that fish are caught in a sustainable manner. Unilever pledges that all its fish products will meet the Council's requirements by 2005. This means ▶

▶ changing equipment and practices so that fewer young fish and unwanted species are caught. Michael Sutton, director of WWF's endangered seas campaign, believes that such equipment is available but: "there's no incentive because competitors won't use it. Enforcement is difficult but the market reaches everywhere."[2]

Certification is a means of applying this market power.

In the long run we need to plunder less and borrow more from nature. Natural cycles involve the production, transport and breakdown of an enormous mass of materials. Borrowing materials from them and returning them at the end of their use (through biodegradation) does not affect the overall "balance of nature." This can reduce overall environmental impacts when synthetic materials involve large amounts of fuels and create non-biodegradable emissions and wastes.

Gentle chemistry

Plants are particularly efficient at converting solar energy, carbon dioxide and water into a variety of chemical intermediates and composite materials. They do this very slowly compared with modern reactive chemistry and cannot usually compete on the raw material to product stages of chemical and material life cycles. Environmentally too, the use of plant chemistry for large scale production for simple molecules such as cellulose or starch is questionable because of large water needs, soil erosion and potential competition with food in the long term. The most eco-efficient options are production of relatively small volumes of complex molecules such as surfactants, fragrances and pharmaceuticals.

Increasing regulatory and other constraints on the processes and products of synthetic chemistry may create niches for "gentle chemistry."

Nature has niches for slow-moving tortoises and peaceful rabbits as well as cheetahs. We would not want to call Ecover or Henkel either tortoises or rabbits, but their cases, which follow, show the potential of natural raw materials.

▶ MINERALS AND FOSSIL FUELS

Sand, gravel and some other minerals are so abundant and easily extracted that they will never be scarce. But it is different for fossil fuels and many metals and other minerals. We use them far more quickly than they can be "manufactured" by geological processes.

The result? Production from more difficult sources: giant oil rigs in 400 metres of water in the storm-lashed North Sea; mines working ores with much lower metal concentrations. Technical innovation has made it possible. But for how much longer? And at what cost of capital and material intensity?

Forever, some say. So when a material becomes scarce the price rises, and lower grade resources become economical. Or new technologies are developed to make them so. Or, if neither is possible, substitutes are found. And there is no doubt about who has won the arguments over the last century. From the Victorian economist Jeavons forecasting the imminent depletion of coal to the Limits to Growth doomsters of the 1970s, there has been a succession of pessimists about energy and mineral prices and availability. Within a few years they have been proved wrong as prices fell and supplies became plentiful.

The laws of thermodynamics set ultimate limits

On the other hand, the laws of thermodynamics set some ultimate limits. It does not pay to use more energy to produce oil than it provides to users. Mining ever lower grades of ore may be technically feasible but is prohibitively expensive because of the energy and material intensity of the process. This point could come sooner rather than later. If government policies are moving towards internalizing full environmental costs, resource production will be one of the first industries to be affected.

This makes potential resource depletion into a business risk as well as an environmental one. Think carefully. How sensitive are your plans to rising costs of energy or material inputs?

When we calculate the eco-compass, we generally assume that fossil fuel and many mineral resources will become scarce and rise in price. But the context is all. Crude oil is worth a lot to a chemical company which uses only a little to make high value products. It is worth much less to burn for energy for substitutes are readily available. So oil is a less scarce resource for a chemical or polymer use than most others.

The following boxes give details of current assumptions about resource depletion and our scoring of Papyron.

● RESERVES OF SCARCE RESOURCES

The French life cycle assessment specialist, Ecobilan, makes the following assumptions about how long resources will last at today's rates of depletion:

Crude oil	44 years
Natural gas	58 years
Coal	250 years
Copper	50 years
Phosphate	78 years
Bauxite	90 years
Iron ore	200 years

● SCORING PAPYRON ON RESOURCE CONSERVATION

Papyron uses 315 tons per annum of nonrenewable fossil fuels. The oil-fired base case consumes 1228 tons per annum. This is a decrease of 74% and merits a score of 4.

Consumption of nonrenewable resources (tons per annum)

	Base case	*Papyron*
Heating oil	872	170
Fossil fuels for electricity generation	<u>356</u>	<u>145</u>
	1228	315

▶ BRITAIN'S NO. 1 DIY RETAILER WILL ONLY SELL CERTIFIED TIMBER

B&Q

> The UK's largest DIY retailer audits and works with its suppliers to reduce environmental impacts. It tracks the source of all its timber to ensure that it is from well managed supplies. Its target is 100% independent certification of timber origin by 1999.

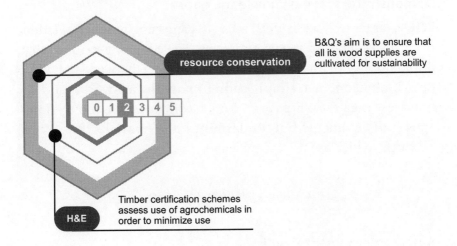

resource conservation

B&Q's aim is to ensure that all its wood supplies are cultivated for sustainability

Timber certification schemes assess use of agrochemicals in order to minimize use

H&E

Contact:

Alan Knight, B&Q plc, Portswood House, 1 Hampshire Corporate Park, Chandlers Ford, Eastleigh, Hants SO53 3YX, UK

1 B&Q reacts to public criticism

Which organization sold 130 cubic metres of timber from the MB Hill farm in Natal in a six month period in 1993? Or 123 cubic metres of rubberwood in flooring imported from Thailand in 1995? And publishes these and other data about the source of all of its wood supplies each year? And does it not only through a report but in full page spreads in leading British newspapers?

The answer is the UK's biggest DIY retailer, B&Q. It spent the early 1990s tracking down the source of all its wood (a total in 1995 of 278,449 cubic meters). It does this in order to meet the World Wide Fund for Nature proposal that companies should source timber and wood products only from well-managed forests after 1995.

Demonstrators reveal knowledge gaps

B&Q's target was set in 1991, after an increasing number of letters from customers and media enquiries. The company realized that it had no way of answering the questions. In the words of CEO, Jim Hodkinson, "we simply didn't know the answers – and do not know means do not care." Public controversy not only damages B&Q's image but undermines the markets for wood products, which are its core business.

> **"Don't know means don't care."**

A new environmental policy

In 1990 the board appointed an environmental coordinator, Alan Knight, and gave him the brief of devising an environmental policy and gathering more information about wood sourcing.

The policy now in place addresses B&Q's own environmental performance with energy efficiency, waste minimization and other internal schemes. However, it was clear that B&Q's most significant environmental impacts were those occurring upstream in the suppliers of the products they sold. Working with these suppliers became the policy's major focus, the aim being to raise their awareness of environmental issues as a prelude to improvements, and to generate the information B&Q needs to comply with its wood supply policy.

● FIGURE 20.1
DIY retailer B&Q audits and works with its suppliers to reduce the
environmental impacts of the products it sells.

2 B&Q's supplier environmental audits

B&Q now conducts an annual environmental audit of its suppliers. It assesses two topics:

● their overall environmental commitment, and

● whether they comply with B&Q's timber policies.

Relevant data come from an environmental questionnaire and suppliers' own environmental policy statements. B&Q environmental staff also communicate their policies and gather data at their environmental supplier seminars and on regular supplier visits.

An A-F rating

The overall output of B&Q's assessment of supplier environmental commitment is a grading of A,B,C,D or E and F. An A rating means that:

> Suppliers demonstrate environmental excellence. A systematic, mature and well-documented environmental programme is in place. Suppliers have developed innovative responses to environmental issues.

As of 1995 only four out of B&Q's 500 primary suppliers had received this rating (Robert Bosch, Philips Lighting, Monsanto

> **B&Q rates all its suppliers from A to F.**

Garden Chemicals and Kew Cleaning Systems).

An F rating is given when suppliers have not provided data and an E when: "Suppliers have returned a questionnaire but expose B&Q to severe liability in one or more specific areas."

The mid rating of C is given when:

> Suppliers have identified the key issues associated with their products and have a framework policy in place which commits the company to achieving broad objectives. Specific targets need to be developed and implemented to address these objectives.

At the end of 1993 only 35% of B&Q suppliers were rated C or better. The board set a target that the remainder must achieve grade C by the end of 1994. 94% did so. Of the 29 who didn't, ten were delisted, eight were given extensions because they had a valid reason for not complying and the remainder, which were of strategic importance to B&Q, were given a final chance, which they took during 1995.

> *Ten suppliers were delisted for failing to meet B&Q's environmental requirements.*

B&Q's timber audit

B&Q's timber audit rates suppliers of wood and wood products, who get marks out of 100. Only those providing independent certification that the wood is from well-managed sources can achieve full marks. B&Q is playing a leading role in establishing certification schemes. It works closely with the Forest Stewardship Council, a collaboration between the World Wide Fund for Nature, timber importers, retailers and other bodies.

Those without certification can gain up to 30 marks for evidence of general commitment, 30 for actual performance (as assessed by B&Q) and 25 for quality of information provided.

In 1994 B&Q set a target that all its suppliers of wood and wood products must achieve a minimum score of 50 on the timber audit. 76% had done so by May 1995, so as a result, B&Q was able to trace 53% of the timber used in products during 1994 to a named forest and a further 46% to a named processing mill.

> *97% of the timber used in B&Q products in 1994 can be traced back to a named forest or mill.*

Suppliers are pressured to improve

The auditing system provides general pressures for suppliers to improve. Around 10% of B&Q's direct suppliers have changed their own suppliers in order to meet the company's environmental requirements. B&Q also provides more specific assistance by publicizing best practice through annual supplier environmental awards, supplier conferences and publications. Within the limits of its resources it gives individual advice, and it puts resources into demonstration projects.

Demonstration projects with suppliers

One demonstration project is pilot certification of Malaysian rubberwood doors to Forest Stewardship Council standards. Another is support for a community forestry project at Bainings, Papua New Guinea.

A third project is at an Indian supplier of brass door handles. B&Q's audit revealed that poor conditions at the foundry made the handles one of the most environmentally damaging of B&Q's products as well as creating hazardous conditions for employees. Delisting was the easiest option. But B&Q now donates the equivalent of $80,000 in consultancy services from its health and safety and environmental specialists to help the company improve. The actions include installing new equipment and adopting new processes. The unexpected result? Not only does the Indian company still have western markets, it is achieving higher product quality and cost savings – and its workforce is highly motivated.

> *An Indian supplier of brass door handles has better safety and environmental performance, improved product quality and reduced costs.*

3 B&Q protects image, anticipates future trends

B&Q began its environmental programs because of the threat to its image. Image is important to a retailer and it makes commercial sense to protect it. This is still a strong driver. But B&Q's initiatives are taking it well beyond most other retailers, in DIY or other areas. Alan Knight and others believe that environment will increasingly shape the values of its customers, and the products it can sell. It is possible, for example, that the UK and other governments will require certification of some or all wood products. If this happens B&Q will adapt at minimal cost. Few of its competitors will be in the same position and some might lose their timber business as a result.

4 Improvements in supplier's environmental performance

B&Q's internal environmental actions create energy savings and reduction or revalorization of packaging materials. The general pressure it puts on suppliers through its rating schemes also encourages them to improve in most if not all dimensions of the eco-compass.

Its timber initiatives encourage timber production from well-managed forests. This protects biodiversity, cuts out excessive use of potentially harmful pesticides and fertilizers and helps preserve soils. The benefits should increase substantially over the next decade. B&Q's new target of all timber suppliers being certified puts more pressure on its own suppliers, and, by example, the entire forestry industry, to move towards sustainable means of production.

5 Benefits for B&Q's corporate image

B&Q is saving money from its internal environmental measures. But the biggest, if most intangible, return is in reputation. According to CEO Jim Hodkinson:

> Through our environmental policy we have been recognized as a responsible retailer and there is no doubt that our corporate image has benefitted. On my travels around the country, whether I'm speaking to fellow businessmen, staff or customers, there is a recognition of what we are trying to achieve and applause for the action we are taking.

> *"There is no doubt our corporate image has benefited." –*
> *Jim Hodkinson, B&Q CEO*

Alan Knight sees three additional benefits:

> One is improved morale. You never should underestimate the importance of the feelgood factor in business. Another is confidence in our buyers. A few years ago they'd go into defensive mode about environment, like some of our competitors still do. Now they have the confidence to face the issues and discuss them. And we're getting a long-term advantage over competitors by influencing the process of timber certification and forging good relationships with suppliers of certified timber.

6 All timber must be certified

One challenge for B&Q is to make environment even more mainstream by integrating it with its other business processes. In 1994 it merged its quality and environmental departments. In other companies which combine the two, environment is sometimes marginal. In B&Q's case the environmental coordinator, Alan Knight, was appointed as Controller of Quality and Environment. He has a brief of extending the environmental audit procedures into the area of product quality and safety as well as meeting environmental targets.

B&Q now has new targets. Since 1995 no new timber products are purchased without the approval of the Quality and Environment department. And the company is the world's first retailer to set a target of 100% of its timber supplies coming from independently certified sources by the end of 1999.

> *All B&Q timber will be from independently certified sources*
> *by end 1999.*

7 Market leaders have responsibilities ... and even small suppliers will respond

The B&Q experience shows that it is possible to stimulate small suppliers, even in other countries, to take an improvement course. The key is explaining why environmental improvement matters, setting clear targets and auditing compliance.

B&Q also provides an example for other purchasers of commodity materials, who often claim they are unable to monitor the environmental impacts of supplies purchased on world markets. The Forest Stewardship Council scheme which B&Q helped bring about proves them wrong. It demonstrates too that win–win partnerships can be forged within international supply chains.

The case also shows that the point in the supply chain closest to the end user can play a critical role in changing customer behavior. This is especially true if companies have a high market share. Alan Knight believes that . . .

> it's a fundamental responsibility of a market leader to lead markets. It has to do more than its competitors. Inaction not only abdicates this responsibility, it blocks actions by others who're nervous about competitive advantage. Some of the other companies in our industry are pleased about B&Q's initiatives. It means they can do the same without looking over their shoulders.

▶ ECOVER MAKES GENTLE CLEANING PRODUCTS

Ecover

A small Belgian company with a ecological vision has established a small but commercial niche for 'gentle' cleaning products – and influenced the entire industry. It believes that gentle products now match synthetic ones in performance and is therefore planning to enter the mainstream.

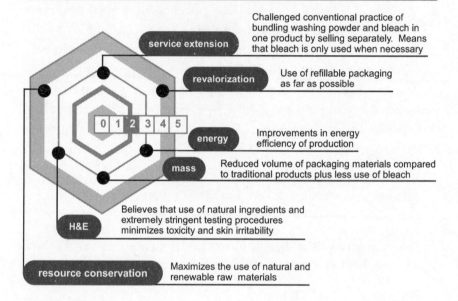

service extension — Challenged conventional practice of bundling washing powder and bleach in one product by selling separately. Means that bleach is only used when necessary

revalorization — Use of refillable packaging as far as possible

energy — Improvements in energy efficiency of production

mass — Reduced volume of packaging materials compared to traditional products plus less use of bleach

H&E — Believes that use of natural ingredients and extremely stringent testing procedures minimizes toxicity and skin irritability

resource conservation — Maximizes the use of natural and renewable raw materials

Contact:
Ecover,
Industrieweg,
B-2390 Malle, Belgium

1 Ecover as environmental pioneer

In the late 1980s the United Nations Environmental Program created the "Global 500 Roll of Honour" award to give recognition to environmental pioneers. The list was mainly individuals but contained just a few companies. One was Ecover, a Belgian manufacturer of "gentle" cleaning products made from natural materials.

Why was it singled out? One reason was its success in creating a "green" niche in the unpromising area of fast moving consumer goods. The other was its impact on the multinationals such as Procter & Gamble and Unilever which dominated the market. While these companies were already taking environment seriously, the fear of losing market share to Ecover, and the ammunition which its example gave to environmental groups campaigning against phosphates, excess packaging and other issues, gave them an extra stimulus to do so.

From smallholding to supermarket

Fittingly, Ecover was born on a farm. The year was 1979, the place a small soap-making unit on a smallholding near the north Belgian town of Malle. The founder was Frans Bogaerts, a Belgian concerned about environmental issues such as the effects of excess phosphate on water courses.

Ecover's first product was a phosphate-free soap which it sold through local health stores. During the 1980s it began international distribution and introduced further products such as washing powders and toilet cleaners. Although most of its sales continued to be through health shops, the upsurge of the "green consumer" phenomenon in the late 1980s led some supermarkets to stock it. In the UK, for example, Ecover could be found on the shelves of several leading supermarkets and its market share briefly rose to almost 10%.

The green consumer brought Ecover into the supermarkets.

A controversial takeover

Rapid growth meant that Ecover required more production capacity and capital. To provide the latter, its shareholders sold the company in 1992 to Group 4 Securitas. The new owners were in the business of providing security for premises and people and saw Ecover's brand of "ecological security" as a logical extension of their activities. Unfortunately, the sale and its consequences has proved controversial. Some environmentalists have become hostile to the company because its parent, Group 4, provides security for some nuclear power plants and road construction sites in the UK. Ecover has also been involved in legal action against its previous managing director over some aspects of the sale.

The ecological factory

Ecover's core business of cleaning products has been unaffected by these controversies and both sales and the product range have continued to expand. In 1992 Ecover took possession of a new 5300 square metres "ecological factory," adjacent to its existing site at Malle. The factory was based on completely closed production cycles so that no emissions and wastes are generated and there is maximum energy efficiency and maximum use of natural materials. Its most distinctive feature is its lawned roof, which helps cool the building in summer and warm it in winter.

The ecological factory – with a lawn on its roof.

2 Gentle products from natural ingredients

Ecover believes in "gentle" or "soft" chemistry. This utilizes only simple reaction processes on renewable or abundant raw materials. The aim is to create products which are effective but involve the least possible interference with the original nature of the raw material. Ecover contrasts this with "hard" chemistry. This is based on nonrenewable materials (primarily petroleum) and utilizes complex reaction processes to break the materials down into their constituent atoms and molecules and then combines them to create specific products. Ecover sees such processes as being unsustainable, too energy-intensive and as carrying a risk of undesirable effects and dangerous by-products.

Gentle chemistry utilizes only simple reaction processes on renewable or abundant raw materials.

Maximum biodegradability

Ecover also ensures that the constituents of its products are biodegradable, minimally toxic and nonirritating or allergenic to skin and other tissue. Rapid biodegradability is an important issue for cleaning products. This is partly to break down harmful ingredients and also to avoid any lowering of the surface tension of watercourses, which can adversely affect aquatic creatures. Ecover considers that the standard tests for this are flawed because they only measure primary biodegradability – that is, breakdown of the original substance to the point where it has lost its original function (washing action in the case of detergents). It believes that some of the breakdown products from conventional cleaning chemicals are only biodegraded slowly and can therefore be actually or potentially harmful. Hence it prefers to test for complete biodegradability, ie complete breakdown of a substance to the point where it can be utilized by organisms.

Most substances can be toxic in sufficiently high amounts and concentrations but Ecover tests to ensure that risks are minimal (see next section). It also believes that many products of "hard" chemistry are skin irritants or allergens. It screens all ingredients for their skin tolerability, using scientific publications and tests on red blood cells – but not animal tests, which the company believes to be unethical.

Do gentle products work?

So far, so green. But do "gentle" cleaning products work? When we spill coffee or get muddied in sport is some aggressive stain removal not required? Certainly gentle cleaning products have gained a reputation for not being as effective as conventional alternatives. Ecover acknowledges that there was some – albeit exaggerated – truth in these claims a few years ago but sees them as part of the "teething troubles" of the first generation of products. It is now confident that its products clean just as effectively as competitors.

> **Ecover is now confident that gentle products clean just as effectively as others.**

No to optical brighteners ...

Clean but not whiten – for one dark area in the washing powder wars is that of optical brighteners. These do nothing for cleanliness but make washing appear whiter by reflecting a blue light which, when merged with the natural yellow hue of newly washed clothes, appears sparkling white to the human eye. Ecover eschews these on the grounds that they are petrochemicals which have only cosmetic value, and accepts the consequence that many mainstream consumers will see its products as inferior.

... But compromise on fragrances

In reality, Ecover's purism is tempered by its desire to bring gentle cleaners to as many people as possible, which means distribution through supermarkets. Hence, while it considers optical brighteners as too serious an issue to compromise on, it is more open-minded about the other cosmetic issue of fragrance. Most consumers expect their cleaners to have a pleasant, fresh, smell, but this is difficult to create using only natural substances. So, whilst its core health shop range continues to utilize only these, the supermarket range makes sparing use of nature–identical or, *in extremis*, synthetic molecules provided that they are made from sustainable raw materials.

3 An ecological vision

Ecover's primary driver was Frans Bogaert's vision of ecologically compatible "gentle cleaning products." This remains the case, although Ecover has now established itself as a commercially viable company serving a small but stable niche. The company was a co-founder, and remains an active member of, the Social Ventures Network. This brings together companies such as Ben and Jerry's and Body Shop which operate commercial businesses on the basis of a strong ethic of environmental concern and social responsibility. Legislation has not been a major driver, although, as when some countries banned phosphates in cleaning products, it has sometimes been helpful.

4 Natural materials and lower toxicity

Ecover clearly scores high on the eco-compass for its use of natural materials. Both it and many environmentalists, but not, of course, mainstream manufacturers, also believe that its approach avoids the problems of toxicity and negative effects on environmental quality which are created by the ingredients in conventional products. It calculates that the critical value volume (that is, the amount of water needed to render 100 grams of substance completely harmless) is 3400 liters for Ecover washing powder compared with 10,400 liters for the market leader.

> **Ecover says its powders are less toxic.**

One ambiguous dimension for Ecover is that of service extension, particularly with regard to multifunctionality. As bleach is only required for white washes, which comprise under a third of total washloads, it prefers to sell this separately so that customers can use it only when necessary. This contrasts with mainstream products, which include bleach in the washing powder with the consequence that it is often used unnecessarily. The example reinforces the point made in the next chapter on service extension. Common sense has to be used when interpreting this, and all other dimensions of the compass.

5 A valuable brand

Ecover's business would not exist without its environmental vision, which has allowed it to establish a strong niche in one of the most competitive of consumer markets. The "green" niche accounts for around 4% of overall sales of cleaning products, and Ecover has 50% of it. This was a profitable niche until the early 1990s, when recession and the costs of building its ecological factory forced it into a loss. It is now back in profit and there is little doubt that, should Group 4 ever wish to sell, the strength of its brand name would result in a high price.

6 Overcoming negative publicity

So far approximately 10% of the population who think "green" buy Ecover products. The company wants to build sales among the remaining 90% and build its presence in North America and Japan.

One barrier is negative publicity about gentle cleaners. Another is confusion about what is and is not environmentally beneficial, a confusion which will not be dispelled, in Ecover's view, by eco-labeling, which it believes to be too dominated by the large manufacturers. A third is price, although the company believes that when the cost per washload is compared its products are usually competitive with others of similar quality.

Convincing mainstream customers

Peter Malaise, Ecover's R&D director, believes that there is also potential for a considerable increase in sales to environmentally concerned customers. But "they can't be convinced in the same way as greens. We have to do it with facts. To prove that actually there is no reason any more *not* to buy green."

Ecover also feels a responsibility to develop knowledge about emerging environmental issues, both for itself and society generally. Its key issue of the moment is genetic manipulation, where it is working with a New Zealand doctor and Greenpeace member in order to build understanding and develop a policy.

7 Slow evolution

Peter Malaise characterizes Ecover's progress as "a slow evolution with lots of compromises. Mistakes are inevitable. What's important is to keep the final destination in mind. Even one and two per cent improvements create progress and build confidence in the company." However, he does not feel that every enterprise has to become an Ecover. "You can improve in many different ways," he says. "Ecover is like yeast in bread. You do not need a lot of it but the example is needed to expand the awareness of a whole industry."

> *"Ecover is like yeast in bread – you do not need a lot of it but the example is needed to expand the awareness of a whole industry."*

▶ HENKEL'S NATURAL MATERIALS LUBRICATE NORTH SEA OIL PRODUCTION

Henkel

> Henkel's chemicals business is based on natural oils and fats. It has proactively developed a drilling fluid, Petrofree, based on these materials rather than petroleum. This is not only environmentally superior but is safer and can also reduce overall drilling costs.

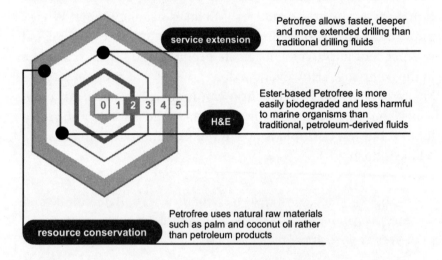

Petrofree allows faster, deeper and more extended drilling than traditional drilling fluids

service extension

Ester-based Petrofree is more easily biodegraded and less harmful to marine organisms than traditional, petroleum-derived fluids

H&E

Petrofree uses natural raw materials such as palm and coconut oil rather than petroleum products

resource conservation

Contact:

Dr Claus-Peter Herold and Dr Stefan von Tapavicza, Henkel KGaA, Henkelstrasse 67, 40191 Duesseldorf, Germany

1 Background

Few environments are less natural than a North Sea oil rig. What creatures other than humans could survive the biting cold, hurricane-force winds and giant waves of a North Sea winter? Only technology can conquer them – and offshore technology is built on artificial materials such as concrete and steel.

Yet it is in these hi-tech circumstances that a product based on renewable natural materials is replacing a synthetic equivalent for a critical task. This task is performed by the drilling fluid, which is constantly pumped down to the drill head as it bites into the rock at distances up to eight kilometers away from the drill site. The fluid is vital both to lubricate the head and to remove the two to three tons of rock debris it creates every hour.

Henkel's natural products

The company which has developed "natural drilling fluid" is Henkel, a German manufacturer of chemical intermediates and products such as cleaning materials and lubricants. It is an unusual player in the chemical industry because of its strong bias towards using natural raw materials. This bias is partly historical. The company was founded to produce detergents using chemicals from natural oils and fats and is now the leading business in the field. It now sees the environmental advantages *vis-à-vis* petroleum-based products as a major competitive strength. Certainly it has allowed the company to become a supplier to "alternative" businesses such as Ecover as well as mainstream customers.

> *Henkel sees its core business as products made from natural materials.*

Henkel's R&D develops effective and sustainable products for markets shaped by environmental considerations. Its zeolites substitute for phosphorus in detergents and chromium in leather tanning. Special nutrient solutions make it easier for microorganisms to degrade oil contamination in soil. And its APG surfactants are 100% based on renewable resources.

These R&D efforts are matched by operational environmental initiatives. Water consumption at its main Düsseldorf site has been halved over the last two decades and waste generation reduced by 40% since 1984. Henkel was also one of the first German companies to introduce environmental auditing and introduce an environmental management system which is compatible with EMAS and ISO14000.

2 Developing a natural drilling fluid

Henkel entered the oil field supply business in the 1970s when it acquired several US companies. The company has traditionally been organized on the basis of customer segments rather than products, so in the early 1980s, when the oil industry was booming, it established an oil field chemical division. The new division soon identified offshore drilling fluids as a huge market where environment was becoming an issue and therefore an opportunity for Henkel chemistry.

> *Offshore drilling fluids were a huge market with growing environmental concern – and therefore an opportunity for Henkel's green chemistry.*

The fluids being used at that time were based on diesel or other mineral oils. Although the fluid is constantly recycled at the surface, the rock debris is filtered out. This inevitably retains an oil coating, equivalent to about 10–15% of the total volume of fluid used. The platforms have no space to store the many tonnes of coated debris generated in every day of drilling and it is prohibitively expensive to transport this material to shore. The solution in the early years of offshore development was sea dumping. Over time this resulted in substantial oil contamination of the seabed and surrounding ocean. By the early 1980s pressure groups and some governments around the North Sea basin were expressing concern about the pollution.

Years of R&D

Henkel believed that legislation would eventually be introduced to limit pollution from drilling fluid. In 1985 it began a search for a technically acceptable, reasonably priced and environmentally benign product. The environmental brief was minimal toxicity to marine organisms and biodegradability in both aerobic and anaerobic conditions.

Drilling fluids have to meet exacting specifications. They must be of low viscosity and capable of performing at both surface temperatures and pressures and the much higher ones at the drill tip. They must be stable in the presence of natural gas, which is often found with oil, and other potential contaminants such as alkaline materials. They must also be safe for rig workers to handle.

The program had three stages. The first was finding the base substance for the drilling fluid. The second was combining this with additives to provide complete functionality. The third was test drilling to ensure that it worked in North Sea conditions.

Stage one involved screening a number of substances. The search began with fish and vegetable oils but these were either unstable or too viscous. It then moved on to complex esters. These result from the reaction of a fatty acid (from vegetable or other sources) with an alcohol in the presence of a catalyst. Finding the best vegetable oil and alcohol combination was a lengthy business and the right ester was only found after three years, in 1988. Combining this with the necessary additives was more straightforward and the first trial wells were sunk in the Norwegian North Sea in 1989 and 1990.

Henkel took three years to find an optimal drilling fluid.

A collaborative strategy

As the research developed Henkel began to put a marketing strategy into place. As its own resources were insufficient to capitalize on the product it looked for a strategic alliance with a major supplier of off-shore products and services. This was Baroid, who had been loosely involved since the project's inception. Henceforth Henkel focussed on the chemistry of the product and Baroid led the field testing.

By the time the first test wells were sunk the Norwegian government had announced restrictions on the oil content of drilling fluid debris, limiting it at 4% after 1991 and an ultimate 1%. As a result three quarters of Norwegian wells are now drilled with pseudo oil-based muds (POBM) such as the Henkel and Baroid product, now called Petrofree.

It is more expensive to buy than conventional fluids but it lubricates more effectively so that drilling can be quicker and reach greater lengths than previous systems. As a result total drilling costs are often reduced even before the (high) costs of disposing of alternative products are taken into account. Petrofree has also enabled Statoil to establish a new record, drilling a well of around nine kilometres in length. Finally, the product has a higher boiling point than alternatives and is therefore safer and more friendly to work with.

> **Petrofree is safer and often reduces total drilling costs.**

3 Long-term commitment

Henkel's actions were ultimately commercial in that natural drilling fluid is an extension of its existing product range. It was also driven by the vision (which proved correct) that legislation would create a large market in the medium–long term. However, the long time scale for the R&D effort – and that originally anticipated for commercialization – deterred other companies who lacked Henkel's long-term commitment to nature-based products.

4 Benefits to marine life

Petrofree greatly reduces the risks of poisoning, affecting the buoyancy or other harmful effects on marine organisms which are created by less biodegradable mineral-oil-based products. It also substitutes petroleum-derived products by renewable raw materials such as palm and coconut oils. Hence there is only borrowing from, rather than permanent effects on natural cycles such as that of carbon dioxide.

5 Business, environmental and safety gains

Petrofree was the first pseudo oil-based mud in the market and therefore quickly won a reasonable market share. This should grow substantially in future. Most customers benefit from the lower total drilling costs and new technical possibilities it creates. Workers also enjoy greater safety and a less polluted atmosphere on the drilling platform.

> *Petrofree has given Henkel market leadership in a fast growing area.*

6 Sustainability and market leadership

The challenge for Henkel and Baroid is to maintain their market leadership. The new legislation has brought forward competing fluids based on oil-derived chemicals such as paraffins. Henkel believes that they are less biodegradable than Petrofree and that this together with their nonrenewable origin makes them less environmentally sound. It is pressing for standardized deep sea biodegradability tests to establish Petrofree's advantages.

In the long term Henkel must also ensure that its production chain is sustainable. At present Henkel buys oils and other raw materials on the international markets and it is currently difficult to determine and influence the production methods. But in the long run it may be necessary to do this, possibly through a certification scheme such as that developed by the Forest Stewardship Council (see Chapter 20).

7 A service not a product

The Petrofree experience has reinforced Henkel's existing feeling that it is now selling a service rather than products. According to Dr Claus-Peter Herold, product development manager for oil field chemicals, "today you do not sell chemicals any more but suggestions about solving problems. Doing this often involves working with other suppliers to create an integrated package." Henkel's collaboration with Baroid is an example of this.

> *"Today you do not sell chemicals any more but suggestions about solving problems."*

Herold also believes that innovations such as Petrofree require a strong product champion but also time for doubts to be aired and resolved. Although its early development was not blocked, some involved in the process were not totally convinced of its merits. Herold comments, "you have to show management the full opportunities, and problems, of a product. We were lucky in having people who didn't lose their faith, who didn't say 'they're never going to understand it and give up'."

Notes

1 Quoted in Brown-Humes C. "Certificates for Swedish Forests," *Financial Times*, 28 February 1996.

2 Quoted in Maitland A. "Unilever in Fight to Save Global Fisheries," *Financial Times*, 22 February 1996.

Chapter 21

Service extension

Eco-efficiency is not only about energy and material flows. It is also about delivering more service to customers from a given amount of environmental inputs. We call this *service extension*. It can be achieved in many ways, including:

- increased durability

- repairability and upgradeability

- multifunctionality

- shared use.

▶ DURABILITY MEANS FEWER REPLACEMENTS

Long-lasting, or *durable* products avoid the environmental impacts involved in making replacements. The case which follows focusses on Kyocera's laser printers. They have permanent toner cartridges which seldom need replacing, thus avoiding the energy and materials required to make the large number of cartridges needed over the lifetime of competing printers. It also saves money.

▶ UPGRADEABILITY ALLOWS REUSE OF COMPONENTS

The Rank Xerox case in Chapter 16 demonstrates the advantages of repairability and upgradeability. It now designs its copiers on a modular basis which means that key components, such as electronic controls, can easily be replaced. This allows the basic carcase and other components of the copier to go through a number of cycles with great cost savings.

▶ MULTIFUNCTIONALITY CAN SAVE ENERGY AND MATERIALS ...

One product serving two functions usually needs less materials and energy over its life cycle than two separate products. The Swiss Army knife provides one example of such a product. Another, described in the Azurel case, is about building insulation panels which are strong enough to replace masonry or timber walls and roofs. Combining the two functions of insulation and load-bearing eliminates the energy and materials used to make bricks or concrete or to grow and process more timber.

▶ ... AS CAN SHARED USE

Shared use of the same product can also reduce environmental impacts. Most cars are driven, on average, for under an hour a day. If two people make use of one car instead of having separate ones, all the materials and energy going into the second vehicle are saved.

▶ DON'T ASSUME TOO MUCH

As ever you must be careful not to assume too much. Durability is not better if old products are heavy polluters or energy users. What is the quickest way to reduce air pollution in most countries? Take the "old bangers" off the road and replace them with new autos. Old products are no good if they cannot provide the desired service. Computers are surprizingly durable, but even last year's model struggles to run this year's software. Consequently only a small number last for more than a few years.

Multifunctionality is also useless if one or more of the functions is not well met – this was a problem with some of the early models of copier/fax/printer/scanners. Shared use occurs infrequently for a reason: many prefer the control and convenience that comes with exclusive use.

Overcoming these obstacles is the challenge for eco-innovators. It can be done. You don't have to make the whole product durable. As Rank Xerox has shown, if it is a modular design individual components can be replaced. We already have working models for shared use of cars with taxis and shared-ride schemes. The rising cost of car ownership and use means that someone, somewhere, will find a way of extending these services.

Service extension is the most difficult dimension to score. Judgments must sometimes be made on a qualitative rather than quantitative basis.

● PAPYRON PROVIDES THE SAME SERVICE

Papyron provides exactly the same service – space and water heating – as the base case of oil-fired heating. There is no improvement. Hence it scores a 2.

This completes the full Papyron compass, which, to remind you, looks like this.

▶ AZUREL* DOES AWAY WITH CONVENTIONAL WALLS

Azurel*

The Azurel* house uses Styrofoam™ insulation boards for walls and ceilings. This drastically reduces its lifetime material requirements and recycleability compared to masonry or timber framed homes. It's also quicker to build, creating higher value for builders.

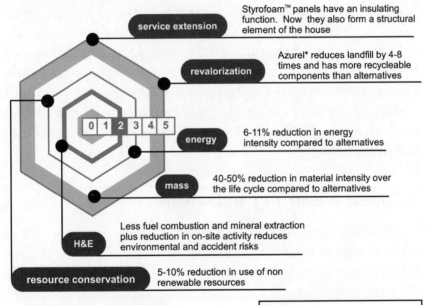

service extension — Styrofoam™ panels have an insulating function. Now they also form a structural element of the house

revalorization — Azurel* reduces landfill by 4-8 times and has more recycleable components than alternatives

energy — 6-11% reduction in energy intensity compared to alternatives

mass — 40-50% reduction in material intensity over the life cycle compared to alternatives

H&E — Less fuel combustion and mineral extraction plus reduction in on-site activity reduces environmental and accident risks

resource conservation — 5-10% reduction in use of non renewable resources

Trademark of The Dow Chemical Company

Contact:
Dow Deutschland,
Jean-Daniel Dor,
D-77834, Rheinmuenster,
Germany

1 Traditional construction is slow and mistake-prone

House construction methods have changed little over the centuries. Most European homes use heavy masonry materials to resist weather and the weight of materials, particularly in the roof, means that walls have to be strong and foundations deep. This adds further to materials requirements.

> **Current house designs are very material intensive.**

The variety and mass of materials make construction a complex, time-consuming and mistake-prone activity. This was a source of frustration to architect Jean-Philippe Deblander when he began his career in the 1980s, because he wanted to build his own house but was dissatisfied with existing techniques and materials.

Deblander joined Dow in 1985. He thought he was abandoning his career as an architect to find new high value applications for Dow's Styrofoam™ (polystyrene) insulation materials. Instead he is the pioneer of a new housing design which provides a better cost:performance ratio and is less environmentally damaging than conventional alternatives.

2 Foams are strong and cheap

Styrofoam™ has similar insulation values to alternatives such as mineral wool or glass fiber but better mechanical and water resistance properties. However it is derived from a nonrenewable resource, petroleum.

Styrofoam™ is also surprisingly strong. Deblander soon realised that it could be a load bearing material. It can be manufactured to a variety of densities and strengths and when encased in a composite timber panel it can substitute for masonry or timber walls.

> **Styrofoam™ can be made sufficiently strong to replace conventional walls.**

Ten years of development

Invention is hard. For Azurel, the ten years of subsequent development show that development and commercialization can be even far more time-consuming. The key stages are:

- 1985, construction and initial testing of panels
- 1986–87, cost analysis and further testing for fatigue, fire resistance and creep
- 1987, first protoype house built in Alsace
- 1988, official confirmation that Styrofoam™-based houses meet French building regulations
- 1989, patents awarded
- 1990, eight houses built and extensive testing for air tightness and energy consumption
- 1992, extra storey using Styrofoam™ panel walls added to existing block of flats to create 80 new apartments
- 1996, over 40 houses built, launch of Azurel as a construction system "brand" in France.

An integrated system

Now Azurel provides more than a house which happens to be built from Styrofoam™ panels. In the words of the Azurel Commercial Development Manager, Jean Daniel Dor:

> It's building a house as an integrated, made-to-measure system. Many of the Azurel components are designed in the engineering office and assembled in the factory, rather than this being done on-site. This makes it much quicker to build.

Azurel's strategy is to stress these advantages to existing builders rather than market the concept independently.

3 Designing houses with wings

Azurel is the result of Jean-Phillipe Deblander's vision of a home which is simple and cheap to build, comfortable to live in, and based on aeronautical principles. Deblander applied "the same mindset that aircraft designers have when they go about building a plane: to make it durable, lighter and more energy efficient."

> *Objective – a durable, lighter and more energy efficient home.*

Ten years have been needed to achieve this vision – a great deal of personal as well as work time. He has overcome both internal and external skepticism. Now Dow sees great commercial potential in the concept for both developed and developing countries.

4 Azurel scores on revalorization and material intensity

The Azurel concept was scored on the eco-compass in 1995 (see Chapter 15 for scoring details). The comparison is with a timber frame system and the base case of masonry. The scoring uses data from an LCA by Ecobilan. The functional unit is provision of 100 square metres of living space over a 50 year period.

Under half the mass of equivalents

Polystyrene is a strong, light, thermally insulating material. A home with Azurel uses under half the mass of a timber frame or masonry equivalent over the whole life cycle. This is a more than 50% decrease and therefore merits a 4 on the eco-compass.

Less energy too

Home heating accounts for over 90% of the lifetime energy consumption of all three houses. Azurel has the lowest energy intensity over the life cycle but the difference is less marked than with mass.

There is a 12% decrease from the masonry base case, which only merits a 3. A timber frame house is also given this score.

Health and environment risks are at least unchanged

The main health and environmental risks from the houses are those generated by the production of their materials and their heating. Azurel's lower energy and material intensity reduces its risk potential. So too does its transfer of activity from building sites, which have high accident rates and considerable dust emissions, to factories. However, this is offset by the potential health and environmental effects of oil and gas winning, refining, cracking and polymerization. So Azurel only receives a conservative score of 2 on this dimension, as does the timber frame system.

Less use of nonrenewable resources

Azurel's lower energy consumption means that it conserves some nonrenewable fossil fuels. Its use of nonrenewable materials is about 11% less than masonry. It receives a 3 for this dimension. The timber frame gets the same.

Revalorization is excellent

The Azurel polystyrene panels are both easy and cost-effective to recycle. They can also be incinerated for energy recovery. Even if neither happens, the lower mass means less generation of landfill. This is five times lower than with a timber frame and eight times less than masonry. Azurel receives a 5 on this dimension, a timber frame 3.

Azurel provides two functions

Azurels' scoring for service extension depends upon whether it is regarded as a home or a construction system. All houses provide the same service to users so if it is defined in this way a score of 2 is appropriate. However, if defined as a construction system, it generates considerable economic and environmental benefit from its multifunctionality. That is, adding a new function (structural support) to the existing one of insulation and thereby replacing conventional walls. As this has been the basis of Azurel's development strategy, we adopt the construction system definition and score it as a 5.

Figure 21.1 shows the eco-compass profile. It is clear that Azurel provides a significant improvement over the masonry house and provides better environmental performance than the timber frame.

5 Easier to build, more comfortable to live in

Azurel houses have similar or higher production costs to conventional alternatives. But they are quicker to build and so increase builders' productivity.

● **FIGURE 21.1**
Comparison of construction systems in the six dimensions of the eco-compass

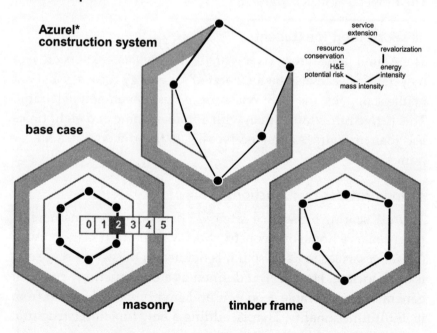

Azurel house owners are also happy. They appreciate the warmth and reduction in draughts, and worry less about subsidence. According to Deblander:

> We went to check a house to see if everything was OK. The owner was telling our engineer he had the only house in the neighbourhood without any cracks in the walls. All the other houses were made out of bricks. The problem of this area is that the ground's not very good. Because of the weight of the bricks, cracks got in the walls of the traditional houses. This didn't happen with Azurel. The skeptics who said "it'll fly away with the first wind" have changed their minds!

6 Overcoming conservatism and improving functionality

Building is a conservative industry. This conservatism is sometimes justified for not all new technologies have lived up to

● **FIGURE 21.2**
Azurel buildings use Styrofoam™ insulation boards for walls and ceilings. This dramatically reduces their lifetime material requirements.

expectations in recent decades. But it does make it difficult for genuine innovations such as Azurel to be taken seriously. Overcoming such conservatism is one key challenge for the future.

Deblander also intends to improve Azurel's technical features. One route to this is integration and pre-assembly of other subsystems such as electrical, sanitary and ventilation equipment. And concrete pouring on-site will be eliminated by development of custom made blocks for foundations.

7 Perseverance and environment-related branding

After more than a decade of working on Azurel, Jean-Philippe Deblander knows that breakthrough innovations take time and perseverance:

> You can't do everything at once. It has to be step by step. And companies and people are very attached to their own ways. If you want to be innovative, you have to establish a goal and steer your path towards it. After some years the same companies who were skeptical at the start will come to you and say, "By the way, we realize that your idea is good. Why don't you work with us."

Understand the whole channel

Jean-Daniel Dor also stresses the importance of . . .

> Understanding the whole channel, including builders and end users. That way you can find the best way in. For Azurel, that's working with rather than cutting out established construction firms. In effect, they'll become our franchisees. We're bringing branding and image-based marketing to housing for the first time. Our selling points are the lower cost, convenience and energy and environmental advantages of the building.

But even obvious environmental benefits will not sell without a well designed business concept. All actors in the channel must find value in the project. The final home owners must benefit from a lower cost of ownership and avoid capital penalties at the start. When all these conditions are met quality of living and the environment will improve ... one house at a time.

▶ KYOCERA BUILDS TO LAST

Kyocera

> Kyocera's laser printers use durable drums which last for the machine's lifetime. This creates a lifetime cost advantage and, compared to less durable alternatives, eliminates the materials and energy used in manufacturing replacements.

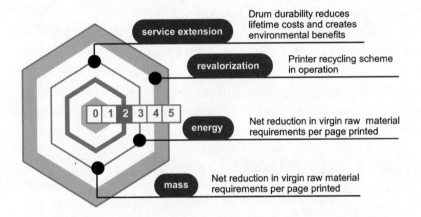

service extension — Drum durability reduces lifetime costs and creates environmental benefits

revalorization — Printer recycling scheme in operation

energy — Net reduction in virgin raw material requirements per page printed

mass — Net reduction in virgin raw material requirements per page printed

---

Contact:

Detlef Herb, Kyocera Electronics Europe, Postfach 2252, 40645 Meerbusch 2, Germany

---

1 Kyocera's business is ceramics-based

Cut the costs of printing and help the environment! That's the eco-efficient message which Kyocera has been using to win market share for its laser printers.

Kyocera is a Japanese company with a $5 billion turnover. Its core business is ceramic-based products such as integrated circuits and artifical bones, but with its materials and electronic expertise it is now building new businesses in cameras, computer games and printers.

Visionary leadership

Kyocera's success is generally attributed to the vision and business skill of its chairman, Kazuo Inamori, one of Japan's most iconoclastic business leaders. He founded the company in 1959. Its mission since then has been to "contribute to the betterment of mankind and society" as well as making money.

Kyocera recently boosted its environmental activities and now has a high level "green committee" and auditing and waste minimization programs. It sees the environmental attributes of its products as a growing competitive advantage. Ceramic-based products are durable, use abundant materials and require few toxic substances to manufacture.

> *Utilizing the generally favorable environmental characteristics of ceramic-based technologies is central to Kyocera's long-term strategy.*

2 Durable printer drums lower lifetime costs

Kyocera launched its first laser printer in 1986. All laser printers work by using light to create charged areas on a rotating drum. The charged areas correspond to the text to be printed. They attract toner (ink) which is then transferred to paper.

Plastic versus metal–silicon drums

Most printers, including those produced by Hewlett Packard which controls over half the market, are based on a Canon technology. This combines the drum and toner cartridge in a single plastic component. When the toner cartridge is empty the whole component is removed and replaced by another. Although the major manufacturers operate recycling schemes for the cartridge drums, many end up in landfill.

Kyocera has its own technology using an aluminium drum coated with amorphous silicon. It is more resilient than plastic and lasts for longer – often the whole life of the printer. Only the toner cartridge needs to be removed when empty. It can then be disposed of or returned to Kyocera for recycling or reuse after filling with new toner.

Kyocera's lifetime cost per page is lower

Kyocera printers do have some disadvantages compared to equivalent products using Canon technology, however their usage costs are lower because their drums are more durable. As the lifetime costs of printer consumables usually exceed those of the printer's purchase price for most users, this translates into a lesser total cost per unit of service, ie a single printed page. A 1994 test by the

● FIGURE 21.3

The durable drums used in Kyocera's laser printers create a lifetime cost advantage. They also eliminate material and energy consumption used in the production of replacements.

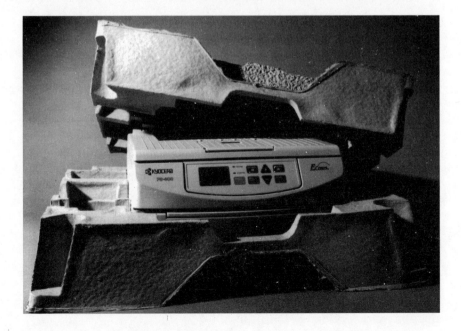

297

independent British testing organization Pira International found that the cost of ownership of a Kyocera machine was just over half that of a Hewlett Packard equivalent. A recent comparison by a British computer magazine found that the Kyocera printer cost 0.5p per page compared to 1.1–2.4p for others tested.

> *In tests, Kyocera's lifetime costs per page were 0.5p compared to 1.1 to 2.4p for competing products.*

This cost advantage allowed Kyocera to establish a small bridgehead in high volume printers (more than ten pages per minute). By 1992 it had around 6% of the world market – but wanted more. It needed to extend into low volume printers and differentiate itself from other manufacturers.

Environmental differentiation

Kyocera's problem is that the cost of use is not prominent in most customers' minds. So when it launched a smaller printer range in the early 1990s it stressed its environmental as well as its cost advantages. The range was branded as Ecosys and the UK campaign ran under the slogan "How to save the world from your office." Its advertising cited the claims of Living Earth International, an environmental education charity, that, by the end of 1994, rivals' printers would have consumed over 300 million cartridges of which only 5% were likely to be recycled. Kyocera UK branded the residue as a "new variety of noxious, nondisposable, landfill."

The initial campaign brought in new, environmentally committed, customers and made Kyocera's name better known. It did not meet its hopes of a sales breakthrough. One commentator noted that "green is not yet the colour of the month for hardheaded equipment buyers." The best results came in countries such as Germany where, because of skepticism about product environmental claims, the cost message was highlighted more than the environmental one. As a result, all Ecosys advertising is now focussed on the printer's cost advantages, with environment featured as an additional benefit.

To strengthen Ecosys' environmental credentials Kyocera now has a return scheme for its own printers and components. The drums can be easily separated into their aluminium and silicon components for recycling.

3 Environment contributes to market share

Kyocera's initiative is largely commercially driven. It is using the cost and environmental benefits of an existing technology to build market share in a new product area. The company also has a tradition of social responsibility and sees the environmental attributes of its core materials as an important part of its long-term strategy.

4 Durability reduces materials, energy needs and waste

Kyocera's aluminium–silicon drums are more durable than the plastic equivalents. This translates into reduced lifetime requirements for materials, and the energy used in their production, and lower generation of waste. These outweigh the greater energy and materials used in manufacturing the Kyocera printers.

> *Durable printer drums use less materials and energy, reduce waste – and cut costs.*

5 Kyocera now has significant market share

Kyocera has built a new product line on the basis of eco-efficient technology. It now has a significant share in all segments and is second only to Hewlett Packard in many countries, including Germany. Its success is largely due to the high durability of its printer drum and the consequent reduced costs for customers.

6 Educating customers about lifetime costs

Kyocera's future challenge is educating customers about lifetime printer costs. Most still buy on the basis of initial purchase price. In addition, many corporate buyers of printers are not responsible for purchasing consumables, so lifetime costs tend to be a less important issue.

7 Price and functionality remain critical

Kyocera's experience has valuable lessons for the marketing of eco-efficient products in mainstream markets. They must demonstrate their superiority on conventional criteria such as price and functionality before environment can come into play as a buying factor. But once these hurdles are overcome, products offering a "green bonus" at no extra cost – rather than using environmental performance to justify a "green premium" – will be preferred by many customers.

> *Products offering a "green bonus" at no extra cost will be preferred by many customers.*

Part 5

USING THE ECO-COMPASS

Thus far we have demonstrated a number of useful, albeit rather educational, applications for the eco-compass. Now we are developing deeper applications which pose fundamental questions about both environmental and product strategy and drive the "super innovation" described in Part 1.

In Chapter 22 we describe how to integrate the compass with existing innovation processes to create an "eco-innovation" methodology. We describe this in some detail so that you can run one if you wish. Alternatively, you may prefer to move straight to Part 6 for the conclusions to the arguments developed in previous Parts.

The methodology uses an "eco-innovation workshop." Its aims are to move beyond incremental product development to imagine – and then implement – radical new options. Ones which can create steps towards environmental improvements and long-term competitive advantage. We use a storyboard approach to describe the five "moves" which take place in the workshop.

All our uses of the eco-compass, and particularly the eco-innovation method, are tuned on a case-by-case basis. We simply describe our experience so that you can learn and hopefully become interested in the approach.

In this section you will get:

- *a detailed guide on how to use the eco-compass to communicate key environmental issues and choose the most sustainable of alternative products;*

- *a unique process combining environmental and business parameters to stimulate breakthrough innovation and create, screen and shape new ideas;*

- *a confidence that you can create competitive advantage for the long term while making a significant contribution to sustainable development.*

Chapter 22

Driving eco-innovation

The eco-compass is not a business-as-usual approach, and should not confirm conventional answers. Competition has already found them. Use it to find breakthrough solutions that will satisfy fundamental needs and put your company ahead.

Innovation is more than creating new ideas. It is a structured business process that plays out at the analytical, strategic and creative levels. It only adds value when it combines three operational disciplines:

● response to future market needs and openings,

● creation of genuinely new ideas for meeting these needs and

● achievement of outstanding implementation of the ideas.

Ideas which react only to current needs will be but incremental improvements (see Figure 22.1). Those which do provide creative solutions to future needs but are not implemented forcefully will be dreams that do not happen. The dreamers too will fall back into incremental improvements. Only the three disciplines together lead to success.

> *Eco-innovation is outstanding implementation of radical ideas which will meet future needs.*

● FIGURE 22.1
Value growth depends on three combined operating disciplines

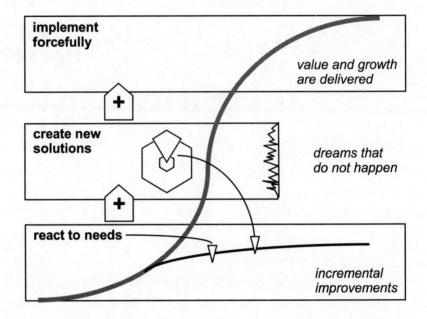

The eco-compass forms the basis of eco-innovation workshops.

▶ ECO-INNOVATION WORKSHOPS

Their objectives are to:

- help to identify and shape new, unexpected and useful ideas;

- select ideas that contribute to significant quality of life and environmental improvement advantages;

- focus on those ideas that will deliver bottom line value to the company in the shortest time – the economic side of eco-efficiency;

- define a long-term business development scenario that builds on and stretches the company's capabilities.

The five innovative moves

The workshops involve five innovative moves.

- *Accept the eco-efficiency challenge and assemble key data.* You need environmental, product and marketing information to identify needs and ground ideas. You must also define your expectation of value and the criteria you will use to assess it.

- *Identify eco-efficiency opportunities for each compass dimension.* The central question is always how can environmental impacts be reduced so that customer value is increased?

- *Organize the ideas* emerging from stage two.

- *Harvest the value options* that emerge at stage three to identify potential eco-efficiency "winners."

- *Prepare and commit to implementation* of the most promising proposals.

As Figure 22.2 shows, each stage has one or more tools to achieve the desired outcomes. We will now take you through these stages and tools by following a recent Dow case history as a guide.

● **FIGURE 22.2**

The eco-efficiency innovation workshop in five moves

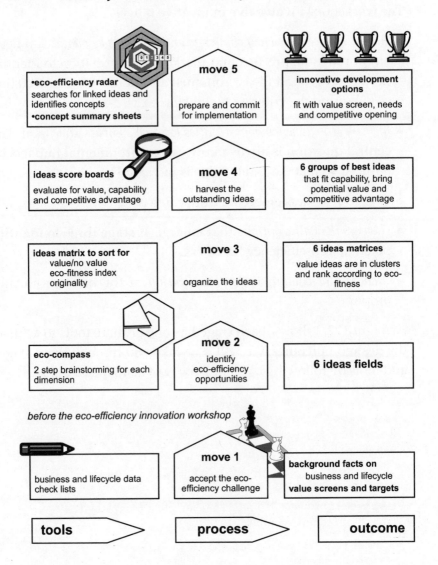

● NAT AND MIN: WHICH IS THE MOST ECO-EFFICIENT?

Dow wants new products which combine high customer value and positive contributions to sustainable development. It has an opportunity to develop one using natural organic materials (NAT) instead of minerals (MIN). Successive boxes describe the decision process to illustrate the practical use of the eco-compass and eco-innovation workshop.

MIN uses inorganic materials. These are abundant but require mining and processing. There are competing products made from organic materials. These are expensive and have only a tiny "green niche." The new proprietary process for making NAT offers a great improvement in functionality. For the first time a natural product can compete broadly on both price and performance with mineral products in this particular application.

So NAT has potential business value. The next stage is a life cycle analysis of the two products conducted by Daniel Halder. Following this he scores the data on the eco-compass. A pre- workshop seminar discusses its validity and implications.

Surprising results

Several results shock participants. NAT has a material intensity some 400 times greater than MIN. The main cause is the inclusion as a mass input of the rainfall which is required by the crop. NAT is recyclable but this makes little difference to its overall mass intensity. NAT's energy intensity is also much higher than MIN. This reflects its dependence on six successive agricultural processes to prepare its raw materials, and a drying stage in its manufacture. By contrast, MIN requires no great movement of overburden and limited processing.

A rounded picture

Dow project manager Paolo Lucchini feels that using LCA data and presenting it in compass form:

> makes it easier to get a rounded picture of the product's overall performance and see the key issues. At the start we thought that the revalorization potential of NAT was so great, and the energy intensity of MIN so high, that it was obviously better for the environment. We were wrong about both. The compass also makes us give equal weight to the other dimensions, which turn out to be very important. Already we know that the product is not quite as green as we thought – but we know why and that we can make it better.

Move 1: accept the eco-efficiency challenge

What is the eco-efficiency challenge? As Figure 22.3 shows it is two questions that are simple to ask and have the potential to bring long-term competitive advantage.

● **FIGURE 22.3**
The eco-efficiency challenge

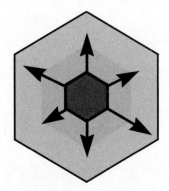

*How can you redesign
your offering
of services and products
to significantly improve it
in several dimensions of the eco-compass?*

*Which redesign options
will you implement
to create the maximum value
for the company?*

Clarify objectives, assemble key data

Before answering these questions and before starting the workshop you must clarify objectives and assemble key data.

- *Define the target products or services.* These can be new possibilities or existing ones to rejuvenate your offering for sustainability and competitive advantage. Start with well identified business lines or specific product applications, not your complete aggregated company.

- *Gather classical marketing data.* Get or review the information on the market channel from your business to the final customer. This includes the number and nature of intermediary business partners and the demographics and loyalty of your end users. Also note key trends in the marketplace, the number and nature of competitors and your relative strengths and weaknesses. Consider inviting suppliers, distributors and/or customers to your workshop.

- *Identify the customer needs* that are satisfied by your target business line. Understand potential developments by answering the Need Test (see Chapter 8).

- *Get the basic life cycle data.* A thorough LCA is helpful but even a simple one based on a few days' work can be useful. The important thing is to qualitatively identify the main impacts for each stage of the life cycle and to generate sufficient data to identify when new ideas are genuine improvements.

- *Understand the functionality* of the product or service. What is its technical lifetime (before it breaks down beyond repair)? How does this compare with the effective economic lifetime (before its use is discontinued by the last user). How many usage cycles does it have? How many functions does it serve? What other functions does it operate in conjunction with and could therefore replace or be optimized to?

- *Define the functional unit.* This will be important in comparing life cycle data and competitive options (see Chapter 14).

- *Define your strategic intent.* What counts for the company? To be the lowest cost player? The technology leader? Focussed on customer needs? The innovation process must preserve and enhance your strategic intent. Remember that if you try to be a leader in every field you will probably end nowhere. This may be a good time to clarify and reorient your positioning.

- *Define your value criteria.* These are likely to include at least one financial criterion (for example, return on investment, earnings per share or net present value), and at least one for marketing (for example market share, customer satisfaction or customer loyalty). Companies wishing to become eco-efficient will also consider the value they can deliver to stakeholders such as employees and society. Social criteria such as job security, earning power, standard of living, distribution of benefits and costs and cultural enhancement are often forgotten but are an important feature of a sustainable enterprise.

These value criteria will prove an important screen for the final stages of the eco-innovation process. The best options will be those which meet them and deliver environmental improvements.

A diverse, creative team

This preliminary work brings the challenge into a finer and quantified perspective. Now you must assemble an eco-efficiency innovation team (see Figure 22.4). The ideal team combines:

- expertise from different sections of the organization;

- expertise from different stages of the life cycle;

- members who will be involved in the ultimate implementation of eco-efficiency ideas;

- a mix of thinking styles – analytical, emotional, conceptual and others.

● FIGURE 22.4
The eco-innovation brainstorming team

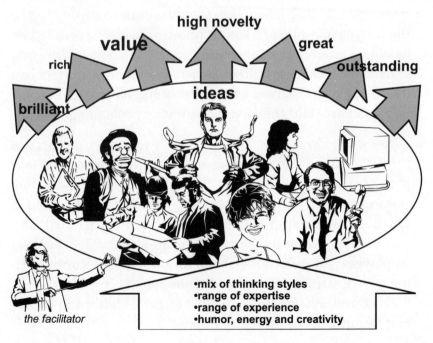

The objective is the right mix of perspectives, expertise and thought processes to create sparks of creativity. Ideas no-one has had before. Ideas that could launch your business on a unique course for success.

What is important is that all accept the challenge, that they are willing to put aside prejudices and organizational turf and that they are willing to undertake the time investment. This is helped if team members contribute to the first move. Each can be responsible for gathering particular data.

> PROCESS TIP: the more you circulate and discuss data beforehand – as at Dow's pre-workshop seminar on NAT and MIN – the more successful the workshop will be.

Good organization, adequate time are essential

But while all should participate, there has to be a teamwork facilitator. As you will see, there is a lot to get through at the workshop and someone must keep the discussions on course. It should be someone who understands both business and environmental issues, and is open-minded about possible ways of improving them.

Consider too using a trained facilitator for the workshop and spend time on the timetable and agenda. The ideal is one and a half or two days. What follows assumes this duration. If there is only one day you'll have to be less ambitious. It is much more difficult to get breakthrough ideas without the space for reflection and greater opportunities for informal interaction which the extra day allows. But it can still be worthwhile especially if you make it so successful that people want it run again to get new ideas or apply it to other products !

Move 2: identify eco-efficiency opportunities

The second innovative move is taking a flight with the eco-compass. This provides six directions for improvement from your current position – six opportunities to innovate in the design, delivery, usage and disposal of every aspect of your product or service.

The team should move around the compass and successively address the following six questions (see Figure 22.5):

How can we maintain the functional unit performance but significantly:

- *reduce the mass intensity?*
- *reduce the human health and environmental potential risk?*
- *decrease the energy intensity?*
- *increase the degree of reuse and revalorization of wastes?*
- *increase the conservation of resources and use of renewable materials?*
- *extend service and function?*

PROCESS TIP: spend a few minutes at the start of the workshop discussing the main findings of the preliminary analysis. The objective is not only to communicate information but also to test that everyone is operating on the same assumptions. Try also to bring everyone into the discussion to get early involvement and buy in.

Start with material intensity, end with service extension

Material intensity is a good place to start. It brings in all life cycle stages and is the most tangible of all the dimensions the team will consider. As the measure, material intensity per unit of service (MIPS) is easy to understand and a good entry to the concept of the functional unit.

Service extension is the best place to end. This involves a discussion of durability, repairability, upgradability, multifunctionality. They are all aspects that provoke out-of-the box thinking. They not only offer tremendous potential for product diversification but they lead as well to complete service and business redesign. They also involve customers and therefore lead into the later, more business-focussed, stages of the workshop.

The route between the two is up to you. Some dimensions may not seem relevant. We usually cover three or four if it is a one day workshop. Nor is it necessary to spend equal time on every dimension. Have an advance discussion about which areas seem the most important or promising and focus on these.

● **FIGURE 22.5**
Second innovative move – the six opportunities to innovate

How could we maintain the functional unit performance and significantly

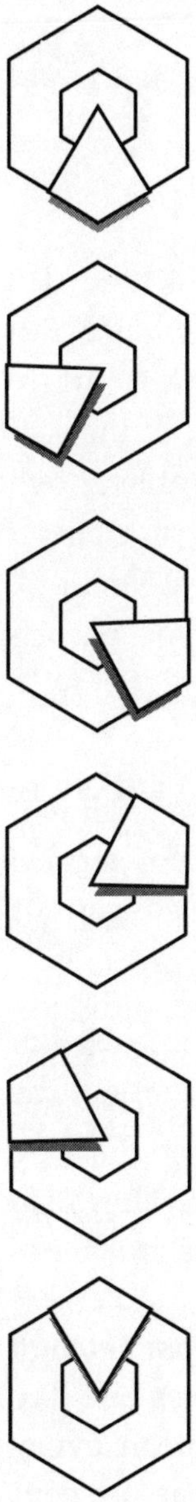

1 reduce the mass intensity

2 reduce the human health and environmental potential risk

3 decrease the energy intensity

4 increase the degree of reuse and revalorization of wastes

5 increase the conservation of resources and the use of renewable materials

6 extend service and function

You can also choose whether to conduct moves two, three and four sequentially for each dimension, or whether to consider all dimensions in move two before proceeding to move three.

The ideas field encourages creativity

Take the first question:

How could we maintain the functional unit performance but significantly:

- *reduce the mass intensity?*

Get the participants to write their ideas on large stickers. One idea per sticker in as few words as possible but in a clear sentence. Put the stickers into an "Ideas Field" (a large board or wall) but do not discuss or censor ideas at this stage. This is brainstorming.

Experience suggests that the process works best with at least two rounds for each dimension (see Figure 22.6). The first produces a downloading of obvious but not necessarily really creative ideas. After a few minutes introduce some prompt questions. Ask participants to read the first round ideas and reflect on them. Bring in pattern breakers and unsettling questions. Have fun.

When the flow of suggestions from this second round of brainstorming dries up start the third move of *organizing the ideas*.

Move 3: organize the ideas

You must now judge the eco-efficiency improvement potential and the business value of the ideas. Remind participants of the challenge they have taken on:

- *How can we redesign our offering of services and products to significantly improve it in several dimensions of the eco-compass?*

- *Which redesign options will we implement to create the maximum value for the company?*

● FIGURE 22.6
Second innovative move – the two brainstorming rounds

Ideas matrix assesses business value, environmental improvement

To find the best proposals we use an Ideas Matrix (see Figure 22.7). The vertical scale is environmental improvement. It has six levels, corresponding to the 0–5 scale of the eco-compass.

The horizontal level has three zones. Those proposals thought to bring no business value go to the left of the vertical scale. Those with value you place on the right. Those of high novelty value are put on the far right side.

> PROCESS TIP: make clear which base case is being used to assess ideas against. If the aim is to develop new or improved products the base case will be the existing one.

The task now is to make "first order" judgments in order to sort the ideas produced during the brainstorming move. Pick up the stickers one by one from the Ideas Field and rank them according to the teams' best judgment of eco-efficiency score. If they bring no business value they go on the left. If they have high novelty, plausible new technology or business solutions, they go on the far right. If they are similar to other ideas assemble them and at the end replace them with one single sticker that adequately summarizes the idea.

This exercise is not about splitting hairs. There is neither enough time nor data at this stage. It is about good judgment and some educated guesses, and the objective is to sort rapidly the mass of ideas into the various horizontal levels and vertical zones.

Move 4: harvest the outstanding areas

Once every idea is positioned you come to the point of having to harvest only the outstanding ideas. A good rule of thumb is to limit the harvest to 10% (at maximum 15%) of the total ideas found in the right hand value zone.

There are a couple of ways to do this. One is to ask participants to vote and pick the top cut of this "hit parade". Another practical way is to let participants go to the Ideas Matrix and pick the idea

● FIGURE 22.7
Third innovative move – organize the ideas fields

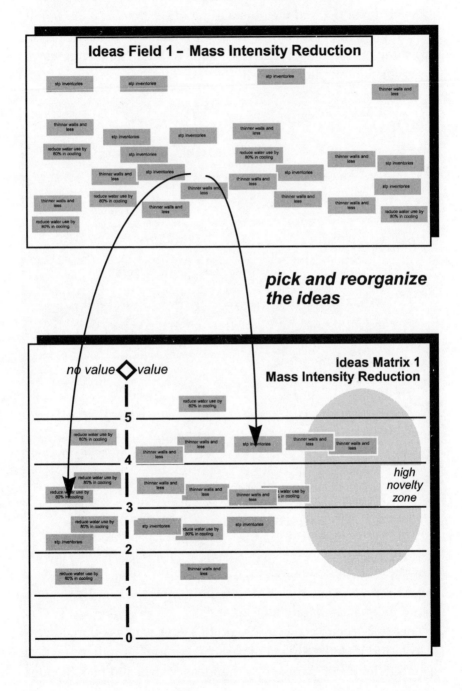

they are most impressed with. If necessary a second pick is allowed to catch any brilliant idea left behind.

By whatever method the outstanding ideas are now collected. It is essential to tag them at this stage with their eco-efficiency level and compass dimension – M4 or H&ES or SE3 – to keep track of the assessment made in move 3.

● IDEAS ON IMPROVING NAT

An eco-innovation workshop considers the opportunities to:

- improve the environmental performance of NAT, and

- increase its business value, both by lowering cost and improving performance.

Energy recovery

The second move – identifying opportunities for improvement in the six dimensions – generates many ideas. The energy discussion focusses on two issues: eliminating the energy-intensive drying stage; and incineration of waste straw which is presently ploughed back into the soil. If this took place NAT would have a lower energy intensity than MIN.

Another raw material?

Another idea which surfaces in both the energy and material discussions is basing NAT on another natural raw material. Several ideas suggest that the optimum is a plant with higher yield, lower water requirements and less need for herbicides. This would have a lower energy and material intensity and be cheaper to produce. It could also be grown on drier land.

Is service extension possible?

As usual, service extension induces exceptional creativity. One first round idea which generates a number of second round "follow ups" is that of integrating NAT with other systems and products in its area of application. Participants perceive an opportunity to make NAT multifunctional so that it can replace more complex systems while providing better service.

You now need to analyze the business attraction of the outstanding ideas in greater detail. For this we use an ideas score board (see Figure 22.8). This brings in a finer discrimination of value and

● FIGURE 22.8
Fourth innovative move – the ideas score board

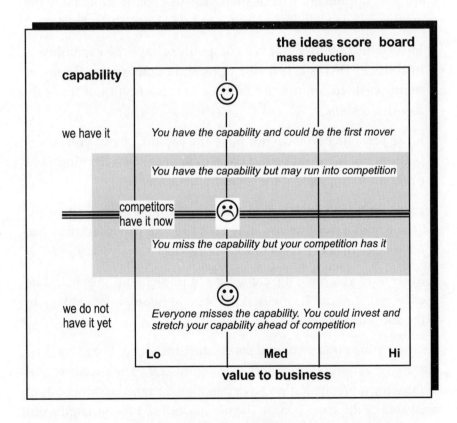

The ideas score board serves as a business screen to select those ideas that can create value and competitive advantage

the ideas score board
mass reduction

capability

we have it

☺

You have the capability and could be the first mover

You have the capability but may run into competition

competitors have it now ☹

You miss the capability but your competition has it

☺

we do not have it yet

Everyone misses the capability. You could invest and stretch your capability ahead of competition

Lo   **Med**   **Hi**

value to business

The ideas score board defines two zones of opportunities:
1   short-term as a first mover
2   longer term as a leader in capability development

an additional question: do we have the capability to introduce the idea? It also introduces a key element: do our competitors have the capability?

The Ideas Score Board: assessing capability and competitive advantage

The horizontal axis is business value, defined in three ranges, low, medium and high where medium corresponds to the level you defined in move 1 during the preparation work.

Capability forms the vertical axis of the ideas score board. There are two broad divisions – do we have the capability or not? But there is a supplementary question: do your competitors have the capability? The result, in ascending order, is four vertical zones:

- Ideas which neither you nor competitors have the capability to introduce. This is a zone for potential business development that invests in unique capabilities. It is however not for early low risk results.

- Ideas for which you do not have the capability but your competitors do. It would be too risky to venture on a development program to implement the ideas in this zone.

- Ideas for which both you and competitors have the capability. This is bad news but you may take the risk provided that you are confident you have a unique approach.

- Ideas only you have the capability to implement. This could be excellent. You can be the first mover and maintain advantage in the short term at least.

Position your outstanding ideas on the ideas score board by then discussing value and capability (see Figure 22.9). The strongest candidates for implementation have percolated to the top and bottom right side of the score board. The other ideas all have strengths but their potential for competitive advantage is doubtful.

● FIGURE 22.9
Fourth innovative move – pick the premium ideas

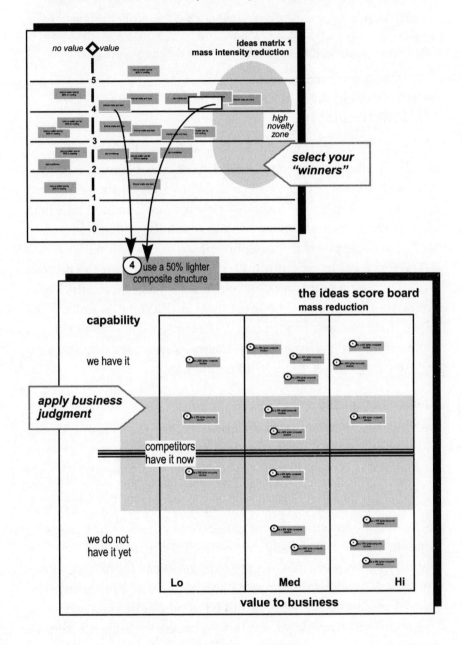

PROCESS TIP: it is easy to spend a lot of time on the Ideas Matrix and Ideas Score Board. You want to be fair to team members' work and discuss their ideas properly. But remember that this is just the screening stage. Make sure that you allow time for detailed discussion of the best ideas in the fifth move.

Move 5: prepare and commit for implementation

When you have repeated the Ideas Matrix and Ideas Score Board for all six dimensions you should have around ten to 20 idea "winners." Some of these will probably overlap as they represent different dimensions of the same new option. The next task is to identify the links and synergy and to distill the winners into clear business concepts worth development.

The top level ideas should be kept separate from the bottom level. The first are the ideas for which we have a capability. These can be implemented in the short term with the potential advantage of first movers. For the second group you need to develop a capability. This is a longer term business development scenario that may have larger strategic implementations.

The eco-compass

We map the winners onto an eco-compass (see Figure 22.10). Remember how you wrote the dimensional score – such as M3 – on each idea? Now you use this to simply position each idea on the compass, in this case on the mass axis at level 3.

Now examine the compass and consider the obvious or potential connections between the different winners. Are some just different aspects of the same innovation? A breakthrough in mass intensity can present a synergy with a proposal for energy intensity reduction and optimum recycling of obsolete equipment. The three ideas should therefore be linked as part of the same concept. The team will draw a strong line between the idea stickers in question. When no improvement is expected for the other dimensions the line will pass the status quo level 2 in the other sectors.

● FIGURE 22.10
Fifth innovative move – look for the eco-efficiency linkages

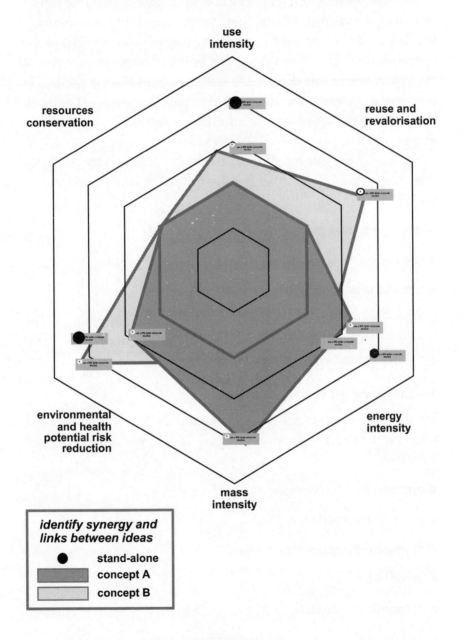

Develop integrated business concepts

The different ideas will therefore end up as either linked to others or as true standalone. On the first, current capability eco-compass, the linked ideas represent comprehensive redesign options of the business line. The standalone are breakthrough improvement opportunities in one dimension of the current business line. On the second compass, for ideas where capability needs to be developed, the linked ideas represent future generations of the business line as well as a new mix of competencies.

You now have integrated business concepts which are ready for implementation. Remember the disciplines of successful innovators? They:

- respond to real market needs and openings,

- create new solutions, and

- achieve outstanding implementation.

In theory you now have answers for the first two disciplines. The compass has enabled you to see some of the long-term trends that the short sighted competitors could miss.

Prepare concept summary sheets

But there is a final stage before this handover. You should produce a summary of each concept (see Figure 22.11), covering the following items:

- opportunity description

- value to the market

- main eco-efficiency dimensions

- capabilities

- economic potential.

These form the basis of the further steps of the concept development. Now it is time to turn the concepts into profitable business.

● FIGURE 22.11
Fifth innovative move – commit to implementation

4 Business launch

3 Opportunity development

2 Opportunity analysis

1 Concept summary   *title* **the designed timber insulation structure**

✎ **opportunity description**

✎ **value to the market**
  • who needs it
  • what if nothing is done
  • importance of this solution
  • its value expectation

✎ **main eco-efficiency dimensions**

✎ **our capabilities**
  • to deliver
  • to differentiate
  • to protect

❖ **economic potential**   **5years**   **10**   **15**
  revenue
  profit

concept B

You are back to the good business skills that characterize technology and market developers. They include a detailed analysis of the market opportunity, the risks, the environmental fit. Financial projections, life cycle impact improvements, technical feasibility and target customers' response must be validated before the redesigned business line is launched.

The process also makes participants aware of the importance of this target and means of achieving it. It builds a specific commitment to the new concepts by team members. And it demonstrates that opportunities can be found which both add business value and fit the larger needs of sustainable development.

> *The eco-innovation process is only the trigger of a wider development and implementation process. But it can generate the breakthrough ideas which form the basis of tomorrow's sustainable business.*

● AN ALTERNATIVE RAW MATERIAL FOR NAT?

The NAT workshop creates a number of concepts. Three are selected for implementation. One is energy recovery from waste straw from the existing raw material. This will improve energy intensity and reduce costs. The second is to make the product in a way which will provide multiple functions. This will fit a market gap identified by a marketeer at the workshop. His insight sparked team members' creativity in finding a way to fill it.

A different raw material?

The most far reaching concept is moving immediately to a new raw material. NAT's high energy and material intensity is not only an environmental problem but will be a financial vulnerability in the long-term.

▶

▶ Can NAT be based on a different raw material? Yes, it can use a variety. Is there a raw material which can achieve "factor four" or even "factor ten" improvements in energy and material intensity? And uses less herbicide? If so, it will not only be environmentally superior but almost certainly cheaper to make.

There is such a material, but supplies are not yet reliable. NAT's inventors have always seen it as a long-term replacement for the current raw material. But they discounted it for the first generation product. The workshop – and the life cycle analysis and eco-compass calculations which informed it – challenges this thinking. The outcome is an implementation concept to develop sources of supply which are reliable.

The eco-compass can highlight breakthrough options

The final decision on NAT has yet to be made. Whatever it is, the eco-efficiency compass and eco-innovation workshop will have made it easier. They have pointed to the obstacles and ways around them at an early stage. Finding that out later would be costly. All the final concepts had previously been identified by one or two team members. The discussion built a general awareness that they are priority topics which require detailed examination. It also challenged key assumptions and brought in alternative perspectives. Overall, it provides a means of bringing in breakthrough as well as incremental options for product development.

Looking back, workshop co-facilitator David Russell also feels that the compass-based process . . .

> allows us to simplify life cycle data for decision making. Using it for NAT brought a quick realization amongst everyone concerned that agriculture is a material-intensive process compared to using abundant minerals. This gave us plenty of time to consider if the material differences are significant and how we can reduce them. We'd have got to this point more slowly if the compass hadn't highlighted it. And we might have missed the breakthrough opportunities.

Part 6

AT THE GREEN EDGE?

Successful eco-innovation depends upon the integration of environmental issues with the whole of the business.

In Chapter 23 we outline a model of sustainable business development. This has three orbits.

The first orbit involves the marketing domain. Immediate bottom lines are addressed. But sustainability will only be considered as long as it is driven by customer demand and short-term value creation.

The second orbit introduces management excellence and the quality culture. It requires leadership at all levels, results oriented goals and employee empowerment. It sets a higher vision of success that introduces the concerns for ecological, resource and social–economic security.

The third orbit extends horizons and reduces barriers both within an organization and between it and stakeholders. It involves cooperation with policy makers and nongovernmental organizations, a life cycle perspective and an articulated vision of a sustainable future.

Chapter 24 defines six simple themes and rules to guide companies along the path to sustainability: eco-efficiency, customers, objectives, empowerment, care and "out-of-the-box" thinking. Their first letters make the mnemonic ECO/ECO. This reminds us that sustainable development and sustainable business are about integrating ecology and economics.

In this section you will get:

- *a management model to embrace sustainable business development;*

- *an understanding of external stakeholders and the value of partnerships with them;*

- *six rules to follow in your journey towards sustainability.*

Chapter 23

Sustainable business development

We are near the end of the journey – and yet just beginning.

As we evaluated the material provided by all the companies for our case studies we kept looking for the lessons. Is there some unifying principle that explains the dynamics, the success or the difficulties of each case? How can we reconcile cost and market advantage with legislative push? Where does the eco-compass fit? And what about ethics?

We have an answer – our "three orbits" model. It explains how you can move towards the higher state of sustainable development without losing sense of the basics of good business management that secures a healthy bottom line.

▶ THE FIRST ORBIT: SUSTAINABILITY IN THE MARKETING DOMAIN

A sustainable business, like any other business, must first orbit around the monetary domain, its centre of gravity. However good "sustainable" products or services might be, they will not change the world if companies cannot make a profit from them. They will be stillborn or, worse, will bankrupt the company. Profits are essential to reward shareholders and employees, and to provide funds for investment in future breakthrough innovations.

The first, central orbit is within the marketing domain (see Figure 23.1). It is the key factor. Sustainable business development is the same as any business development. It must identify market opportunities and innovate to seize them. This has two dimensions:

● to balance customer *needs* with the *affordability* of products and services, and

● to create innovations to provide leverage of existing *capabilities* without excessive *costs*.

● **FIGURE 23.1**
Sustainable business model – first orbit

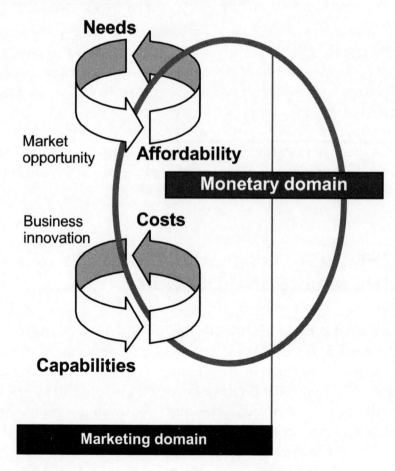

Match needs and capabilities, costs and affordability

What are the secrets of success? A good fit between needs and capabilities; and a good margin between the costs of producing goods and services and the affordable price for customers.

Eco-efficient innovations can come just from the marketing domain. They do not necessarily require high levels of environmental leadership or awareness. One example is "win–win" waste reduction schemes. Another is "unintended" improvement. The performance of computer chips now doubles about every 18 months. This means less energy and fewer materials per calculation. The driver is not sustainability but rather the escalating demands of customers, and the aggressive determination of manufacturers to meet or go beyond these demands.

▶ THE SECOND ORBIT: MOVING TOWARDS EXCELLENCE

The move towards sustainable development will often be similarly "unintentional". But sustainable business development makes the process intentional since it seeks and creates opportunities to force the pace.

By doing so it moves into the second orbit (see Figure 23.2). There management excellence is the key factor. There you need a leadership capability that not only masters the success rules of the market but sets results oriented goals – ambitious goals. A leadership that empowers employees, aligns resources with strategy and drives a process of continuous improvement.

● **FIGURE 23.2**
Sustainable business model – second orbit

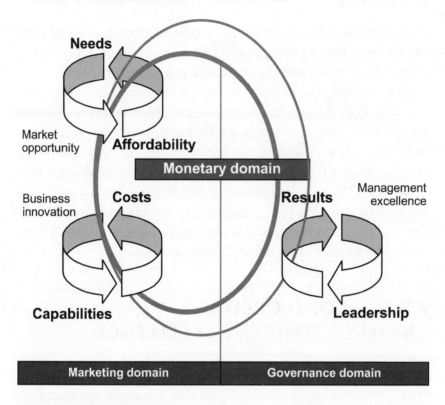

Above all ... passion

It is not only leadership at the top but a passion and determination throughout the enterprise to be an outstanding company in the mind of your customers, your employees and all your associates.

When a larger vision sets in, the company merges into a broader governance culture. It brings in focus its role in society, its responsibilities towards the communities where it operates and the environment at large. Ecological, socio-economic and resource securities become relevant to the business development strategy.

A genuine commitment to management excellence requires consideration of environmental and other impacts on society.

An environmental policy is adopted, the quality culture and discipline are extended into environmental management systems, improvement targets and public reporting (see below).

● QUALITY APPROACHES TO SUSTAINABILITY

Many companies are adopting a total quality management (TQM) approach to issues of sustainability. There are many connections between the two:

- TQM emphasizes the customers, defined in a larger sense than mere purchasers of a product. It prepares to respond to external stakeholders.

- TQM is continuous improvement. It helps to move beyond mere compliance with legislation.

- TQM eliminates the root causes of problems rather than their symptoms. It supports pollution prevention approaches.

- TQM asserts that quality is everyone's responsibility. It fits the awareness that all employees must contribute to sustainability.

- TQM calculates the cost of (non) quality. This is a useful framework for considering the total costs and benefits of unsustainable performance.

US and European initiatives

The US Global Environmental Management Initiative (GEMI) brings leading US companies together to share experiences of quality-based approaches to environmental management. A transAtlantic equivalent is the European Foundation for Quality Management (EFQM).

European quality award scores impact on society

The EFQM has a template to assess the overall performance of an organization. The template allocates points for different aspects of

▶

▶

performance, such as customer satisfaction and resource management. Up to 6% of the overall points are for positive impacts on society.

Companies applying for the EFQM's annual European Quality Award – the equivalent of the US Baldridge Award – must demonstrate good performance in both environmental management and social responsibility.

Are the disciplines of the first orbit, the marketing skills, a burden of the past? Not at all: they remain at the core. They are now enhanced by the discipline of management excellence and a well earned image amongst environmentally aware publics.

▶ THE THIRD ORBIT: EXTENDING THE HORIZONS, STRENGTHENING THE VISION

The third orbit involves four crucial changes (see Figure 23.3). All require that business stretch from the familiar domains of marketing and management and enter the *terra incognita* of public policy and nongovernmental organizations (NGOs). The changes are:

- Working with policy makers and NGOs to develop regulations which drive towards sustainable development but also maximize flexibility and opportunity for business.

- Establishing dialog and partnership with NGOs and other stakeholders to learn, influence and gain early warnings of how public opinion and customer values might shift.

- Considering the whole life cycle of products and services and working with suppliers and others to minimize the total burden you put on the earth.

- Building your own long-term vision of a sustainable future and the role of your business.

● FIGURE 23.3
The model of sustainable business development

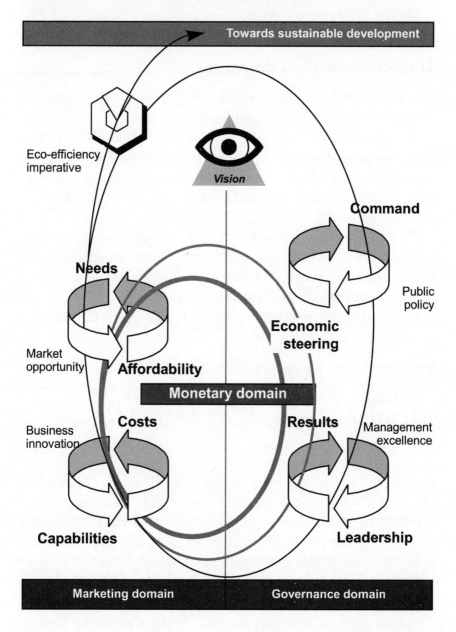

> *The third orbit builds partnerships with governments and stakeholders, a life cycle perspective and a long-term vision of sustainable business.*

The orbits work in harmony

This third orbit does not replace the first or second orbits but incorporates them. The marketing domain remains crucial. One cannot discount the rules of the monetary domain. New public policy initiatives will only work if they allow business to create new sources of customer value and improve their cost effectiveness in the long run. If this does not happen the third orbit will collapse from within its core.

Without satisfied customers there is neither business success nor a contribution to sustainable development through changed purchasing and consumption behavior. The drive to management excellence becomes more important rather than less. However, new issues become relevant and horizons must extend further.

▶ THE THIRD ORBIT: FROM COMMAND AND CONTROL REGULATION TO ECONOMIC STEERING

Sustainable business development cannot be achieved without government action. Our coolant case shows this (see Chapter 19). But what kind of action? The US President's Council on Sustainable Development, which brings together industry, NGOs, policy makers and community representatives, makes this assessment of traditional "command and control" regulation:

> Over the years, the value and limits of this regulatory approach have become clear. There is no doubt that some regulations have encouraged innovation and compliance with environmental laws, resulting in substantial improvements in the protection of public health and the environment. But at other times, regulation has

imposed unnecessary and sometimes costly administrative and technological burdens and discouraged technological innovations that can reduce costs while achieving environmental benefits beyond those realized by compliance. Moreover, it has frequently focussed attention on cleanup and control remedies rather than on product or process redesign to prevent pollution.[1]

From command to economic steering

It calls for more flexible and diverse approaches, using market incentives and producer responsibility initiatives. Their essence is economic steering. This provides positive incentives to encourage innovation such as fiscal incentives or award schemes, and negative incentives to continue with the status quo, in the form of environmental taxes or expensive takeback requirements.[2] These should make it easier for business to benefit from sustainable development and so encourage breakthrough innovation.

Uneven standards and implementation

Domestic environmental regulation is often partial. Some sectors can be under pressure while others are lightly treated. Uneven standards and implementation are even more of a problem at international level. McKinsey conducted several environmental case studies for a report on Legislative and Administrative Simplification within the European Union.[3] This highlights the risk of a "three speed" implementation by the various member states. It also shows that industry wants more not less harmonization and evenness.

The same points apply with even greater force between continents.

Driving out free riders

This variation of standards and implementation allows free riders to flourish. These free riders are barriers to sustainable development as they not only pollute and waste themselves, they make others ask: why should I take action when that company or country isn't? Especially when it might put us at a short-term competitive disadvantage.

Business can take independent initiatives to deal with free riders. The Marine Stewardship Council will use the buying power of Unilever and other processors to favor sustainable fishing practices. But anti-trust regulations and the dynamics of competition mean that there are limits to independent business initiatives.

Government intervention is necessary to create a framework for making your decisions, and a base line you may not fall below. If we want to get the benefits from free trade without mortgaging the environment in some regions of the world we will need minimum global standards together with harmonized commitment and enforcement. Of course, there is a danger of business seeing these as a maximum as well as a minimum standard. Eco-innovators must work with NGOs and policy makers to ensure this does not happen.

Aligning business and public policy objectives

The third orbit involves alignment between public policy objectives and business leadership. They merge into a governance consensus. They have common long-term priorities and do not work against or past each other anymore.

One means of implementing this is explicit agreements between business leaders and policy makers. These set exacting long-term goals for business but provide flexibility and responsibility in achieving them.

The Dutch process of environmental covenants between government and industry associations provides a leading example of consensus-based but still demanding policies.

▶ THE THIRD ORBIT: FROM CONFLICT TO PARTNERSHIP WITH STAKEHOLDERS

Stakeholders are the organizations and individuals whom your actions affect and who can help or hinder the pursuit of your objectives. The third orbit is smoothest when you identify who they are and talk with them. Sometimes this means recognition of stakeholders who have always had an interest but have previously been excluded, such as NGOs or community activists. On other occasions you must identify "neutral" stakeholders who have the potential to advise and coach you.

The value of NGOs

Stakeholders can be recognized, involved and informed in many ways. Corporate and site environmental reports are one obvious way. A few companies such as Body Shop are extending this to reporting on ethics and social impact.

But the third orbit goes beyond reporting or establishing liaison panels. The objective in this orbit is partnership with stakeholders. This means identifying areas of common ground and then working together to take action.

NGOs are the key partners for eco-innovation. They represent aware and motivated citizens. They shape public opinion, customer values and policies. Dialog with them can provide early warnings of how this might shift.

The role of NGOs is crucial in maintaining the issue of sustainable consumption and production on the policy

NGOs and other stakeholders can provide "out-of-your-box" challenges, the stuff breakthroughs are made of.

agenda. Their vitality and creativity is a source of inspiration and ideas. They can help in exploring new product and service avenues. They can validate consumer reactions in advance and decrease the risk in new business launches. And they can provide reliable insight into some of the more difficult sustainability criteria like danger to species or social impact in developing countries.

The power of dialog

Dialog is a two-way process. It also creates an opportunity to shape your partners' thinking. They may better appreciate the powers of business as a change agent, a creator of jobs, a mover of technology and know-how.

UNEP has summed up the benefits of partnership – and the challenge of making it work:

> Multistakeholder partnerships are not an answer to every problem, nor are they easy. They require a difficult balance of idealism and pragmatism, creative vision and practical hard work, a strong commitment to principles and a willingness to compromise. Most are extremely complex and many fail to live up to their expectations.
>
> However if they can be made to work, multistakeholder partnerships can be a powerful force for change and a vital tool for developing efficient and equitable solutions to sustainable development. They can offer a sense of common purpose and a compelling vision – locally, nationally and internationally – for a more sustainable future.[4]

The European Partners for the Environment we described in Chapter 6 is one such partnership. Groundwork provides another example of this dynamic (see box). And Figure 23.4 gives examples of who potential partners might be.

● FIGURE 23.4
Potential partners

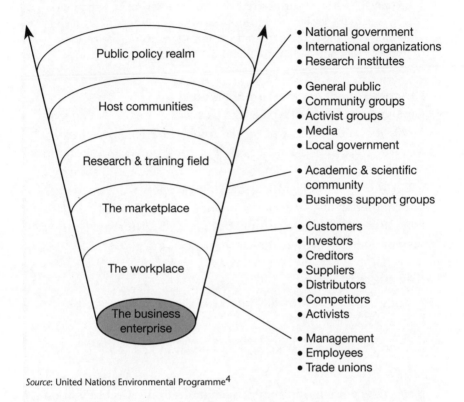

- National government
- International organizations
- Research institutes

- General public
- Community groups
- Activist groups
- Media
- Local government

- Academic & scientific community
- Business support groups

- Customers
- Investors
- Creditors
- Suppliers
- Distributors
- Competitors
- Activists

- Management
- Employees
- Trade unions

Source: United Nations Environmental Programme[4]

● **THE GROUNDWORK PARTNERSHIP**

Britain's Groundwork Foundation is a national charity for environmental improvement. It operates through over 30 local Groundwork Trusts in all parts of the UK. Both the Foundation and the Trusts have boards which bring together central and local government, business and NGOs.

▶

▶
Groundwork's mission is . . .

> to bring about the sustained regeneration, improvement and man-
> agement of the local environment by developing partnerships which
> empower people, business and organizations to maximize their
> impact and contribution to environmental, economic and social
> well-being.

Reaching small business in Blackburn

Groundwork Blackburn typifies the partnership's work. Founded in
1990, its initial focus was working with the local community
to restore degraded landscapes. But local small and medium
sized companies, of which there are many, see it as a source of
expertise on environmental issues. It now offers them a low cost
environmental review and consultancy service. Several hundred
companies have made use of it and spent several millions of
pounds on implementing the recommendations.

Key success factors

A study summarizes the key factors in Groundwork Blackburn's
success as:

- strong local business leadership and strong support from the
  elected local government;

- an independent and impartial organization – Groundwork –
  that is not part of the regulators or government, but is seen as
  being supported and trusted by both;

- a multiagency partnership at the local level – to act as a catalyst
  and an enabler;

- a coordinating, networking body to share ideas and provide
  support;

- a shared vision;

- committed staff with drive, creativity and the ability to cope
  with uncertainty.[5]

▶ THE THIRD ORBIT: A LIFE CYCLE PERSPECTIVE

A life cycle perspective leads naturally to greater cooperation with customers and suppliers to minimize overall impacts. Large companies have a particular opportunity, and a responsibility to support their small and medium sized suppliers for environmental improvements and social responsibility. This creates a dynamic network of creative enterprises that stimulate one another in continuous improvements.

B&Q's work with the Forest Stewardship Council demonstrates that this is achievable across as well as within national boundaries. /

A life cycle perspective requires internal changes. Sustainable development requires redesign of products and processes. Designers must integrate the customer knowledge of distributors and marketers, the operational knowledge of site managers and maintenance staff and many others. Our eco-innovation process provides one tool for doing this.

> *A life cycle perspective means cooperation with internal and external suppliers and customers to minimize impacts from the cradle (origin) to the grave (final disposal) of products*

▶ THE THIRD ORBIT: A VISION OF SUSTAINABILITY

Vision is critical in the third orbit. A vision of:

- shared responsibility by business and political leadership to create a better legacy,

- a stronger social sensitivity in business, and

- a long-term perspective of the sustainable development imperative.

You must create a process which shifts people's horizons from the short term, the current product, today's processes. Lets them see with their own eyes rather than yours the long-term trends and the threats and opportunities these trends create. Give them space and incentive to consider the arguments for "factor four" or "factor ten" improvements and the need to provide socio-economic security for the disadvantaged. Allow them to explore the implications for long-term competitive strength, for products and services, jobs and personal contributions.

▶ TOWARDS THE FOURTH ORBIT ...

The three orbit model is an ideal construction. It emerged from our own lessons and those we observed in the case histories of Part 4.

The three orbits are also interlocked. Sustainable business only occurs when they are synchronized. That is not to claim that there is a smooth transition in the periodic table of business models from one orbit to the other. Like electrons around the nucleus, business development is a vibrant, energetic process. There are jumps forwards and there are setbacks. There will always be short-term tradeoffs between profitability and sustainability. But in the long term there is a relationship as stable as the electronic structure of elements. This relationship is one of complete compatibility.

Remember too that scientists are always discovering new particles in new orbits. The same will be true of sustainable business development. Such a long-term change will create many surprises. It may even require a fourth orbit to meet them.

Time flies

But for the moment, maintaining a steady third orbit is challenge enough. The challenge to share more quality of life among more people and reduce significantly our resources throughput. A 30 year transition. A generation. A very short time.

Meeting the challenge requires business skills, leadership capacity and a governance model that operate in full synergy with our sights continuously on the eco-compass to lead business development with a long-term purpose.

Notes

1 The President's Council on Sustainable Development *Sustainable America.* Washington, DC: US Government Printing Office, 1996, p.28.

2 Porter M. and Van der Linde C. "Green and Competitive", *Harvard Business Review*, September–October 1995, pp.120–134.

3 McKinsey & Company *Environmental Regulation: Case Illustrations.* Amsterdam, 1995. See also Commission of the European Communities *Report of the Group of Independent Experts on Legislative and Administrative Simplification.* Brussels, 1995.

4 UNEP Industry and Environmental Programme, The Prince of Wales Business Leaders Forum and Tufts University, *Partnerships for Sustainable Development.* London: The Prince of Wales Business Leaders Forum, 1994, p.51.

5 UNEP *op cit.*, p.59.

Chapter 24

Simple "sustainability rules"

Science and mathematics have shown that complex systems are often influenced by a few variables and governed by a few simple "rules". One of the difficulties with the ideas of sustainability at present is that they are often dauntingly complex. It can seem that any individual action is futile because an entire system needs to be changed.

▶ COMPLEXITY IS A CONSTANT

This complexity is real and cannot be wished away. But we believe it is possible to summarize the themes of our book into some simple rules for you to follow.

The rules will work best when they are supported by policy initiatives. For example, ones which internalize environmental costs or set long-term emission or energy targets for products and processes. But even in their absence the rules build awareness and move your organization towards sustainability and the breakthrough innovations which are necessary over coming decades.

There are six rules, whose one word summaries form the mnemonic ECO/ECO:

Eco-efficiency	Empowerment
Customers	Care
Objectives	Out-of-the-box

ECO/ECO reminds us that sustainable development, eco-efficiency and cleaner production are about integrating *ecology* and *eco*nomics. The *eco*nomic imperative is to provide goods and services that people value because they bring them better quality of life. The *eco*logical imperative is to reduce the environmental impacts and resource requirements of providing them. Both are equally important (see Figure 24.1.).

Figure 24.1 Six simple sustainability rules

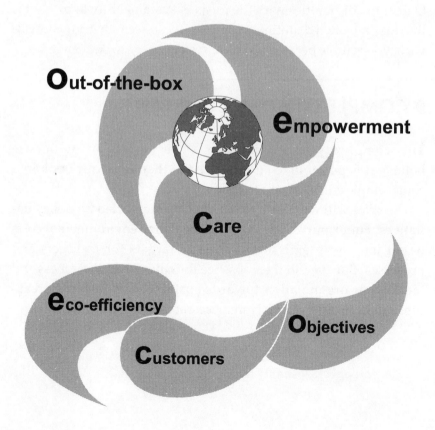

Eco-efficiency

Wastes, emissions, products which deliver poor environmental performance are not just in conflict with sustainable development. They represent business inefficiency and a failure to convert expensive inputs into useful products.

The remedy to this is eco-efficiency. As the World Business Council for Sustainable Development (WBCSD) puts it:

> The vision of eco-efficiency is simply to "produce more from less". Reducing waste and pollution, and using fewer energy and raw material resources is obviously good for the environment. It is also self-evidently good for business because it cuts companies' costs.
>
> Resource productivity is fundamental in the eco-efficiency approach. The potential for step-by-step improvements in resource productivity, to match the increases in labor productivity in recent years, is greater than often perceived.[1]

And this does not just apply to your own operations. You need a life cycle perspective to identify opportunities for improvements in downstream or upstream sections of the product chain.

> **Rule 1: You must achieve more from less.**

You can use the eco-compass and eco-innovation workshop to help implement this rule.

Customers

WBCSD's concept of eco-efficiency also links environmental concerns with adding value for customers. The Council writes:

> The goal is to create value for society, and for the company, by doing more with less over a life cycle ... To achieve long-term success, companies must create value for their shareholders and customers. Over time, customers will increasingly demand more than a product that simply fulfils a function.

How to maximize your value added and your customers' satisfaction in this eco-efficient world? In the short term you have to provide your customers' wants. But in the medium to long term the demands of sustainable development will reshape them. They will want goods and services which are both sustainable and provide quality of life. So stay close to your customers to find out what their real needs are. Apply the needs test to innovate products and services that will enthuse them.

> **Rule 2: Consider your customers' long-term needs even before they do.**

Objectives

Becoming sustainable is difficult. It encompasses a diversity of impacts from long-term global problems to local nuisances, requires cooperation between a wide range of internal and external stakeholders and needs clear objectives.

To be successful your objectives must be:

- *comprehensive*, covering not only processes but the life cycle of products, and issues of socio-economic security as well as ecology and resources;

- translatable into *targets*, so that you can measure progress;

- *clear*, so that they are easily understood and communicated;

- capable of *implementation*, either immediately or by stretching your capability.

A quality approach is essential to meet all of these.

But surely this is a book about breakthough innovation? Does this conflict with total quality management (TQM)'s stress on continual improvement? Some certainly think so. In fact, continual improvement has many definitions and interpretations. We prefer radical ones. The key question is improvement towards what? If targets are unambitious, then improvements will be incremental at best. But if they are stretch targets, backcasted from sustainable development, the prospects are better. How do you achieve continual improvement towards a goal of "factor four" or greater improvements in energy and mass intensity? You obviously need both breakthrough innovations as well as year on year incremental improvement. Base your definitions around this – and take into account the need for socio-economic security as well, and continual improvement becomes a radical philosophy.

> **Rule 3: Set ambitious objectives and targets for sustainability.**

Empowerment

A quality approach requires the breakdown of organizational boundaries. The operational levels of an organization share the best knowledge. Quality programs try to unleash that knowledge by providing tools to analyze and shape it, and opportunities to act independently to implement solutions. They also reduce barriers between functions, and between an organization and its customers and suppliers, in order to move knowledge and create solutions.

When TQM fails, as it often does, it usually happens because organizations treat it as a set of tools and techniques to achieve incremental change, not wanting to embark on the radical change to the established order which excellent management requires. But that is exactly what is needed. Real TQM, in the words of George Binney and Colin Williams, involves a ...

> holistic approach to change: focussing on customers *and* practicing fact-based management *and* creating an environment in which people bring to work the same energy, ability and commitment that they display in their life outside work.[2]

But empowerment is not just a route to sustainable development within organizations. It is critical to achieving sustainable communities. The English city of Leicester ran a European Union-supported Environment City project between 1990 and 1995. The aim? To move the city towards sustainable development and to draw lessons for future initiatives, and for other European towns and societies. One conclusion was . . .

> Providing increasing opportunities for individuals to influence the development of their communities is a fundamental aspect of local sustainability. Ultimately, individuals' pride in, and personal responsibility for, the local environment, coupled with adequate resourcing of local initiatives will ensure a shift towards a more balanced, sane and sustainable society.[3]

Empowerment is also critical on a global scale, to provide the disadvantaged with an ability to influence the forces which shape their lives.

Empowerment at all these levels is a key requirement for sustainable development. To make it happen, people's belief in, and aspirations for, more sustainable lives must match the sustainability agendas of the communities they live in, the businesses they work for and the planet they share.

Business can play a part in these processes by providing opportunities, joining partnerships, supporting local initiatives and many other means.

Rule 4: Sustainability means empowered employees, citizens and communities.

Care

Sustainable development is a complex issue. To understand it fully, and to respond appropriately to its demands, you must extend your horizons. You have a duty and a moral responsibility to care for a wider range of people, organisms and natural systems. This caring has an ethical and spiritual as well as a utilitarian dimension.[4]

The President's Council uses the term stewardship to describe this. In its definition the word:

> calls upon everyone in society to assume responsibility for protecting the integrity of natural resources and their underlying ecosystems and, in so doing, safeguarding the interests of future generations. Without personal and collective commitment, without an ethic based on the acceptance of responsibility, efforts to sustain natural resources protection and environmental quality cannot succeed. With them, the bountiful yet fragile foundation of natural resources can be protected and replenished to sustain the needs of today and tomorrow.[5]

But the economic sphere also cares for human needs. The duty of care gives a deeper purpose to your business and a sense to your individual career. It provides your lifetime's chance to make a difference. For yourself. For the billions who do not yet have their basic needs for food, water, shelter and medicine met. And for future generations.

> *Rule 5: Sustainability is about ethics and socio-economic security as well as environment.*

Out-of-the-box

Cleaner production, eco-efficiency, life cycle assessment and the eco-compass are all thinking tools. They are designed to challenge mindsets. To create discomfort with today's solutions. To provoke curiosity about the future. To excite with its opportunities. To introduce new, holistic ways of thinking about the world. To encourage dialog, and sometimes uncomfortable partnerships, with the forces which are reshaping it.

You must operate in the present and not be constrained by it. Remember that we are in a period of innovation lethargy, merely running to stand still. Get out of today's box and think of the coming decades. Think in the 30 year timescales over which intergenerational obligations, long-term trends and the innovative pathways to the future become clear and actionable. Think in terms of the minimum "factor four" and ideal "factor ten" improvements in performance which sustainability requires.

On these timescales our innovation lethargy will end and sustainability breakthroughs will happen. There is a practical and a moral imperative and an opportunity to create new markets and profitable business. Our cases show that this is possible. The future equivalents of Bill Gates of Microsoft will emerge and build value from them. Do not be part of the problem of business-as-usual, incrementalist thinking. Create value by being part of the solution, which is a long-term vision of sustainable business.

> *Rule 6: Sustainable development is imperative, possible, and value creating. Someone will make it happen. The choice is yours.*

Notes

1 World Business Council for Sustainable Development *Eco-Efficient Leadership*. Geneva, 1996, p.4.

2 Binney, G. and Williams, C. *Making Quality Work: Lessons From Europe's Leading Companies*. London: Economist Intelligence Unit, 1992, p.vii.

3 Environ Trust *Summary Report on Local Sustainability: Turning Sustainable Development into Practical Action for Our Communities*. Leicester, 1996, p.vii.

4 For a discussion of this point, from a radical perspective, see Welford R. "Hijacking Environmentalism ? Corporate Responses to Sustainable Development", in Ulhoi, J. and Madsen, H. (eds) *Industry and the Environment*. Aarhus, Denmark: University of Aarhus School of Business, 1996.

5 The President's Council on Sustainable Development *Sustainable America*. Washington, DC: US Government Printing Office, 1996, p.110.

Index